Turning
Wood
with Richard Raffan

Turning Wood
with Richard Raffan

Richard Raffan
16·11·86
Overlake School

T The Taunton Press

Cover photo by Rod Shone,
courtesy of Pilot Productions Ltd.

Text photos by Mark Alexander, John Cederquist,
John Lascelles and Richard Raffan.

Gallery photos by Richard Raffan,
except where noted.

First printing: April 1985
Second printing: April 1986
International Standard Book Number: 0-918804-24-8
Library of Congress Catalog Card Number: 84-052130
Printed in Denmark

A FINE WOODWORKING Book

FINE WOODWORKING® is a trademark of The Taunton Press, Inc.,
registered in the U.S. Patent and Trademark Office.

The Taunton Press, Inc.
63 South Main Street
Box 355
Newtown, Connecticut 06470

Acknowledgments

I would like to thank Roz Lovett, Leigh Williamson and Maggie
Long (who each suffered my handwriting and typed various bits of
manuscript) and John Cederquist, John Lascelles and Mark
Alexander (who took most of the action photographs).

For Eleanor

Contents

Introduction

On January 1, 1970, I removed myself from London big-city life and a well-paid job that exercised the nebulous skills of middle management. Watching the encroachment of technology on the business world, I concluded that the sooner I learned to do something more practical, the better—but it had to be something that could not be improved upon by a machine. For the previous six months I had considered other ways of making a living that would allow me to return to my native west of England. Picture-framing, pottery, plumbing and furniture-making were all possibilities, but on a whim, I eventually chose woodturning.

I had absolutely no knowledge of the craft other than the notion that it involved lathes and tools with rather long handles. I chose woodturning not because of a long-standing love affair with wood or trees, but because I felt I could learn the basics of turning more quickly than I could learn almost any other hand skill. (And a small internal voice told me it was the right thing to do.)

My intuition proved correct, and I learned enough during five months working in a small country shop to produce a well-made bowl, lamp base or eggcup. I was able to sell enough of these almost immediately to craft shops, galleries and gift shops to cobble together a livelihood. Even so, this was a time of relative poverty for me. My income plunged 90% as it dropped a zero. I had prepared for this by ensuring that I owned my own small house, car and other basic essentials so that little cash was needed to maintain life. I changed gears: I ceased to dine out or spend money on entertainment. I drove around hawking my wares off the back of my car. (And this is still basically what I do, although for the last ten years I have been fortunate in not having to approach new customers.) The unexpected revelation was that, perhaps because I had been so concerned with finding an alternative way of earning a living, I was surprised by the immense pleasure and satisfaction I was gaining at the same time that I was developing my skills at the craft.

If I had a problem, it was that by working in isolation I had no mentor to ask for advice. I had to discover almost everything the hard way—buying poor lots of wood, ruining nearly completed bowls and so on. On the positive side, there was nobody to tell me I was doing things the wrong way, so my approach was uninhibited and I pursued the best techniques as I saw them. If one technique failed, I tried another. In fact, I must have tried just about every conceivable way of cutting, scraping and hacking wood on the lathe. Pieces often flew off and bounced around the workshop in the early days (and still do occasionally), but I learned a great deal in the process.

The techniques, tools and systems I have set down in these pages are the ones I use now. They are the result of a 14-year odyssey, charted by my trial-and-error meanderings. They serve me well, but are subject to instant alteration should anything better come along. In my years as a full-time woodturner, I feel I've sorted out most lathe problems (mine anyway), and have found methods that are quick, efficient and relatively safe. Over the past three years I've conducted many short workshops for beginners, advanced amateur, and semi-professional turners. I've tried to keep in mind the difficulties they commonly encounter. If I repeat myself in the text, it is because I've found that these particular points tend to be forgotten in the mass of things to remember.

This is primarily a manual of hand techniques. I have tried to explain how to cut any internal or external surface and what problems and hazards to expect. To make the book comprehensible to readers everywhere I have converted all standard measurements to metric. And, for the sake of expediency, all metric measurements greater than 50mm have been rounded to the nearest 5mm. Also, all action photo sequences have been set off with red edge bands to make them easy to locate if you are thumbing quickly through the book. The novice should be able to work steadily through the exercises in centerwork and facework, practicing the cuts and just enjoying the shavings while developing control. I hope that those who know a little more will also find much that is new and useful as well as gain an insight into one professional's approach. Most people know vaguely what they want to make, but the projects at the end of the centerwork and facework chapters, the photos in the gallery and references throughout the text underline my own approach to design.

If you have never turned wood before, I'm sure you'll enjoy it. Shapes develop in seconds as the shavings fly away, and I have a hunch that the ability to remove so much wood so quickly satisfies some basic destructive urge and gratifies the vandal in us all.

Richard Raffan
Mittagong, NSW
Australia
March 1985

The Lathe

This is a brief guide to the lathe, the essential tool of the woodturner.

I begin by examining the qualities you'll want to look for, or avoid, when you purchase a lathe and I suggest ways of modifying commercially available models to enhance their performance. My comments are based on my own experience and what I have found useful or essential in my own shop. Attachments for the lathe—drives, faceplates and chucks—are described in Chapter 2 (p. 12). Cutting tools, such as gouges, scrapers, chisels and parting tools, are examined in depth in Chapter 3 (p. 28) and safety gear is dealt with in Chapter 4 (p. 40). Refer to the drawing of a typical lathe on p. 4 to locate its various elements as they are discussed in the text.

The wood lathe is the heart of the turner's craft: It is the machine that spins the wood. If you are serious about woodturning, the care taken in choosing (or making) this most important tool of the trade will return handsome dividends of satisfaction for years to come. Nothing is more frustrating than struggling against limitations imposed by an ill-conceived or poorly constructed lathe.

Although lathes have been endlessly adapted to suit the specific requirements of many trades, there are characteristics common to virtually all of them. The business end of the lathe is called the headstock, a stationary housing containing a belt-driven step-pulley on a drive shaft. Power from an electric motor is transmitted to the headstock by rubber V-belts running in the pulley. The motor is usually mounted below or behind the headstock and is securely bolted to the frame or base of the machine. The pulley rotates the shaft in a counterclockwise direction, and a drive center, faceplate or chuck mounted on one of the threaded ends of the shaft transmits power to the work. The belt's position on the pulley may be changed to vary lathe speed. The tailstock assembly slides up to the headstock along the horizontal lathe bed to provide tail-center support, and is adjustable at any point along the bed's length. Lathes are designed so that as you stand facing the front of the lathe, the headstock will be on your left, the tailstock on your right.

The maximum diameter that can be turned on any lathe is determined by the distance between the point of the drive center (on the headstock) and the bed. Turners describe this distance in terms of what a lathe will swing; for example, a lathe with a center height of 6 in. (150mm) will swing 12 in. (305mm). The length of work that can be turned is determined by the distance between the drive and tail centers when the tailstock is moved to its outermost position on the right end of the bed.

Woodturnings fall into two categories—centerwork or facework. Most people think of centerwork as chair legs and rungs, newel posts or other long, thin projects turned between two centers. Bowls and platters and other large-diameter work turned on a faceplate are considered standard facework. While this is often the case, there are frequent exceptions, which I will describe in greater detail in Chapter 2. Essentially, whether a job is centerwork or facework is determined by the orientation of the grain of the wood in the piece to be worked, rather than the way in which it is held on the lathe. In centerwork, the grain runs the length of the work and lies parallel to the rotational axis of the lathe, while in facework, the grain lies at a 90° angle to the axis.

For most centerwork, a 12-in. (305mm) swing is sufficient and a 3-ft.- (915mm) to 4-ft.- (1220mm) long bed is desirable. For most facework, the center should be about 10 in. (255mm) above the bed, which will allow a 20-in.- (510mm) diameter disc to be turned. A short bed, about 18 in. (455mm) long, will allow you to move with the tools and work from all angles across the face.

The classic manufacturer's solution to the different requirements of centerwork and facework has been to put the faceplate for large-diameter turnings on the outboard (left-hand) side of the headstock with the centerwork fixings mounted on the inboard (right) side. Large-diameter work can then be mounted and worked unhindered. But I don't like working on the outboard side. Apart from the fact that I'm right-handed, I feel it is always safer to approach the lathe (and rotating wood) from the same angle. Also, many of my tools are ground to be used on the inboard

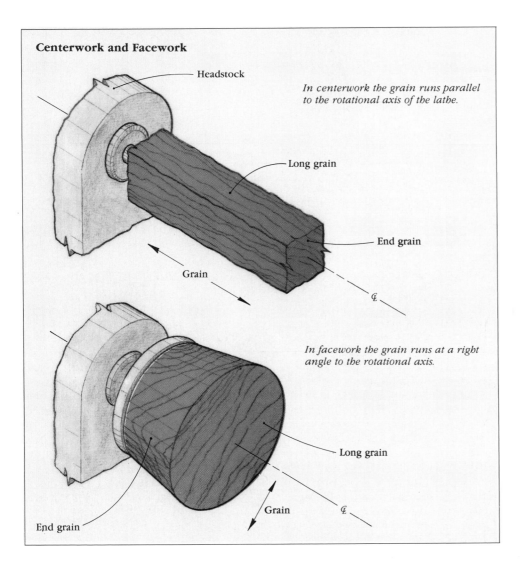

Centerwork and Facework

Headstock

In centerwork the grain runs parallel to the rotational axis of the lathe.

Long grain

End grain

Grain

₵

In facework the grain runs at a right angle to the rotational axis.

Long grain

End grain

Grain

₵

side. Instead, I keep a 4-in.- (100mm) diameter faceplate mounted on the outboard shaft as a handwheel. I use it to rotate a job for close inspection while the motor is switched off, or I grip it to slow the lathe to a stop rapidly. Lathe beds are occasionally recessed in the area inside the headstock, as shown in the drawing of the lathe, to permit larger-diameter turnings to be made inboard.

My lathe, a Harrison Union Graduate, is nearly ideal. It has a good center height of 9½ in. (240mm), with a short bed and a removable tailstock. With the tailstock in place, the lathe will accept work up to 16 in. (405mm) long between centers. With the tailstock removed, I can work with complete freedom around the lathe.

For long centerwork, I have a second Harrison lathe with a swing of only 12 in. (305mm) but a maximum length of 4 ft. 6 in. (1370mm) between centers. In business I need both lathes and could not function efficiently without either.

The type of lathe you need depends on the kind of work you do, but there are certain features to look for in any lathe.

This Harrison Union Graduate short-bed lathe is ideal for facework and short center-work. It has a 19-in. (480mm) swing and can take work up to 16 in. (405mm) long between centers. The pedestal contains a four-speed pulley that provides speeds of 425, 790, 1330 and 2250 rpm. A cam lever adjusts the belt tension. The center height has been raised from 40 in. (1020mm) to 48 in. (1220mm) by bolting two 8-in. (205mm) steel *I*-beams to the base.

The Lathe

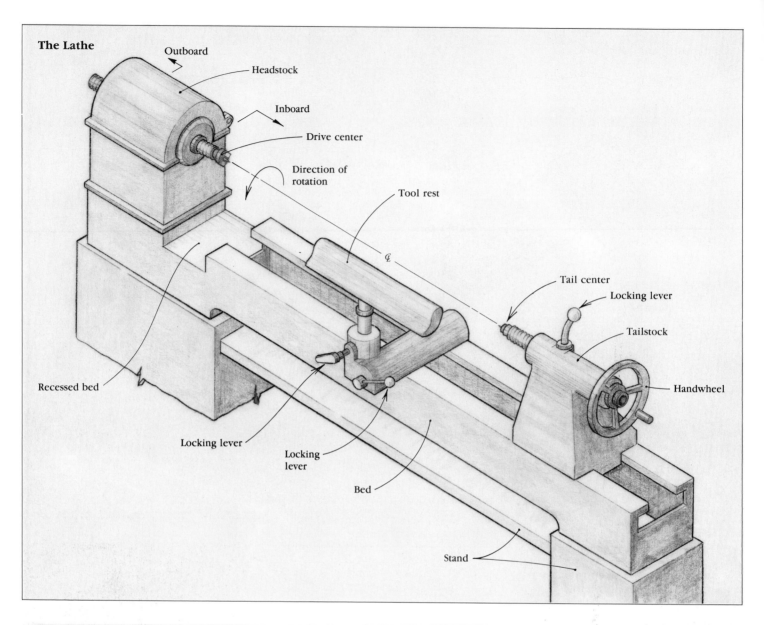

Outboard

Headstock

Inboard

Drive center

Direction of rotation

Tool rest

Tail center

Locking lever

Tailstock

Handwheel

Recessed bed

Locking lever

Locking lever

Bed

Stand

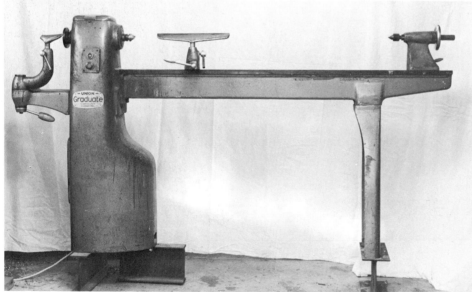

This Harrison long-bed lathe is used for longer centerwork. It will swing 12 in. (305mm) inboard and 20 in. (510mm) outboard, and will accept work up to 4 ft. 6 in. (1370mm) long between centers.

The Headstock

I recommend a 12-in.- (305mm) long, 1½-in.- (38mm) diameter drive shaft, mounted at both ends in 3-in.- (75mm) to 4-in.- (100mm) diameter roller or ball bearings. Plain bearings, available on some less-expensive machines, are seldom satisfactory because they rarely eliminate all play, especially in small lathes where the shaft is less than 1 in. (25mm) in diameter. The more robust roller or ball bearings are needed to cope with the rotation of irregular blocks of wood or the stress of knocks against the axis or end of the shaft caused by the mounting of centerwork blanks. When powered by a 1hp motor, this combination of drive shaft and bearings will easily handle a 90-lb. (35kg) block of wood. The smallest shaft I would consider using would be 1 in. (25mm) in diameter, mounted in 3-in.

The Headstock

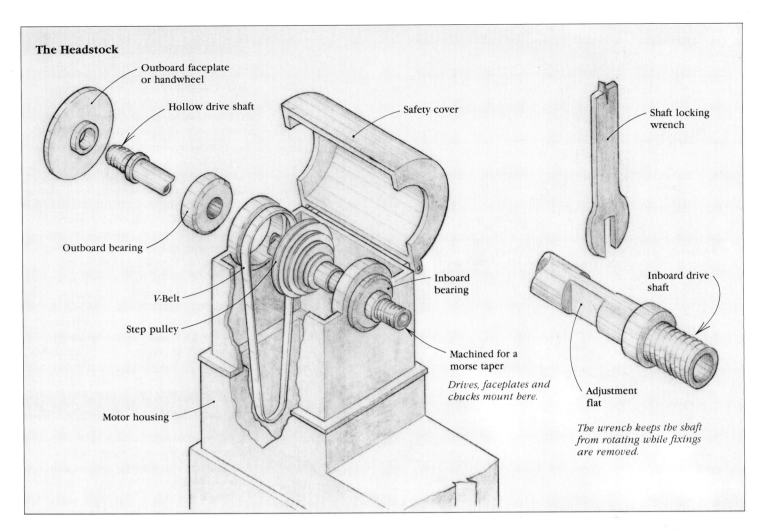

Outboard faceplate
or handwheel

Hollow drive shaft

Safety cover

Shaft locking
wrench

Outboard bearing

V-Belt

Step pulley

Inboard
bearing

Motor housing

Machined for a
morse taper

*Drives, faceplates and
chucks mount here.*

Inboard drive
shaft

Adjustment
flat

*The wrench keeps the shaft
from rotating while fixings
are removed.*

(75mm) bearings. A shaft larger than 1½ in. (38mm) or 2 in. (50mm) in diameter is heavier and would require a larger motor (2hp to 3hp), which would be slower to start and stop and would involve a higher energy cost.

The shaft and bearings should be mounted in a heavy casing, similar to the cast-steel machines shown in the photos on pp. 3 and 4. If the shaft does not run true, or if it is not secure in its bearings, any play will be magnified at the point where the tool is cutting. Not only does this make fine work impossible, but it leads to dangerous vibration. When bearings become worn, they must be replaced to ensure safety. (You will find that new ones run more quietly, too.)

The drive shaft should be hollow and machined to accept morse-taper drives and chucks (p. 13). Some solid shafts are designed to accept a morse-taper drive, which is removed by unscrewing a collar that has been previously wound onto the drive shaft. I prefer the hollow shaft because I can insert a rod through it to knock the drives out quickly. In addition, a hollow shaft can be used as a cup chuck for small work (p. 88).

Drive shafts are usually threaded at both ends to accept faceplates and chucks. Lathes rotate in a counterclockwise direction so the threads on the outboard end of the shaft must be opposite to the ones on the inboard end, which are right-hand, so that attachments will screw on tighter with the machine's rotation. If the threads are both right-hand, attachments on the outboard end of the shaft will unscrew. (Some lathes are equipped with a reversing switch to aid in sanding and finishing and care must be taken to ensure the chuck or faceplate doesn't become unscrewed [p. 128]).

You must be able to lock the drive shaft to aid in the removal of lathe attachments. This is done either by using a wrench on a flat section of the shaft or inserting a rod into a hole in the shaft. Most rods will bend easily while a wrench will not.

With the hinged cover plate removed, the step-pulley and V-belt are easily reached to change speeds. To unscrew faceplates or chucks from the lathe, lock the drive shaft in position either with a wrench on a flat section of shaft or by inserting a rod through a hole in the shaft.

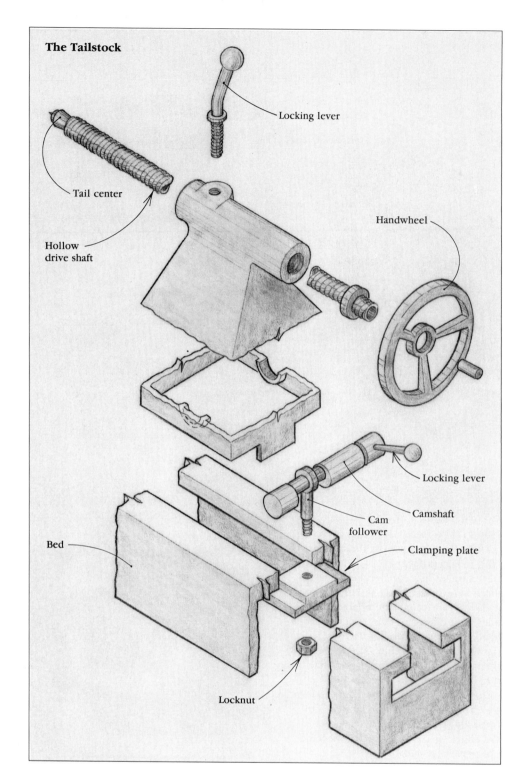

The Tailstock

Locking lever

Tail center

Hollow
drive shaft

Handwheel

Locking lever

Camshaft

Cam
follower

Clamping plate

Bed

Locknut

The Tailstock

The tailstock slides along the lathe bed
and is locked in position before the tail
center is wound in to support the work.
The locking operation should be quick and
easy. A locking lever that remains attached
to the unit is better than a nut and bolt
assembly that requires separate wrenches.
A handwheel is turned to adjust the tail
center. It's handy to have at least 4 in.
(100mm) of travel in the tail center so that
work may be mounted or unmounted
without undoing the locking lever and
then moving the tailstock. The handwheel
should be at least 6 in. (150mm) in
diameter or have a handle on its rim to
make it easy to use.

The shaft should be the same size as the
one in the headstock. Likewise, it should
be hollow and machined to accept the
morse taper of centers and chucks so they
can be easily inserted and removed.

Centers

The headstock and tailstock centers should
be in exactly the same plane; in my
experience, this is uncommon on most
woodturning lathes. This is not essential
when the wood is held between two points
(as between a drive and tail center), but it
is when you want to provide tail-center
support for work mounted on a faceplate
or chuck. When the wood is held firmly in
one plane, it will work loose from the
faceplate screws or the chuck if the tail
center is not true. You can check if your
tail center is true in two ways. First, insert
a drive center in the drive shaft and move
the tail center in so that both cones are
point-to-point. If the points don't meet,
adjust the tail center by placing shims
between the bed and tailstock until they
line up. You can also mount a disc on a
faceplate or in a chuck and move the tail
center in so that the point just penetrates
the wood. Then rotate the disc by hand. An
untrue tail center will make a circle on the
wood; a true center will leave a dot. Again,
use shims to adjust the tailstock until the
point of the center is aligned with the
center of the circle.

The Bed & Stand

A common source of vibration, especially in small lathes, lies in the substructure of the machine. The best headstock and tailstock are no good unless mounted on a substantial bed of cast iron or steel, or wood beams fixed to a heavy frame, or, perhaps best of all, a large block of concrete. A solid, well-built lathe eliminates all vibration, and the job of turning becomes much easier. Greater precision is possible and the scope of what you can achieve is broadened.

Many standard lathes have beds and stands of cast steel that provide excellent, rigid support. Buy these with confidence. Other lathes suffer from having a good headstock and tailstock mounted on a flimsy bed. These are often made of round or square steel bars, which are less effective than cast-iron or steel beams at dampening vibration. A 3-ft.- (915mm) long, 2-in.- (50mm) diameter bar will vibrate enough to create a significant loss of control and a safety hazard. Lightweight beds made of cast aluminum or sheet steel are even worse; it takes real skill and determination to obtain decent results using such machinery. The solution is to replace the bed with 8-in. (205mm) steel *I* or *U* beams or 4-in. (100mm) by 12-in. (305mm) wood beams, as shown in the drawings at right. The tailstock can then be attached to the bed with either a cam follower or a machine bolt, as shown in the drawing at far right.

Many good small lathes, with well-made headstocks and tailstocks and solid cast-iron beds, are sold on sheet-metal stands. The vibration in these lathes is so great that they are practically useless. In 1977, as a visiting craftsman in Australia, I was confronted by a lathe on a flimsy sheet-metal stand. Even when bolted to the floor, this lathe vibrated so much that it was dangerous. I removed the lathe from its manufactured plinth and fixed it on about a cubic yard of concrete, after which it proved to be superb.

You can buy a lathe without its stand and make a solid frame yourself from 2-in. (50mm) angle iron (3-in. [75mm] angle iron would make the stand even more rigid). The pieces could then be welded or bolted together, and the entire frame bolted to the floor.

If your lathe rattles about, strengthen the stand with crosspieces. If this fails, you might try securing it to a solid stand of heavy wood or steel beams bolted to the floor. A lathe cannot be too heavy or too well anchored.

Lathe Beds

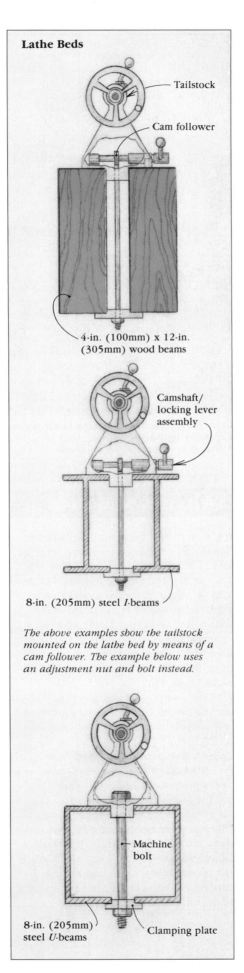

4-in. (100mm) x 12-in. (305mm) wood beams

8-in. (205mm) steel *I*-beams

The above examples show the tailstock mounted on the lathe bed by means of a cam follower. The example below uses an adjustment nut and bolt instead.

8-in. (205mm) steel *U*-beams

Mounting Assemblies

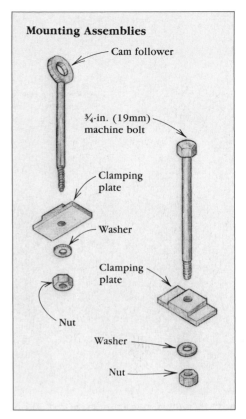

A rear-mounted motor and drive belt. The belt tension is increased by knocking in the wooden wedge under the motor platform and tightening the wing nut—very basic, but effective. The V-belt is readily accessible on this system for changing speeds, but it should be covered for safety.

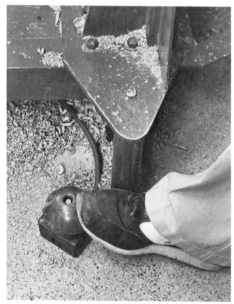

For maximum safety and efficiency, install a foot-operated *on-off* switch.

Switches & Motors

It is vital to be able to turn the lathe off quickly if something goes wrong. Have a switch box with a big red *on-off* button. The button need only be touched lightly to stop the motor. A similar foot switch is available, as shown in the photo at left. Even better, wire your motor with two switches, one on either side of the headstock, so you won't have to cross the firing line of the work in the event of a problem (p. 43).

I have always used a single-phase 1hp electric motor—sealed against dust. This will provide enough power to cope with blocks up to 90 lb. (35kg). If you are unlikely to turn anything larger than a 12-in. (305mm) by 4-in. (100mm) bowl or a newel post, you could get by with ¾hp, but I would still suggest opting for the larger motor. My lathe, with its 1½-in.-(38mm) diameter shaft and 1hp motor, stops and starts in one second. I've used lathes that take 10 to 12 seconds to reach full speed. This is time-consuming and costly if I'm stopping the lathe frequently to inspect progress on a job.

Speeds

Another consideration with any lathe you buy should be the ease with which you can change speeds. On occasion, you may need to slow the lathe down if you're working with unbalanced wood or if you're changing from one type of work to another. On most lathes, the V-belt is moved by hand to change speeds, so be sure that the belt and any tensioning devices are accessible and easy to operate, as they are on the lathe shown in the photo at left. Usually, there are four or five speeds available within the 400 rpm to 2500 rpm range, which should be more than adequate for most turners who will not need to change speeds often. Specific speeds are recommended on p. 69 for centerwork and p. 99 for facework.

Variable-speed systems are better, though they're more expensive. These systems are based on cones or expanding and contracting pulleys that allow you to change lathe speed simply by winding a handle. Some of them run from zero rpm upward, and others give a range of about 1:4 (i.e., 400 to 1600 rpm or 200 to 800 rpm). The advantages of the variable-speed systems are that you can change speeds without stopping the lathe, and you can select the exact speed that you want, rather than having to choose between one speed that's too high and another that's too low. Remember that, to ensure safety, all belts should be kept covered while the lathe is running.

Center Height

I like to be able to see what's happening without bending double, so I prefer to have a center height no lower than my elbow or even 2 in. (50mm) to 3 in. (75mm) above for centerwork. For facework, I prefer the center to be 1 in. (25mm) to 2 in. (50mm) lower. If a number of people are going to use the same machine, it's better to fix the center height high—at, say, 55 in. (1400mm) from the floor—and build up platforms for the short people rather than giving the tall ones backaches. I use green boards that I'm seasoning to stand on, because I have plenty of them around. This is not only for any shorter people who happen to use my lathe, but also to adjust my own height for different jobs. You'll notice that lathe manufacturers cater to turners below 5 ft. 2 in. (157cm) tall, so I've blocked up my machines on 8-in. (205mm) steel beams to correct the problem.

Look for a tool rest that can be positioned completely around and inside a bowl that has been mounted on a faceplate. On many lathes this would present a problem, but on this Harrison short-bed lathe, the 14-in.-(355mm) long rest can be swung around by releasing the two locking levers, and will provide quick support close to any area of the bowl.

Tool Rests

The tool rest is an integral part of the lathe. It is essential for supporting the tool as it cuts the wood. It should be easily adjustable to at least ½ in. (13mm) above and below center height, and at any position along the bed. Easy tool-rest adjustment is important because the rest must be moved frequently to support the tool as close to the work as possible. The farther the tool rest is away from the tool's cutting edge, the greater effect the downward force of the revolving wood exerts on the unsupported tip (see p. 48 for more on leverage). The tool rest must lock down securely when tightened.

Tool rests come in many shapes. The ones I use have two quick-action locking levers; one controls the height and angle of the rest, the other locks it in position on the bed. (Avoid systems that require wrenches and often three hands and a tail. Life is too short.) The rests on my lathes can be positioned ¾ in. (19mm) above and below center height and can be readily moved to work on both the outside and inside of a large bowl held at its base on a faceplate as shown in the photos above. This isn't possible on many lathes but is worth looking for.

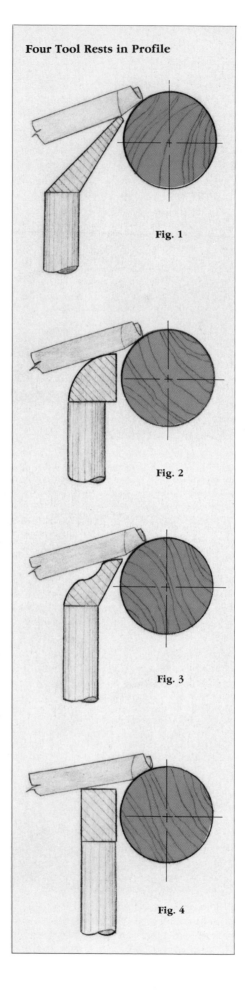

Four Tool Rests in Profile

Fig. 1

Fig. 2

Fig. 3

Fig. 4

The rest at Fig. 1 in the drawing at left is the shape I normally use. Its edge can be moved right into the work, leaving space for fingers below. Leverage is reduced to a minimum, affording the turner more control. With the rests at Fig. 2 and Fig. 3, the fulcrum moves back across the rest as the tool is angled up to cut, increasing leverage against the edge. The advantage of the rest at Fig. 3 is that the groove provides a useful guide along which to slide a finger—this helps control the distance of the cutting edge from the rest. Avoid the square, flat-topped rest at Fig. 4; the moment the tool is angled up to cut, the fulcrum is moved to the edge farthest away from the work. This increases the leverage and results in a loss of control.

The tool rest should be solidly built. The vertical shaft should be at least ¾ in. (19mm) in diameter to provide adequate support for the horizontal rest. Few of the manufactured rests I've encountered are sturdy enough, apart from those on the big patternmakers' machines. The worst are made of pressed sheet steel and are flexible enough to be dangerous. If your lathe has a tool rest of this sort, you could weld a bar to the horizontal member to strengthen it, but it's best to have another made up from more substantial steel. Keep a file handy to smooth nicks on the rest, so the tool can be moved evenly along it.

In general, it is best to work with the tool over the vertical shaft of the rest to minimize vibration. I have two rests, 7 in. (180mm) and 14 in. (355mm) long. You can manage with one rest, 5 in. (125mm) to 7 in. (180mm) long, but be prepared to move it more often. A longer rest is convenient, especially for turning spindles or broad, flat discs (such as platters). For large runs of long spindles, it is common practice to make up a rest with two or more supports to eliminate vibration and avoid endless readjustments. There are also specialized rests available that are curved to fit bowl curves. These are usually flat-topped and are fine to use with scrapers because the tool is held flat on the rest, but I've never found them easy to use with gouges. My standard rests have always served me well, so I have never bothered to acquire a curved one.

This long tool rest has two support shafts, which makes it useful for turning large runs of long spindles.

Choosing a Lathe

Small, well-designed and well-constructed lathes are available that will cope with the demands of most woodturners. Look for a lathe that will swing 12 in. (305mm)— that's a center height of 6 in. (150mm) above the bed—and accept 36-in.-(915mm) long stock between centers. And make sure it measures up to the standards I've discussed. Beware of the many lightweight lathes competing for the amateur market. These have small shafts— less than 1 in. (25mm) in diameter—and flimsy sheet-metal rests, beds or stands that flex and never give the turner a chance. Manufacturers often overlook the stresses involved with turning wood and the vibrations arising from lathe speeds that are much higher than for metalworking.

Until now, I've been referring mainly to small lathes. They do come larger, and it's worth keeping an eye open for a secondhand patternmaker's or metalworking lathe. These often weigh a ton or more and so they eliminate practically all vibration. All you need is space and the strength and ingenuity to move them.

Every lathe will present problems and options that you'll have to consider. The large lathes are wonderful machines for turning large, heavy or off-center work, but frequently they can be adapted to small-scale production or custom work. If you don't need the power of a 3hp (or larger) motor and a mammoth drive shaft, you can easily replace both and end up with a 1hp motor and 1½-in. (38mm) shaft in a good, solid machine.

This is an example of an excellent, custom-built lathe stand. The welded angle-iron frame is bolted to the floor for rigidity. The belt tensioning bracket on the motor is readily accessible and the *on-off* switch is easy to punch at a moment's notice.

If you fail to find a suitable machine in your local tool store or through woodworking magazines or catalogs, try a local engineering works; they may be able to make up the parts for much the same cost as a brand-name lathe. Such a lathe might not look so elegant but could work better than anything you could buy ready-made. I recommend training on a small machine before moving up, if and when you can justify the expense and effort that will be involved.

Fixings:
Drives, Faceplates & Chucks

2

Before a piece of wood can be turned, it must be mounted on the lathe so that power is transmitted to it efficiently.

There should be no play or chatter in the headstock connection or tailstock support. All kinds of attachments are made that purport to achieve this and many do. I shall make no attempt to analyze every weird and wonderful device; over the years I have tried many and find the following ones suit me. Among the vast array of commercially available fixings, I always look for systems that are quick and easy to use, and do not impose too many restrictions on the design of an object.

Devices for holding wood on the lathe are divided into several categories: drive centers, faceplates and chucks. Drive centers always require support from a tail center. Power is transmitted through wedge-shaped spurs that bite into the wood; work is held tightly against these spurs by pressure from the tail center. Faceplates are flat metal discs that screw onto the drive shaft. Wood is attached to the faceplate by one or more screws. Chucks come in many forms: Mechanical chucks grip by expanding into, or clamping around, the work; jam-fit chucks are either turned out of wood to fit work that is jammed into or over them or made of metal, in which case the wood is turned to fit. Always ensure that any chuck or faceplate is wound fully onto the drive shaft before switching on the lathe. Failure to do this can cause the fixing to spin on so tightly that removing it will take a great deal of time, effort and ingenuity.

Most of the fixings I describe in this chapter have applications to a wide variety of work. For example, there are several chucks that can be used to hold centerwork on the lathe by only one end so that the other can be worked (typical jobs include eggcups, goblets and small boxes). And it is often desirable to rough-turn bowls between centers, rather than on a faceplate. As a rule, centerwork (the grain lies parallel to the rotational axis of the lathe) is held on the lathe by drive and tail centers or a chuck. Facework (the grain lies at a right angle to the rotational axis) is held by a faceplate or chuck. Do not attempt to hold centerwork on a faceplate. Screws don't grip well in end grain, as shown in the drawing at right. Faceplates should be reserved for facework, where the grain alignment is ideal for screws.

It is always advisable to cut any wood as close as possible to its end shape—or at least to a symmetrical and balanced form—prior to mounting it on the lathe. Cut discs for facework and squares or octagons for centerwork. If you don't have a bandsaw or hand-held electric jigsaw, cut facework with a series of flat edges so that the blank is as near to round as possible. Square blocks for facework sound like propellers and are about as dangerous. Before starting the lathe, rotate the wood by hand to ensure it is clear of the tool rest and bed. With large blocks, check for balance. If one side gravitates to the bottom when the lathe is stopped, the block should either be trimmed or a slow speed should be selected to cope with the vibration.

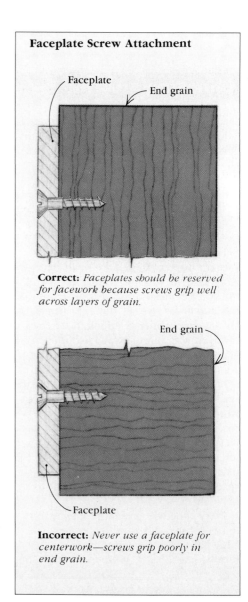

Faceplate Screw Attachment

Faceplate

End grain

Correct: *Faceplates should be reserved for facework because screws grip well across layers of grain.*

End grain

Faceplate

Incorrect: *Never use a faceplate for centerwork—screws grip poorly in end grain.*

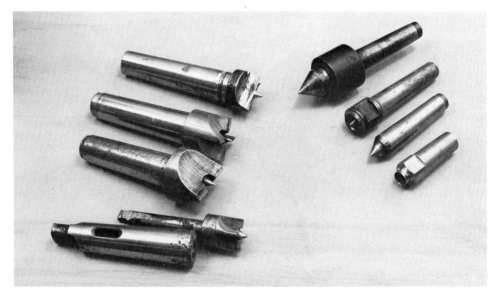

Insert the morse-taper shaft of a spur-drive center firmly into the hollow drive shaft.

At left are two-spur and four-spur drive centers. At lower left is a No. 1 morse-taper four-spur drive and a sleeve. At right are four styles of tail center commonly used for centerwork, from top to bottom: a live center, a cup center, a dead center and a hollow center.

Drives

Spur drives are the simplest and most common way of fixing centerwork on the lathe. The spurs bite and hold well in end grain, but must be used with a tail center that pressures the work against them. Spur drives have a morse-taper shank that is placed in the end of the hollow drive shaft. Drive and tail centers are available with morse tapers in sizes ranging from No. 1 to No. 3 (small to large). If your spur drive center has a small morse taper and your shaft is bored to a larger size, you can buy a sleeve to allow you to use the smaller taper in the larger shaft. Or you could turn a sleeve in wood. Ensure that you can remove the spur drive easily. If the shaft is hollow, you can insert a rod through the shaft and tap the drive out. If your lathe doesn't have a hollow drive shaft, it will probably have a collar that threads onto the shaft before the spur drive is inserted. To remove the drive, lock the drive shaft with a wrench, bar or lock pin and unscrew the collar. If the shaft has no collar (and you can't fit one to it), lock the shaft and rotate the spur drive with Vise-grip pliers to loosen it.

Spur drives come with two or four flat spurs arranged around a central cone, which locates and holds the center of the work. The cone should be sharp and stand proud of the spurs by about $\frac{1}{8}$ in. (3mm) to $\frac{1}{4}$ in. (6mm). The edges of the spurs should be kept sharp, sharpened on one side only and at about a 45° angle. If the angle is too long and chisel-like, you risk splitting the wood when applying tailstock pressure. I prefer to use two-spur instead of four-spur drives. Four-spur drives require a flat surface at 90° to the axis of the lathe to grip satisfactorily, while two-spur drives will bite into almost any kind of surface. Perhaps the major advantage of a two-spur drive is that, when I rough-turn the outside shape of a bowl between centers, I can tilt the wood around the spur to expose certain grain patterns or adjust the plane of a free-form rim.

The job of the tail center is to hold one end of the work and to keep it pressured against the drive center. Tail centers are generally cone shaped, and have a morse taper to fit the tailstock. They come as either live (revolving) or dead (static) centers. Dead tail centers are solid and tend to wear away or burn into the wood, loosening the fixing and causing chatter and play. The likelihood of this happening is greatly increased if the drive and tail centers are not absolutely in line and true. Some of this friction can be reduced by using a little grease or oil on the tip of the cone, but the wood still tends to wear away, which means that the tailstock needs to be wound in constantly. I prefer to use a live center that has the cone mounted in a bearing. This allows the center to revolve with the work, and prevents the burning and loosening that occurs with dead centers. But even the bearings in live centers can wear and develop play. If this happens, it is no good winding in the tailstock because the play is in the bearing. So, if you buy a revolving center, be sure it's a good one. I have used an inexpensive Czechoslovakian live center for ten years without trouble. There are live centers available with removable cones, so that you can have a range of center points for

Two-spur drives work well on irregular surfaces while four-spur drives need a flat surface at 90° to the axis to grip properly.

various purposes. Like many of the fixings on the market, they suffer from poor workmanship. The removable cones tend to wear rapidly and develop play. And the cone has a habit of staying attached to the wood, rather than the tail center, when the work is removed from the lathe.

Cup centers and hollow centers are variations on the cone, as shown in the photo at upper left. The cup center has a greater area to bear on the end grain, and the ring prevents the long point of the cone from splitting the wood if too much tail-center pressure is applied. The hollow center is like a cup center, but without the cone. You'll need a hollow center for such projects as drilling long auger holes in lamp bases.

To mount centerwork on a spur drive, present one end of the stock to the spurs and tap the other end with a mallet. The tool rest supports the hand holding the stock. Then wind in the tail center to the center of the stock.

To mount a length of wood between centers, you can tap the wood against the drive center to wedge the spurs into the wood, or you can apply pressure by winding in the tail center. I favor tapping the wood onto the spurs because it is slightly faster and it puts less stress on the wood which, if it's thin, could bow with heavy tail-center pressure. Present one end of the wood to the drive center and tap the other end with a mallet. (Use the tool rest as a support for the hand holding the wood.) Wind in the tail center as tightly as possible by hand and then ease off a fraction. (Lathe sounds can tell you when the tail center needs adjustment; if the pitch changes, it may only mean that the center needs winding in or backing off.)

Production spindle turners often have their lathes running continuously and have developed a method of mounting stock on a spinning lathe. The end of the spindle blank is rested against the center cone of the spur drive and the tail center is wound in lightly to support the other end. With the stock held between the two centers, the slight friction will cause the wood to revolve, even though it doesn't contact the spurs of the drive. (When doing this, it's important that the drive cone protrudes at least ³⁄₁₆ in. [5mm] beyond the spurs.) If the wood is off-center at this stage, it can be stopped easily with one hand and tapped true. Once centered, the tail center is wound in, forcing the wood into the spurs. When the spindle has been turned, the tail center is unwound to release pressure and the finished piece is jerked off the drive center by hand.

One problem with spur-drive fixings, particularly when turning heavy blocks, is that the drive revolves faster than the wood when the motor is started. This can cause the spur to bore into the end grain, failing to grip. To avoid this, bandsaw a ¹⁄₁₆-in.- (2mm) deep slot in the drive end of the spindle to take the flat edges of the spur. Two-spur drives require only one bandsaw cut; four-spur drives require two. Or spin the stock toward you as you switch on the motor so that the wood is revolving as the motor picks up speed. (Make sure to pull your hand well clear of the wood.) It will be easier for the spurs to grip and rotate the wood without boring in than if they have to start from a dead stop.

The main disadvantage of mounting work between centers is that you can't turn the wood at the points where it is supported. This won't matter for such work as chair rails, where the ends fit in mortises and can remain rough, but if you want a smooth finish, you'll have to sand the wood by hand.

Many turners do not consider mounting facework between centers, even for the initial external shaping. But for many jobs, the disadvantage of not being able to work the tail-center face freely is outweighed by the advantages. It's quick and easy to mount a block of wood between centers, especially if it has natural bark edges or is rough and uneven. Such irregular blocks are much safer if held between centers than when balanced on a faceplate. Perhaps the major advantage is that the block can be aligned precisely. This is essential if you are manipulating grain patterns in a decorative bowl while the outside shape is being turned; it's easy to stop the lathe to adjust the axis of a block, just by shifting the position of the tail center. Once the rough exterior form has been turned, the piece can be transferred to a chuck for hollowing. To ensure a good grip for the spur drive in facework, and to keep the spurs from boring into the wood, cut a shallow, central slot, using a carver's chisel and mallet.

Bandsaw a ¹⁄₁₆-in.- (2mm) deep slot to keep the spur drive from boring into the end grain (above). To grip facework (right), cut a shallow slot using a carver's chisel.

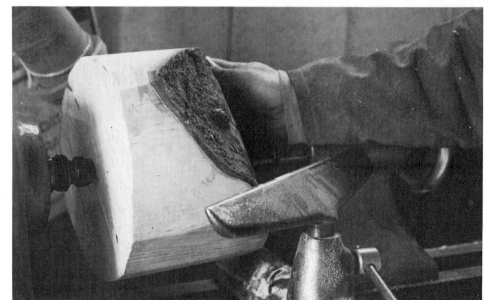

Facework can also be mounted between centers. It's easy to mount blocks quickly and precisely and uneven blocks, such as this 9½-in. (240mm) by 5-in. (125mm) holly bowl blank, are much safer if held between centers than on a faceplate.

Faceplates

Faceplates are flat metal discs with one or more screw holes for attaching work. Faceplates are screwed onto the threads on either the inboard or outboard end of the drive shaft. (All of mine are shown mounted inboard.) Because screws do not grip well in end grain, I always use chucks, never faceplates, for mounting centerwork. Screws grip well across the grain, so facework can usually be held securely by only one face, without the tail-center support, allowing free access to the inside of a bowl or platter.

There are two kinds of faceplates, center-screw and standard. Center-screw faceplates have a single center screw and discs are attached while the faceplate is on the lathe. Standard faceplates, which have holes for two or more screws, are screwed to the wood before mounting the faceplate on the lathe. Because wood is attached to a faceplate by only one face, there are dangers that relate to a basic law of physics: Every force has an equal and opposite reaction. When you sit on one end of a see-saw, for example, the other end will go up just as quickly as you go down. In woodturning, if a tool is cutting with strong forward pressure parallel to the axis on the edge of a large disc mounted on a small faceplate (Fig. 1 in the drawing below), the disc is certain to come loose as it pivots on the small faceplate. If you increase the diameter of the faceplate (Fig. 2) there is much more support for the disc and less danger of its coming loose. The basic rule is to use a faceplate that supports as much of the work as possible. A 10-in.- (255mm) diameter by 2-in.- (50mm) thick disc can be held quite easily on a 7-in.- (180mm) diameter center-screw faceplate with only a ⅜-in.- (10mm) to ½-in.- (13mm) long No. 12 or No. 14 wood screw. A 4-in.- (100mm) diameter faceplate would be much less effective and would require a longer and heavier screw.

Many of the screw holes were drilled in the large standard faceplate (mounted on the drive shaft) for specific jobs, such as 14-in.- (355mm) bread boards or clock frames.

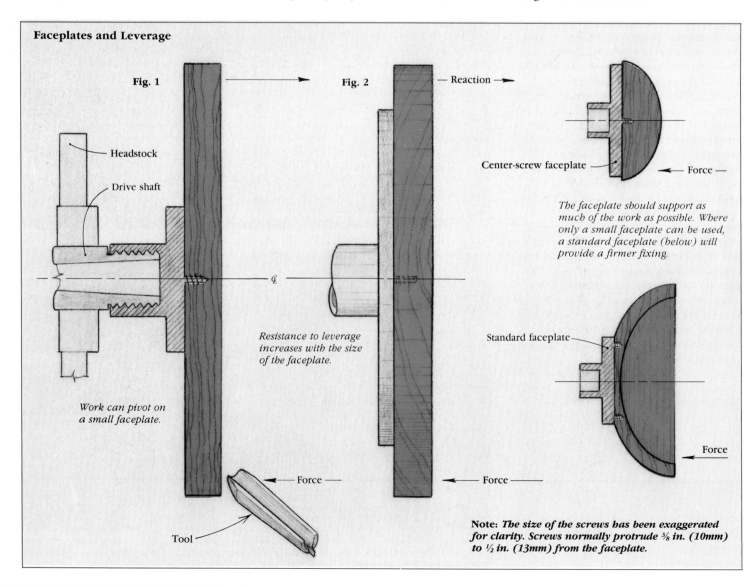

Faceplates and Leverage

Fig. 1

Headstock

Drive shaft

₵

Work can pivot on a small faceplate.

Tool

Force

Fig. 2

Reaction

Resistance to leverage increases with the size of the faceplate.

Force

Center-screw faceplate

Force

The faceplate should support as much of the work as possible. Where only a small faceplate can be used, a standard faceplate (below) will provide a firmer fixing.

Standard faceplate

Force

Note: *The size of the screws has been exaggerated for clarity. Screws normally protrude ⅜ in. (10mm) to ½ in. (13mm) from the faceplate.*

There are two common methods of mounting a disc on a center-screw faceplate. First, drill a pilot hole in the center of the disc (see p. 60 for finding centers) slightly shallower than the length of the screw and the same diameter as the shank. With the lathe turned off, lock the drive shaft to keep it from rotating and screw the disc onto the center screw. Or, you can present the disc to the screw with one hand and rotate the drive shaft by turning the faceplate or handwheel with the other hand until the disc rests tightly against the surface of the faceplate.

A flat or slightly concave surface on the bottom of the disc is essential to prevent it from pivoting on the screw of a center-screw faceplate. Friction between the bottom of the disc and the faceplate will help keep the wood in place. Where there is a gap and the wood can rock on the faceplate, you can use a thin wedge to eliminate play. But this is not a practice for the novice because wedges can loosen and fly out (inviting disaster).

Experienced turners will often mount discs on a center-screw faceplate with the lathe turned on. Though this is a quick method and I use it frequently, it's also not a technique for the novice. Present the disc to the faceplate, lining up the pilot hole with the screw. Don't grip the disc with your fingers but rest it on your flat, open hand (as you would feed a horse), as shown in the photos at right, and give a slight push with the heel of your palm as the revolving screw bites into the hole. The weight of the wood and pressure from your hand will cause the disc to rotate

more slowly than the faceplate, so the screw will feed right in, drawing the disc against the faceplate.

With practice, discs can be flicked onto the revolving screw like this in a moment, but the largest size I would ever mount this way would be 12 in. (305mm) in diameter by 2 in. (50mm) thick. The weight of a larger disc will usually cause the screw to spin in the hole and fail to grip; these discs must be screwed on with the lathe at rest. Very small, light discs can be flicked on the lathe, but they require more pressure from your hand. They can be held on with a very short screw—only ⅛ in. (3mm) long.

I have three center-screw faceplates of 4 in. (100mm), 7 in. (180mm) and 8 in. (205mm) in diameter, all with No. 12 wood screws protruding ½ in. (13mm). I also have plywood discs (⅛ in. [3mm], ¼ in. [6mm] and ⅜ in. [10mm]) to place between the work and the faceplate to reduce the effective length of the screw to as little as ⅛ in. (3mm). These have a central hole that fits loosely over the faceplate screw. This system enables me to turn 10-in.- (255mm) diameter by 1½-in.- (38mm) thick plates on a 7-in. (180mm) faceplate with a single screw protruding ⅜ in. (10mm), which means I can keep the base thin. (A longer screw would require that I leave more wood in the base, which would upset the design.) However, if I have a catch and the plate loosens, I can remove the plywood disc and allow the screw to penetrate further into the base. This might mean a thicker base than intended but it could salvage the project.

To mount a disc on a center-screw faceplate, align the screw with the pre-drilled pilot hole (top left). Then either rotate the disc onto the screw, with the drive shaft locked, or rotate the faceplate to thread the disc on. To flick work onto a spinning lathe, present the disc to the faceplate, rested on your open hand (top). Give a slight push with the heel of your hand as the revolving screw bites into the hole (bottom).

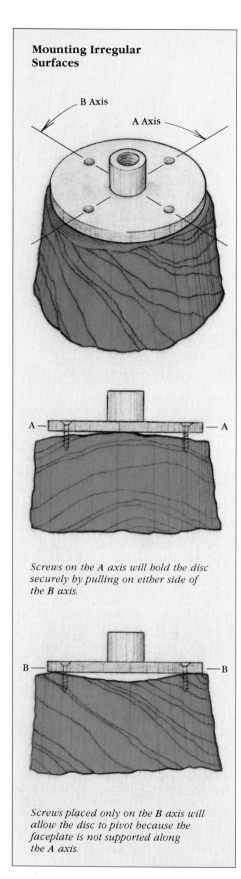

Mounting Irregular Surfaces

Screws on the A axis will hold the disc securely by pulling on either side of the B axis.

Screws placed only on the B axis will allow the disc to pivot because the faceplate is not supported along the A axis.

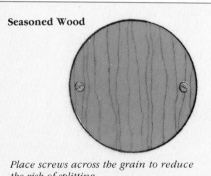

Remove standard faceplates from the shaft to insert the screws. Drill pilot holes to avoid splitting the work (top). Remount the work with washers under the screw heads to reduce the length of the screws.

Seasoned Wood

Place screws across the grain to reduce the risk of splitting.

Green Wood

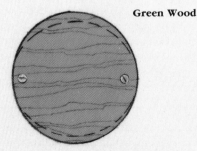

Place screws along the grain, where their position will not interfere with the wood's shrinkage.

A more secure method of attaching facework is to use a standard faceplate. You must remove the faceplate from the lathe to insert two or more wood screws through its back into the wood. I use No. 10 wood screws, which fit the faceplate holes exactly. Usually, I find two screws sufficient, even on blocks up to 15 in. (380mm) in diameter by 6 in. (150mm) thick or 18 in. (460mm) in diameter by 4 in. (100mm) thick. When roughing-down larger pieces, I'll use longer screws to penetrate ⅝ in. (15mm). Large blocks, say 18 in. (460mm) in diameter by 6 in. (150mm) thick, need four screws for safety. Once a shape has been roughed, I remount the work using metal washers under the screw heads to reduce the effective length of the screws, as shown in the photo at left.

A flat surface on the base of the disc is less critical with standard faceplates than with center-screw faceplates because the screws can lie on either side of any high point as shown in the drawing at far left. Screws on the *A* axis will hold the disc securely by pulling on either side of the *B* axis. Screws on the *B* axis only, with no support on the *A* axis, will not secure the disc to the faceplate.

If the weight or shape of a disc make it unbalanced, it's safer to use more screws. Always check a heavy or irregular block by rotating it first by hand. Rotate it toward you and let it swing freely through a couple of revolutions to see where it comes to rest. If the uneven weight of the block brings it rapidly to the same position, use a slow lathe speed and check that the screws are tightened. Large flying blocks are an unpredictable hazard.

When turning seasoned wood, place the screws across the grain, as shown in the drawing at left, to reduce the risk of splitting. However, if you are turning green wood, which will be remounted when dry (as when rough-turning bowls), the screws must be placed along the grain, where the shrinkage will be the least.

Remember that you can always use the tail center with any faceplate to provide extra support, but it must be true. This will restrict the use of many tools, but with heavy blocks it is safer, at least until some of the bulk has been removed.

Three-jaw chucks are excellent for gripping an irregular shape, though the protruding jaws are dangerous.

Chucks

There are a good many chucks on the market that look marvellous but somehow fail to make the grade. Some must be rejected outright while others have only very limited use. Because most are sold to amateur or part-time turners, the manufacturers' main concern appears to be to keep the price down in a competitive market. This is achieved through slipshod workmanship that often results in the chuck's failing to do its intended job properly. There's nothing worse than a sloppy tool that doesn't quite work. Many professional turners have well-engineered copies made and soon recoup the additional expense.

Also, many of the manufactured chucks, even the well-made ones, impose severe limitations on design. What I require more than anything is to keep my design options open for as long as possible so that I can make small alterations. Most commercially available chucks seem to conspire against this. I look forward to the time when some manufacturer comes out with a whole range of lathe equipment that will allow maximum flexibility combined with speed and efficiency of operation. For now, you must be prepared to make many of your own devices. It is more important to decide what you want as an end product and make the tools necessary to achieve it than to work within the limitations imposed by the available chucks.

The Jacob's chuck is the only way to grip thin work such as this ¼-in.- (6mm) square spillikin blank. The tail center only provides stability.

Jaw chucks

The jaw chuck is a metal-engineer's tool with many applications for the woodturner. It has two sets of interchangeable jaws, one internal and one external, that are adjusted with a key to grip the work. Its major disadvantage is that it is dangerous—the exposed jaws can catch clothing and knuckles (which usually means blood). Because the jaw chuck contacts the wood at only three or four points, it doesn't grip nearly as well as a spigot chuck (p. 21) or jam-fit chuck (p. 24), which grip all around the wood. Catches, when they occur, are usually disastrous (with wood flying) because of the tenuous fixing. But most turners I know use jaw chucks a lot, and consider the possibility of the occasional missing hunk of flesh worth the risk. Its advantages are that it's quick and easy to use, it will grip an irregular shape (such as the foot of a rough-turned bowl that has distorted in drying or a small rough-cut disc) and no screw holes will be left in any surface.

I try to avoid working blocks over 4 in. (100mm) long without tail-center support because of the leverage. When I have a long cylinder to mount, I'll often use a three-jaw chuck to grip one end quickly and accurately, and use the tailstock to support the other end. The jaw chuck grips well, with none of the problems encountered with spur drives spinning and boring into end grain. I also use a small Jacob's (or lathe) chuck when turning fine spindles, such as the one shown above. In this case, a spur drive would be too large for the ¼-in.- (6mm) square blank, which would split with the pressure of the drive-center cone.

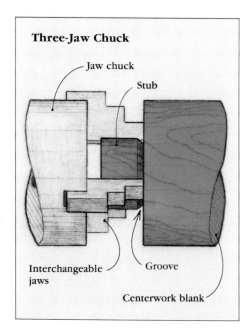

Three-Jaw Chuck

- Jaw chuck
- Stub
- Interchangeable jaws
- Groove
- Centerwork blank

Tightening a self-centering three-jaw chuck on a box blank. The stub will eventually be turned to a tall finial on the lid of the box.

The most commonly used jaw chuck has three jaws and is self-centering. I have two chucks, with capacities of 4 in. (100mm) and 5½ in. (140mm) in diameter. A self-centering four-jaw chuck would be even better, but these are often difficult to obtain and are more expensive. Usually the jaws on a four-jaw chuck are adjusted separately, which is slow and might be fine for metal engineering, but not for any job I've encountered in woodturning.

I have found jaw chucks excellent for all kinds of production work, though I use them less now for centerwork since the advent of the much safer spigot chuck. I used to make all my small boxes, about 2 in. (50mm) to 3 in. (75mm) in diameter, using my 4-in. (100mm) jaw chuck; the photo above shows a lid blank ready for turning. The stub will eventually be turned to a tall finial on the lid. There is a tendency for the wood fibers to pull out of the end grain as the jaws tighten around the stub. To overcome this, I usually turn a groove at the base of the foot, as shown in the drawing at top left.

Generally, I find jaw chucks most useful when making bowls. I rough-out the form between centers and leave a foot, as shown in the photos on pp. 22-23. The bowl is held by the foot in the jaw chuck while it is hollowed. The jaws grip on very little wood, so careful cutting is vital—too much force will put pressure on the jaws and the wood will split away (a flying bowl). The less wood held by the jaws, the greater the

risk, especially as you work farther away from the chuck. Once the inside is turned I can mount it over the expanding jaws to work on the base. I leave a shoulder on the inside of the bowl for the jaws to abut, as shown in the photo at top left on p. 23. When expanding the jaws to grip the inside of a bowl, the wood will flex a little, providing a margin of safety against splitting. Because this will distort the form (it will return to normal when the pressure of the jaws is released), I finish only the foot and lower curve, and leave the shaping of the rim and upper wall until after the bowl has been reversed and remounted for final turning and finishing.

A jaw chuck is also useful for gripping irregular, small-diameter blocks so that the face can be quickly turned to fit another chuck. I use this technique when turning a quantity of small bowls—less than 5½ in. (140mm) in diameter, which is the maximum my chuck will take.

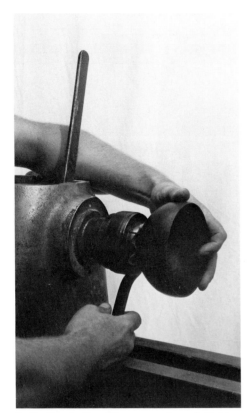

Lock the shaft with a wrench and tighten the spigot chuck with another wrench. Use a piece of cloth between the chuck and the finished foot to avoid damaging the bowl.

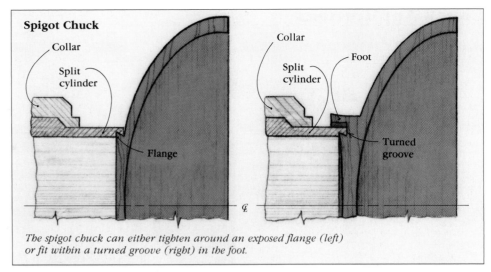

The spigot chuck can either tighten around an exposed flange (left) or fit within a turned groove (right) in the foot.

When fitting a box blank to a spigot chuck ensure that the turned shoulder abuts the jaws to improve the grip.

Spigot chucks

Although spigot chucks were originally designed for small centerwork containers, they are also excellent for small plates, bowls and other facework. A spigot chuck consists of a split cylinder inside a collar that is tightened with wrenches to close around a very short flange. As the collar is screwed on, it meets a taper on the split cylinder that forces the jaws in. It will grip on a flange as short as 1/16 in. (2mm). The spigot chuck works well with centerwork because the long grain runs into the jaws. But it presents problems with facework, when the grain lies at 90° to the axis. Because the grip is around such a small-diameter flange, there is a tendency for the wood to split, so the chuck will not cope with too much weight. I wouldn't mount any facework block larger than 6 in. (150mm) by 2½ in. (65mm) in a 1½-in. (38mm) spigot chuck, or 8 in. (205mm) by 3 in. (75mm) in a 2-in. (50mm) chuck. But even with the larger chuck, the slightest catch or forward pressure while cutting will cause most woods to split from the flange.

The major attraction of the spigot chuck is that it leaves little or no scar on the wood. But on the other hand, the flange must be turned accurately because there is little margin for error. It should be turned to as large a diameter as possible because the farther the jaws are pulled in, the more risk of damage occuring to the wood and, with facework, the greater the likelihood of splitting as the jaws cut into the end-grain surface.

I use spigot chucks regularly, in conjunction with the three-jaw chuck, to make bowls up to 12 in. (305mm) in diameter. I turn the bowls almost completely on the jaw chuck and transfer them to the spigot chuck for finishing the lower curve and foot, as shown in the photos on pp. 22-23. This gives me maximum freedom to shape the foot. With small bowls, up to 4 in. (100mm) in diameter, I finish the foot while turning the outside shape so the bowl can be remounted in the spigot chuck and the inside finished. I place a small piece of cloth (an old wool shirt is ideal) between the spigot chuck and the foot to protect the finished surface. Spigot chucks are safe to use and I wouldn't be without them.

1 You can rough-turn a bowl on a three-jaw chuck first and then transfer it to a spigot chuck for final shaping and finishing. The exterior form of this 6-in.- (150mm) diameter by 3-in.- (75mm) deep black locust bowl has been turned on a faceplate. The foot is then mounted in the jaw chuck so the inside can be hollowed.

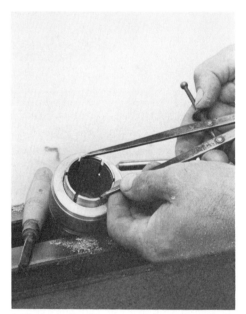

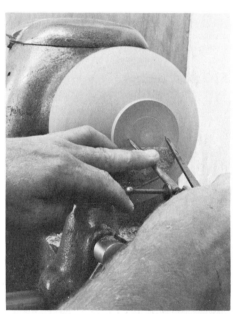

3 Measure the diameter of the split cylinder on the spigot chuck with dividers (above left) and transfer the measurement to the base of the bowl while it's still mounted on the jaw chuck. Only the left point of the dividers should contact the wood, as described on p. 64. The dividers are centered when both points are aligned on the scribed mark (above right).

2 Once the inside has been rough-shaped, the bowl can be reversed for turning the base. Note that a shoulder has been turned on the inside of the bowl (far left) for the jaws of the chuck to abut—creating a firm fixing. Because the expanding jaws of the chuck will distort the shape of the bowl slightly, leave the final shaping of the rim and outside wall until later.

4 Cut a shallow groove, about ⅛ in. (3mm) wide, on the scribed mark using a ⅛-in. (3mm) square-edge scraper (left). Then remount the bowl in the spigot chuck for final turning and finishing of all inside and outside surfaces. The spigot chuck will grip on a flange as short as ¹⁄₁₆ in. (2mm), so the base of the bowl can be turned quite thin, providing maximum flexibility in the design.

The rim of the bowl fits into the innermost tapered recess in the chuck. A slight vacuum is created when the bowl is pressed into the turned groove.

Jam-fit chucks for centerwork can be made from short bits left over from previous turnings. The rim of the work should abut the shoulder of the chuck for the form to run true. The shallow tapered flange on this chuck was turned down until it fit the inside of the box perfectly.

A 12-in. (305mm) ash bowl is mounted in a jam-fit chuck so that the base can be finished. This bowl was held first on a faceplate for external rough-shaping. It was then held by its foot in a three-jaw chuck, hollowed and finished (except for the foot). This multiple chucking technique offers unlimited design options for the base.

Jam-fit chucks

I have dozens of jam-fit chucks and use them frequently for turning the bases of bowls, boxes and scoop handles. The facework chucks are turned from waste discs and bowls or platters that failed to make the grade earlier in their careers. The one shown in the photograph at left is typical. Jam-fit chucks for centerwork are made from short bits left over from centerwork turnings as shown in the photo of the box at bottom left.

I make jam-fit chucks as I need them for a particular project so that the rim of the work fits tightly to a shoulder turned in the chuck. The flanges, or rabbets, on these chucks are turned with a very slight taper (ideally of 1° or 2°) to ensure a good fit. Although I occasionally jam-fit work over a taper because it is quicker, it is preferable to fit the piece inside a turned groove in the chuck whenever possible. In the facework bowls at A and C, and the centerwork forms at E and F in the drawing on the facing page, the grip is around the form, rather than pushing out from within and the work is securely contained. In the forms fitted around a taper (B and D), the rim could easily split if the work is pushed onto a taper of too large an angle. In addition, there is always a risk that work will come loose during cutting or sanding. If enclosed, the rim of the work may rattle around within the groove of the chuck and possibly sustain surface damage, but should remain intact. (Such damage can be repaired easily by hand-sanding.) If fitted over a taper, however, there will be no such external restraint on the rim and the work could fly outward with centrifugal force, possibly disintegrating. For extra security, I arrange the tool rest across the face of the work while turning, as shown in the photo at left, or keep a supporting hand on the work while sanding.

Jam-fit chucks for centerwork are mounted in either spigot, cup or jaw chucks. Facework chucks are attached to center-screw or standard faceplates. My smaller chucks, up to 12 in. (305mm) in diameter, attach to a center-screw faceplate so they can be removed easily. This is especially useful if a bowl is jammed in tightly and needs help entering the world. If this occurs, remove the faceplate from the lathe (so you don't weaken the grip of the screw) and tap the rim of the chuck. (I use a light hammer or the lathe shaft wrench.) The bowl should drop out. With a really good fit, a vacuum is created when the bowl is pressed onto the chuck, and what appears to be a risky fitting is in fact quite strong. Remember that the best fit always comes from a very slight taper. Too steep a taper will either split the work or allow it to jam in quickly and, just as quickly, pop out.

Many people have problems mounting an object in a jam-fit chuck so it runs true rather than wobbling off-center. It's all a matter of practice, as usual. Work is mounted with the chuck on the lathe. It should go easily into the chuck at first and gradually become tighter as it is pushed gently forward. When mounting small centerwork, such as the 2-in.- (50mm) to 3-in.- (75mm) diameter box in the photo at lower left on the facing page, I keep the lathe running, and ease the work onto the taper until the stub grips the work and rotates it. I use one or both hands around the work to center it so that it runs true, and then apply pressure to the end to ease it farther onto the taper until it abuts the shoulder of the chuck, being careful not to split the work. If the rim of the work doesn't quite reach the shoulder of the chuck, I can jerk the work off the rotating lathe, cut away more of the tapered flange and repeat the process. Larger objects, such as salad bowls, are more difficult to center. If you can get the rim to abut the shoulder of the chuck, as shown at *A, B, D* and *E* in the drawing at right, it will run true, but this is difficult to achieve if you can't see what's happening inside. Such jobs *(A, C, E* and *F)* must be fitted with the lathe stopped. I rotate the chuck by hand once the job is fitted and note any eccentricity by watching the top of the form. I tap any higher portion with the heel of my hand to bring that part farther into the chuck. Sometimes this will cause another part to ease out so I have to tap that section. Eventually, the whole form runs true. Another problem can occur when a bowl that has been finished, except for the base, is mounted in a jam-fit chuck. Sanding will often make the form slightly oval because the long grain is removed faster than end grain. Such a bowl will never fit the chuck properly or run absolutely true. Fit it to the chuck as near as possible and fair the new surface into the old as you cut. A slight eccentricity will be difficult to discern, even when you know it's there.

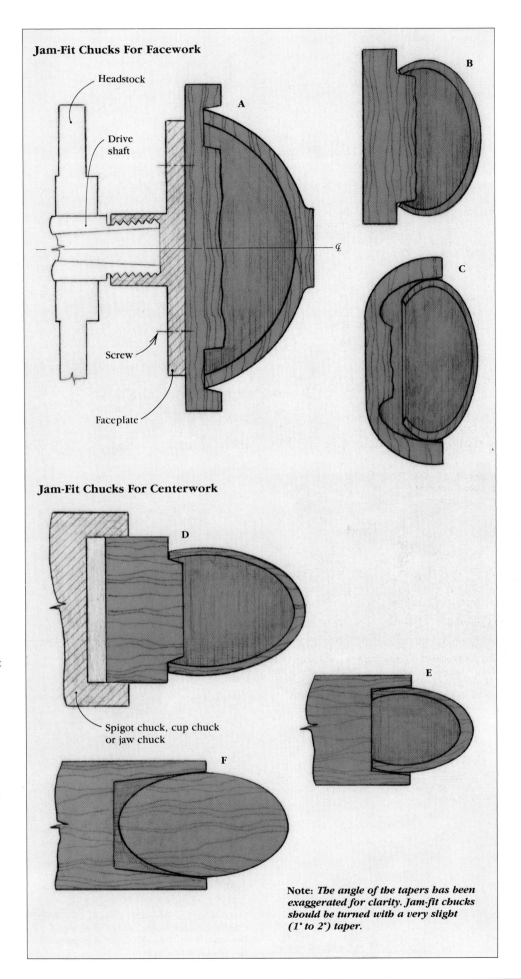

Jam-Fit Chucks For Facework

Headstock

Drive shaft

A

B

C

₵

Screw

Faceplate

Jam-Fit Chucks For Centerwork

D

E

Spigot chuck, cup chuck or jaw chuck

F

Note: The angle of the tapers has been exaggerated for clarity. Jam-fit chucks should be turned with a very slight (1° to 2°) taper.

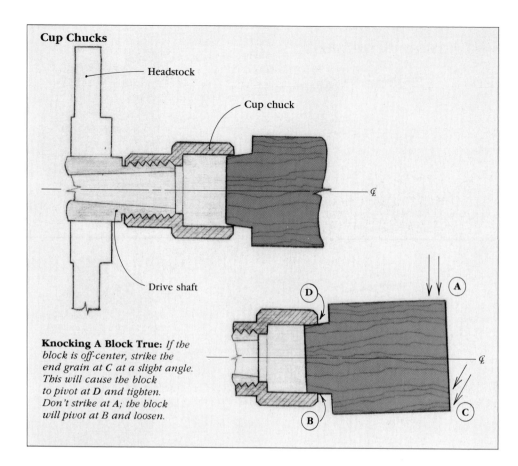

Cup Chucks

Headstock

Cup chuck

Drive shaft

Knocking A Block True: *If the block is off-center, strike the end grain at C at a slight angle. This will cause the block to pivot at D and tighten. Don't strike at A; the block will pivot at B and loosen.*

To fit work to a cup chuck, turn a taper on one end of a blank and drive it into the chuck. The grub screws on this chuck can be used for added strength on large blocks.

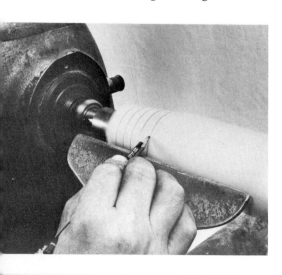

Mark a series of lines around the freshly roughed taper (left). Drive the wood into the chuck so that the lines are parallel to the chuck face (above).

Cup chucks

A cup chuck consists of a cylindrical hole in a piece of metal. It is strictly a centerwork fixing, used to grip grain running parallel to the axis of the lathe and into the chuck. Do not attempt to use a cup chuck for facework; grain at 90° to the axis will shear if any pressure is put against the work. I would not even try to mount a 6-in.- (150mm) diameter by 3-in.- (75mm) thick facework bowl on a 2-in.- (50mm) long flange because the body of the bowl could shear easily from the foot unless mounted absolutely accurately. Cup chucks are safe to use because, unlike jaw chucks, they have no protuberances to catch fingers or snag clothing.

Blanks are turned with a shallow taper to jam-fit in the chuck. They are knocked in with a mallet with the chuck screwed onto the drive shaft. The actual grip is on about ¼ in. (6mm) to ½ in. (13mm) of wood squashed around the circumference. My practice of thumping blocks into cup chucks on the lathe will no doubt appall many people, but I've done it thousands of times over the past ten years on my two short-bed lathes, both of which still have their original bearings in good condition. I feel justified in my notion that good bearings can take it. The fixing is secure enough not to require tail-center support and, with a hollow drive shaft, the waste section can be removed easily with a rod after the work has been parted off—without having to take the chuck off the lathe. If your headstock is lightweight, it's prudent to remove the chuck from the lathe and knock the blank in on the bench or floor. To aid knocking the blank in true, mark a series of lines by holding a pencil against the freshly roughed taper on the revolving wood, as shown in the photo at lower left. Then drive the wood into the chuck so that the lines are parallel to the face of the chuck.

I have two cup chucks that accept 2-in.- (50mm) and 1½-in.- (38mm) diameter work. The larger one has grub screws that can be tightened to grip the wood, though I seldom use them with stock less than 8 in. (205mm) long or less than 4 in. (100mm) in diameter.

Very small square-section material can be knocked into the end of a hollow drive shaft, which then functions as a miniature cup chuck (p. 88). The only problem is that the slightest catch will throw the block off-center or, more likely, send it airborne. I make my production salt and spice scoops this way out of ⅞-in.- (22mm) square by 3-in.- (75mm) long blanks. A hollow shaft is essential so the stock can be easily pushed out with a rod.

The expanding collet chuck needs a large turned rabbet to grip the foot of a bowl.

Expanding collet chucks

These chucks have collets that expand into a ¼-in.- (6mm) deep rabbet turned into the bottom of the work. Although they can be used with either centerwork or facework, expanding collet chucks were developed so the exterior of a bowl could be finished and the piece remounted to finish the interior with no unsightly screw holes. In practice, the self-centering is often less than perfect and the slightest catch or heavy-handed use of a cutting tool will knock the work off-center. I also find the big rabbet far more unsightly than two well-plugged screw holes.

Expanding collet chucks are widely used as a final fixing for bowls and provide a classic example of a tool that imposes severe constraints on design. The principle of a chuck expanding into wood is wrong, and great care is needed to avoid accidents. Wood splits easily and any slight weakness caused by overtightening the collets can result in the wood's flying apart and endangering anyone or anything within 10 ft. (3m). This is generally overcome by having plenty of extra wood around the collet. So 6-in. (150mm) bowls typically have 4-in. (100mm) to 5-in. (125mm) bases to accommodate a 2-in. (50mm) to 3-in. (75mm) collet. If the collet is smaller, you run into the leverage problems inherent in all chucks and faceplates. Too thin a rim around a larger collet will almost certainly break away with the slightest catch or excess pressure from the tool. Because the rabbet has to be between ⅛ in. (3mm) and ¼ in. (6mm) deep, and you have to leave some wood in the bottom of a bowl—about ½ in. (13mm) for an 8-in. (205mm) bowl—you end up with a very chunky base, probably much chunkier than you would really like. I have found collet chucks most useful in limited production runs of small, straight-sided chunky jobs—such as candle holders, eggcups or hand mirrors—where there is plenty of room for a deep rabbet.

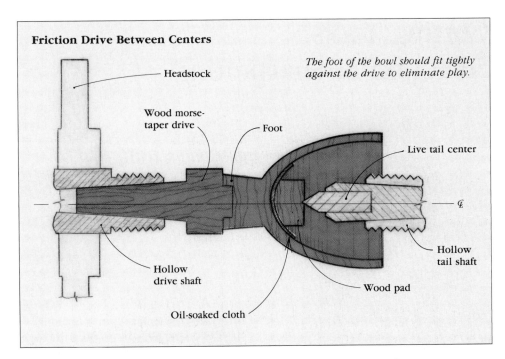

Friction Drive Between Centers

The foot of the bowl should fit tightly against the drive to eliminate play.

- Headstock
- Wood morse-taper drive
- Foot
- Live tail center
- Hollow drive shaft
- Wood pad
- Oil-soaked cloth
- Hollow tail shaft

Friction Drive

This is another technique for finishing bowls and other small facework without leaving fixing marks. I complete the bowl as much as possible on a jaw chuck, with the base having been finished at an earlier stage of the exterior shaping. I then remount the bowl between a morse-taper drive (I made one of wood) fitted into a recess turned in the base of the bowl, and the tail center is wound into the bowl's interior. Use a bit of heavy, oil-soaked cloth or suede and a wood pad between the tail center and the finished inside surface of the bowl, as shown in the drawing. Center the bowl by eye and gently turn and finish the foot. The technique is similar to the combination of three-jaw and spigot chucks shown on pp. 22-23. In both cases the bowl is lightly fixed for finishing. Too much pressure will cause the drive to spin faster than the wood and will lead to burn marks and possible damage to the bowl.

You can use the same technique to finish off a sphere, except that both the drive and tail chucks should be turned with concave ends to fit the convex surface of the sphere to provide a firm fixing.

Cutting Tools: Selection & Sharpening

3

There are four main groups of woodturning tools: gouges, scrapers, chisels and parting tools.

They are used to perform distinctly different operations on the lathe. Accordingly, they are selected for specific qualities and sharpened differently. I'll introduce cutting tools and describe how to sharpen them in this chapter. Their uses are discussed in Chapters 6 and 7.

Selection

All four groups of cutting tools are available in either long-and-strong or standard strength. The long-and-strong tools, as their name implies, are longer, thicker and altogether more robust than the standard, which are about ³⁄₁₆ in. (5mm) thick and less than 6½ in. (165mm) long, excluding the tang. Because of their increased mass and length, the long-and-strong tools flex less than standard tools when the cutting edge is well away from the tool rest or when turning large or off-center objects. Standard tools are better for cutting close to the rest, in hard-to-reach spots or for making detailed cuts.

When I began to turn wood in 1970 the only tools available were made of carbon steel. These tools are still available, indeed widely used, and are much cheaper than the succeeding generation. Since the late seventies, tools have been marketed made of harder, high-speed steels with a tungsten content between 4% and 18%. High-speed steel is better where the tool is heated in use. The name refers to the steel's resistance to softening when used at high speeds (as in jointer knives and drill bits). Unlike carbon steel, which will lose its hardness at about 300°F/150°C, high-speed steel maintains its hardness up to about 1050°F/570°C.

Though high-speed tools are nearly twice the price of similar carbon-steel tools, they hold an edge five or six times longer and so are worth the extra. Any tools I buy now are of high-speed steel, though I still have a number of carbon-steel tools; they work well but need to be sharpened more often. To keep your initial investment small, begin with carbon-steel tools and upgrade as your experience, needs and budget dictate.

While many manufacturers produce a similar range of these tools, the market is dominated by two companies—Sorby and Henry Taylor—both from Sheffield, the traditional home of fine steel in England. Turners benefit from the rivalry between these two because they compete to maintain high quality and good value. Ashley Iles and Marples are also well-known English manufacturers. Increasingly, there are other smaller companies, even individuals, producing high-quality tools. These may be more expensive, but are worth the cost for a serious turner; they usually hold an edge much longer than even the best mass-produced, high-speed tools. There are, of course, cheaper tools on the market. These have thin, almost flexible blades, weak tangs, short handles, thin ferrules and a general air of insubstantiality.

I have always bought tools produced by the well-known manufacturers and these have served me well (the manufacturers' reputations vindicated). I know little of the steels used—only that they hold an edge well. Occasionally I will encounter a tool that dulls easily and wears unevenly, indicating hard and soft patches of steel. Any such poorly forged or tempered tool can always be returned to a reputable manufacturer. Beware of sets of six tools made for beginners, which may only cost as much as one good Sorby or Taylor gouge; they are money down the drain. A list of suggested tools for the beginner is shown at the bottom of the facing page.

Gouges

Gouges are used frequently for roughing large, square spindle blanks to round and for cutting shallow coves or twisted grain in centerwork. They are in almost constant use in facework for cutting bowls of all sizes and shapes. Woodturning gouges have a curved cutting edge with a bevel ground on the outside of the tool. They are made either shallow or deep-fluted (see drawing at the top of the facing page). To confuse the issue, the shallow gouges are often regarded as spindle gouges, used for centerwork, while the deep-fluted tools are called bowl gouges, used on facework.

Don't be misled by these manufacturers' labels into thinking that spindle gouges can be used only for spindles or bowl gouges for bowls. In general, any gouge can be reground and used for any purpose. I favor some shallow gouges for both centerwork and facework because their edges taper from a thick center to a thin top edge, which is easy to grind to a long point or scraping edge. (I use gouges frequently as scrapers, as described in Chapter 7.) A thicker center also puts the weight of the metal in the bottom of the tool, making it better balanced. Some deep-fluted gouges have an even thickness of metal throughout. This creates a thick top edge that is difficult to grind to a long, curved shape.

Gouges can be ground from straight across (square-ground) to a long, fingernail shape, as shown in the drawing. Square-ground edges (either deep-fluted or shallow) are best for roughing-down and for fine cutting of cylinders or tapered spindles in centerwork; the shape allows you to use all of the edge. To cut coves or beads in centerwork and for the shearing and scraping cuts used in facework, you'll need a long, symmetrical fingernail edge (shallow for centerwork and either deep-fluted or shallow for facework), with no corners to catch the work and a point to get into small spaces. If your range of tools is limited, start with shallow, fingernail-ground gouges.

All the gouges I use now are machined from high-speed steel rods and are a joy to use. Their round shape allows these tools to be rolled easily on the rest and they are better balanced than the traditional square-section gouges (usually made of carbon steel). But the high-speed tools are more expensive so, unless you're working with very hard woods or aiming to turn a lot, you might be better off with the less-expensive, carbon-steel models.

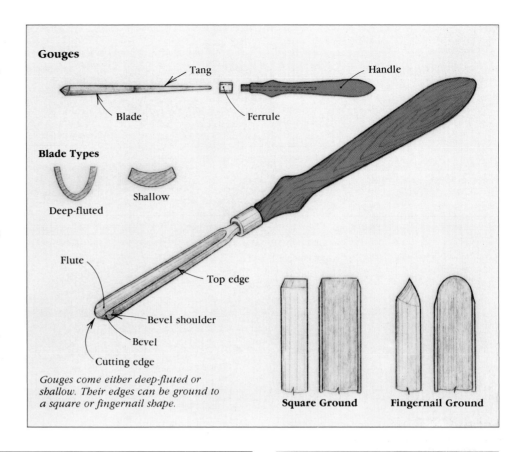

Gouges come either deep-fluted or shallow. Their edges can be ground to a square or fingernail shape.

Basic Tool Chart

- **A.** 1-in. (25 mm) standard gouge: deep-fluted or shallow
- **B.** ¼-in. (6mm) long-and-strong gouge: deep-fluted
- **C.** ¼-in. (6mm) long-and-strong gouge: shallow
- **D.** ½-in. (13mm) long-and-strong gouge: deep-fluted
- **E.** ½-in. (13mm) standard skew chisel
- **F.** ¾-in. (19mm) standard skew chisel
- **G.** ¼-in. (6mm) parting tool: fishtail or diamond-shaped
- **H.** ¼-in. (6mm) standard scraper: square-end
- **I.** ½-in. (13mm) standard scraper: square-end
- **J.** 1-in. (25mm) long-and-strong scraper: square-end
- **K.** 1½-in. (38mm) long-and-strong scraper: round-nose

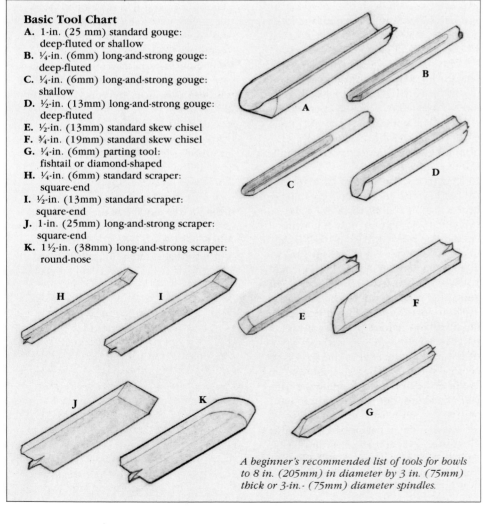

A beginner's recommended list of tools for bowls to 8 in. (205mm) in diameter by 3 in. (75mm) thick or 3-in.- (75mm) diameter spindles.

My high-speed-steel gouges (left) are made from tungsten-carbide rods. They are better balanced than the square-section, carbon-steel gouges (right) and are easily rolled and manipulated on the rest.

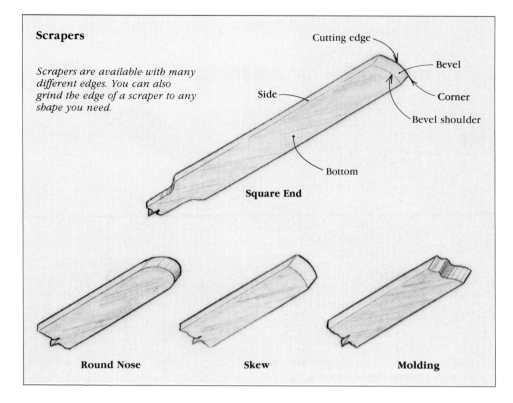

Scrapers

Scrapers are available with many different edges. You can also grind the edge of a scraper to any shape you need.

Cutting edge
Bevel
Side
Corner
Bevel shoulder
Bottom
Square End

Round Nose   **Skew**   **Molding**

Scrapers

To me, scrapers are not generally suited for roughing down, especially for centerwork. The finish they leave when used forcefully is very poor. I regard scrapers mainly as tools for fine finishing, and to use them effectively requires a smooth, flowing and delicate touch that removes only fluff and very small curly shavings. Some hardwoods—mulga, African blackwood or ebony—can come up like glass off the scraper and hardly need abrasives for finishing. Scrapers can also be used to make heavier, internal cuts in facework, where gouges can't reach.

Scrapers are flat tools of square section with a cutting edge any shape you like: round, square, skew or even ground to match the shape of a molding or to cut several beads at once, like a cutter on a spindle molder. Scrapers should have squared, not rounded sides. Often a sharp corner on a scraper is useful for getting into corners on the work, such as the base of a bead or inside a container, and a rounded side precludes the possibility of using the tool this way.

Because scrapers are ground with only one bevel, and are always used with the bevel down, they are not always made of solid high-speed steel. Instead, the cutting edge may be made of a layer of high-speed steel laminated to a lower grade of less expensive carbon steel below, which reduces the cost of the tool. When buying such a tool, be sure that the high-speed steel runs the length of the tool (you can

usually see the lamination seam on the top and side of the tool blade). Many tools have only an inch or so of high-speed steel at the tip. This is not enough if the tool is ground with a long curved edge or if it will be used and ground often.

I've had my old set of carbon-steel scrapers for about six years, but I use them mostly for very light final cuts and they are rarely subjected to heavy sharpening. I'll replace them with high-speed steel tools when they're worn back, but most beginners will do perfectly well with these less expensive scrapers.

If I need a scraper to cut more than 1 in. (25mm) away from the tool rest I use a heavy, ⅜-in.- (10mm) thick, long-and-strong tool. For exceedingly fine work close to the rest, such as on small boxes or to cut coves, even a ⅛-in.- (3mm) thick tool may be too big. For miniature boxes, ¹⁄₁₆ in. (2mm) wide by ¹⁄₃₂ (1.0mm) high, I grind mini-scrapers out of common nails.

If you can't find a manufactured scraper the shape you require, you can always purchase steel by the bar and make your own. Grinding the edge is time-consuming because you must be careful not to overheat the steel, and grinding the tang will be tedious, but it is sometimes the only way to get what you want. I do not recommend the common practice of using old files as scrapers. The steel in files is too hard and brittle and could break easily from the shock of a sudden catch.

Chisels

The chisel is, to me, the best tool for working along the grain. It is the main tool used in centerwork and is used only rarely for facework. It functions best on absolutely straight, knot-free wood and can leave a near-perfect finish with its shearing cut, so that abrasives are needed for only the smoothest of surfaces.

Chisels are flat tools of square section, like scrapers, but they are ground with a bevel on both the top and bottom. For any job up to 3 in. (75mm) in diameter I prefer my chisels thinner than the scrapers, or about ³⁄₁₆ in. (5mm) thick. This creates a shorter bevel, which is easier to grind. For larger centerwork, I like a heavier tool with a cross section similar to that of the heavy scrapers.

Chisels can be purchased either straight or skew and both have straight edges. I have reground all of my own chisel edges to a curve, as shown in the drawing at top right on the facing page. The curve allows a wider range of use for the tool. The bevel can be ground either concave or convex, and there are advantages to both. The concave (hollow-ground) bevel is best for the convex curves I cut when making scoops or boxes. It's also easy to sharpen the edge on an electric grinder, and the shoulder of the bevel can be used as a secondary fulcrum when turning, providing an extra measure of control over the cut (see p. 48 for a description of the tool rest as primary fulcrum). The only disadvantage of the hollow-grind is that it leaves a distinct bevel shoulder, which can mark the concave curves on stair spindles or cabriole legs. This shoulder can be softened with a slipstone, but using a convex-ground chisel is better. The convex-ground tool has a gradual curve from the flat surface of the blade to the cutting edge. No hard shoulder will mark the wood when cutting concave surfaces, but the edge is more difficult to grind.

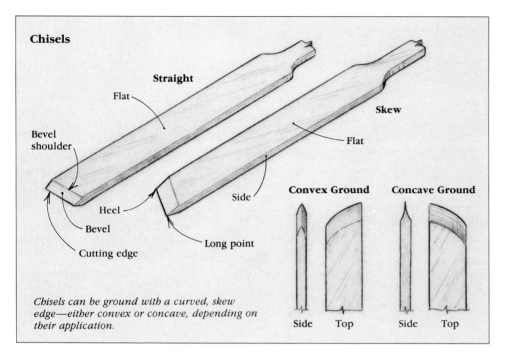

Chisels

Straight

Flat

Skew

Flat

Bevel shoulder

Side

Heel

Long point

Bevel

Cutting edge

Convex Ground

Concave Ground

Side   Top   Side   Top

Chisels can be ground with a curved, skew edge—either convex or concave, depending on their application.

Parting tools

Parting tools are narrow, chisel-like tools used primarily on centerwork to get into odd corners and to cut, or part, turned pieces from the lathe while it's running. They have a long hollow-ground bevel on both top and bottom faces, tapering to a thin edge.

The ¼-in. (6mm) fishtail parting tool (on top in the drawing at right) is a good, solid implement. Its edge is wider than its shaft, ensuring that the tool won't bind as it cuts deeply across the grain. Better still is the narrow diamond-shaped tool, which doesn't waste as much material as the fishtail and is ideal for work up to 4 in. (100mm) in diameter. These are available in high-speed steel and hold an edge well. The diamond shape demands less precision and I forsake it for the stronger fishtail only on large-diameter jobs.

There are standard high-speed steel tools with parallel sides that hold an edge well, cut end grain cleanly and waste less wood than the fishtail parting tools, which have a wider cutting edge. They can be useful, but they require accurate use to avoid binding and levering off the finished piece toward the end of the parting cut.

Beware of the high-speed steel fluted parting tools shown at far right in the drawing. These are used with the flute down and are liable to cut up the rest. They are reputed to cut end grain more cleanly than any other parting tool because of the leading spurs on the edge caused by the flute. But you can grind spurs on ordinary parting tools. These will cut as cleanly as the fluted tool, without destroying the tool rest.

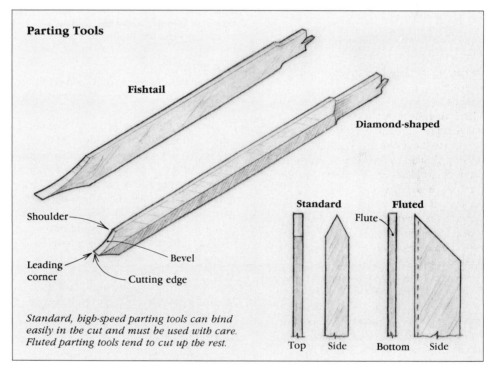

Parting Tools

Fishtail

Diamond-shaped

Shoulder

Leading corner

Bevel

Cutting edge

Standard

Fluted

Flute

Top   Side   Bottom   Side

Standard, high-speed parting tools can bind easily in the cut and must be used with care. Fluted parting tools tend to cut up the rest.

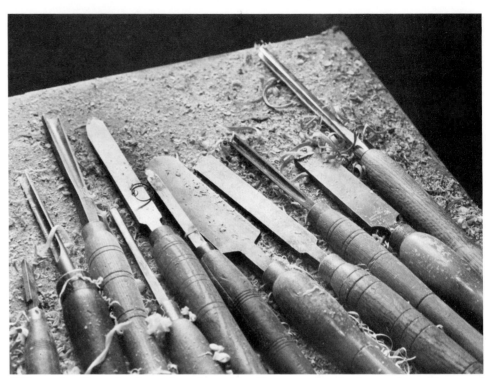

Different handles make the tools easier to identify among the shavings and provide a good turning project for the beginner.

Handles

Tool handles deserve careful consideration. Those provided by manufacturers come in all shapes, sizes and woods. They vary in length from the traditional size of about 12 in. (305mm) to a ridiculous 36 in. (915mm), often bearing scant relation to the probable use of the tool. There is no point in having a long handle on a short or lightweight tool that should not be used more than ½ in. (13mm) to ¾ in. (19mm) from the rest. Likewise, I would never put an 8-in. (205mm) handle on a long-and-strong tool that might be used to cut 6 in. (150mm) or more from the rest. Not only would it feel wrong, it would lack the length to provide the required leverage. My handles range from 4 in. (100mm) long on small tools used for miniature centerwork, to 12 in. (305mm) for the standard-strength tools, and 20 in. (510mm) to 24 in. (610mm) long for the heaviest scrapers. A tool should be balanced, with the weight distributed equally on either side of the ferrule, which makes it comfortable to use. The balance gradually alters as the blade wears. I will grind away a high-speed-steel bowl gouge in about 14 to 18 months of regular use and, with a new tool installed in the handle, wonder how I managed with its predecessor or why I used such an unbalanced tool for so long. I get used to whatever I'm using even though something else might be better (typical of life in general, really).

Although I use some handles provided by the manufacturers, I prefer to make my own so that they fit my hands, which are on the small side. I leave the wood untreated and it develops a patina and a comfortable feel from constant use.

When making your own handles, vary one from another. A set of tools with matching handles looks impressive on a tool rack, but is infuriating to use. It's difficult to pick one tool from the rest of the set on a bench full of shavings. So, have slightly different shapes or colored woods or decoration. Varying sets of grooves or beads are useful identification and good turning practice for the beginner. The procedure for making a tool handle is described on pp. 155-157.

Sharpening

Sharp tools are essential and much easier and safer to use than blunt ones. Any woodworker must not only be able to identify a good edge and whether a sharp tool can be made sharper but must also be able to decide when a tool is sharp enough for a particular job. Obviously, an edge should be free of chips or nicks and should not reflect light, but there is more to it than that. The shape and quality of the edge depends on the tool being used and the species and quality of wood being turned. An edge of ultimate sharpness, with the metal tapering away to nothing, as on a razor blade or cabinetmaker's chisel, may not produce the cleanest cut or be best for roughing wood on the lathe.

I do not subscribe to the widely publicized and accepted sharpening rigmarole involving successive grades of oilstones, waterstones, strops and so on. These techniques are fine for carving and joinery, but excessive for woodturning. Turning tools are called upon to remove enormous amounts of wood relatively quickly, which can dull even the finest edge. There is no point in doing five minutes of sharpening for thirty seconds of cutting. And the edge you so meticulously achieve might not be superior to that which the grinder can produce. Skillful grinding, allowing you to use the tool directly from the wheel, is the answer.

Sharpening is usually done on a grindstone with wheels of between 5 in. (125mm) and 8 in. (205mm) in diameter. I have two grinders, each with 36-grit and 80-grit wheels. One grinder has carborundum wheels, suitable for carbon steel, the other has silicon-carbide wheels, suitable for high-speed steel. I have only recently acquired the softer silicon-carbide wheels; before that I used my carborundum ones, which do the job less efficiently. I have always used the fast-cutting, dry grinding wheels rather than the slow-cutting, wet ones and I use the tool straight from the fine-grit wheel. I keep a can of water handy to cool the tool should it become too hot.

As an alternative to the grinder, you can also sharpen tools on a stationary belt sander using a 100-grit belt, as shown at right. It's difficult to achieve the hollow-ground bevel on the flat surface of the sander, so I use it only for convex-ground skew chisels, on the odd occasion that I require such a tool. The sander can also be used to produce a flat bevel, which is perfectly acceptable and functions much the same as the hollow-ground bevel.

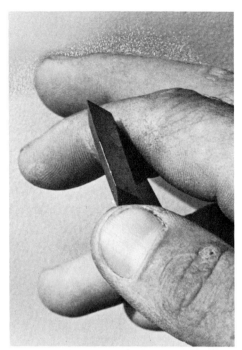

Light reflecting off the edge of a damaged skew chisel indicates dullness. More often, such highlights will be mere nicks and difficult to see. It is impossible to cut with such an edge; it must be reground.

To grind a tool on a belt sander hold the chisel nearly flat, resting on the bevel shoulder. Raise the handle slowly to produce a convex curve, or hold the bevel flat against the belt to produce a flat bevel. This curved skew chisel is being ground in the softer, unsupported area of the belt between the roller and the table, where slight pressure of the tool will produce a convex bevel. The belt sander will not raise a burr suitable for scraping and the tool will have to be honed.

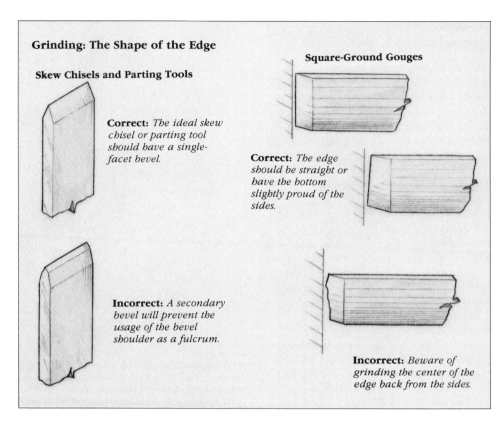

Grinding: The Shape of the Edge

Skew Chisels and Parting Tools

Correct: *The ideal skew chisel or parting tool should have a single-facet bevel.*

Incorrect: *A secondary bevel will prevent the usage of the bevel shoulder as a fulcrum.*

Square-Ground Gouges

Correct: *The edge should be straight or have the bottom slightly proud of the sides.*

Incorrect: *Beware of grinding the center of the edge back from the sides.*

There are two ways of holding a tool while grinding: freehand and jigged on the rest. The long-and-strong scraper (top) is being ground freehand—the tool makes contact with the top edge of the rest but the angle of the bevel is controlled by the position of your hand and fingers. The gouge (below) is being held flat on the rest, which has been fixed at about 30°. It may be easier for beginners to jig the tool on the rest.

Grinding the bevel

I grind most of my tools with the bevel set at an angle of 30° to 45° from the flat surface of the blade. The arc of the bevel matches the circumference of the grinding wheel, so a larger wheel will give you a longer bevel. The precise angle of the bevel isn't critical. The object of grinding is to achieve a single-facet bevel, as shown at top left in the drawing above. If you grind a second bevel at the edge, as on a joiner's chisel, you'll have less surface to rub on the wood, which will reduce your control of the edge.

Gouge edges can be ground either straight across or to a fingernail shape, as shown above. Whichever way you do it, ensure that the point is even with, or proud of, the sides. If the center of the edge is ground back, it will severely limit the tool's cutting capabilities.

You can grind in two ways, as shown in the photos at left: either freehand, using the rest to support the tool at one point (top), or by setting the rest to the appropriate angle and holding the tool flat on it (bottom). Because the angles and shapes of my tool edges differ considerably, I generally use the first approach, though it may be easier for beginners to achieve a single-facet bevel by jigging the tool rest at the desired angle. A high flat rest, as shown at far right in the drawing on the facing page, is ideal for scrapers, which are kept flat on the rest while the handle is moved sideways.

Grinding

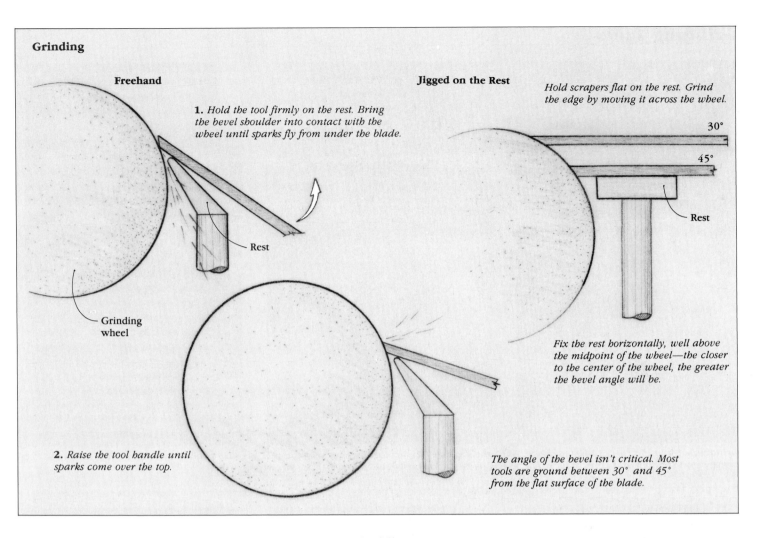

Freehand

Jigged on the Rest

Hold scrapers flat on the rest. Grind the edge by moving it across the wheel.

1. *Hold the tool firmly on the rest. Bring the bevel shoulder into contact with the wheel until sparks fly from under the blade.*

30°

45°

Rest

Rest

Grinding wheel

Fix the rest horizontally, well above the midpoint of the wheel—the closer to the center of the wheel, the greater the bevel angle will be.

2. Raise the tool handle until sparks come over the top.

The angle of the bevel isn't critical. Most tools are ground between 30° and 45° from the flat surface of the blade.

I begin by holding the tool firmly on the rest with one hand, hooking the knuckle of my forefinger under the rest. My thumb and fingers grasp both sides of the tool to control its movement. I grind my tools in two stages, as shown above. First I bring the bevel shoulder into contact with the wheel. Sparks fly from under the tool. Next, I raise the tool handle until the sparks come over the top, at which point the tool should have a single-facet bevel from shoulder to cutting edge. The bevel shoulder should remain in contact with the wheel throughout the process.

Keep the tool moving and the movements flowing, side to side for scrapers, chisels and parting tools, rolling sideways for gouges. Apply just enough pressure to keep the tool from chattering against the wheel. Grind out large chips on the coarse (36-grit) wheel with a fair amount of pressure applied, though not so much as to overheat the tool, turning it blue. The final grind must be made with a light touch on the 80-grit wheel. It's common practice among students to grind too long and too hard. If the tool begins to blue, dip it in the water to cool and use less pressure against the grinding wheel.

The photos on the following two pages show a correct sequence for grinding a gouge or a chisel using the rest as a jig. The scraper with a long, curved left edge and the parting tool are being ground freehand—only the part of the blade closest to the wheel contacts the rest. I keep the blade flat on the rest if I want to maintain a precise bevel angle.

With any tool that has a curved edge, such as the gouge, scraper and chisel on pp. 36 and 37, I swing the handle sideways through an arc to catch all of the edge, rather than push the tool higher up on the wheel. This provides more control, because the edge is nearer the rest.

Grinding a 1-in. (25mm) deep-fluted gouge. Hook the knuckle of your forefinger under the rest, and use your thumb and middle fingers to keep pressure on the tool and control its roll. The tool is simultaneously rolled and swung through an arc.

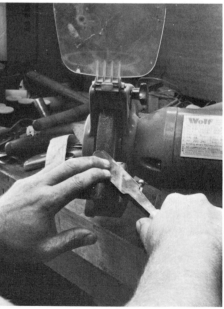

Grinding a 1-in. (25mm) scraper with a long, curved left edge. The shape of a tool can be modified to suit any purpose. The curve on the edge of this scraper will be useful for hollowing scoops and boxes. Because of the severe curve, it is easier to begin grinding with the handle held in the left hand, transferring it to the right as it is swung through an arc. Keep the tool near horizontal on the rest rather than pushing it higher up on the wheel. This keeps the grinding close to the rest and makes it easier to control.

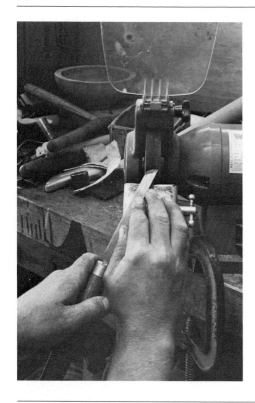

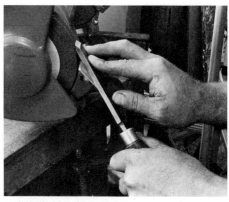

Swing the handle slightly to put a curve on a skew chisel. Note that the chisel can be held flat against the rest to maintain the bevel angle.

To grind a parting tool freehand, first bring the shoulder of the bevel into contact with the wheel (left). Then raise the handle to lower the edge until sparks fly over the top (center). You can also obtain a single, flashing bevel by adjusting the rest to the appropriate angle and pushing the tool straight in so that the shoulder and edge of the bevel contact the wheel at the same time (right).

Test the burr with a stroke of the thumb across—not along—the edge. With experience, this critical test should become a quick indicator of the quality of an edge.

Burrs

When you grind an edge, no matter how delicate your touch, there will be a build-up of metal, called the burr, on top of the edge of the tool where it contacts the rotating wheel. The burr resembles a small hook running the length of the cutting edge. On scrapers, the burr does the cutting and is left on, while on gouges, chisels and parting tools it is often removed using a slipstone, so that the tool will cut exceptionally cleanly. Most of the time, I use my tools straight from the fine wheel and still obtain a smooth, clean cut, though the precise type of edge varies from one situation to another.

There are no hard and fast rules concerning burrs and judging a suitable one is tricky. You can see it but that doesn't tell you enough. It has to be felt by stroking your thumb across the edge, as shown in the photo above. Stroke across the edge, not along it, or you risk getting cut. (Though you would know that the tool is sharp.) Since we all have a different sense of touch, you can learn how a burr should feel only from experience. I feel the edge habitually before using any tool and this almost subconscious spot check lets me know when it's time to sharpen. As you turn, experiment with different edges. Try cutting with burrs that come from the lightest touch on the wheel and burrs from the heaviest grind and see what happens. In turning, as with any other skill, there is no quick route or short cut to proficiency—you must take time to experiment and compare.

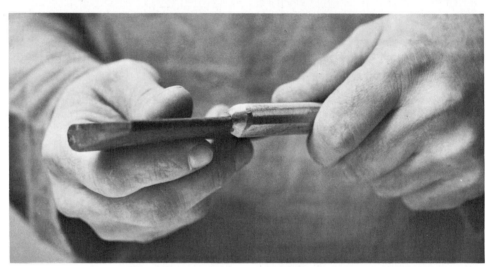

You can use a fine, oil slipstone to remove a burr. Hold the tool firmly and move the stone back and forth (top), keeping it in contact with both the shoulder and cutting edge. Use the curved edge of the slipstone (below) to remove the burr on the inside of a gouge, keeping the stone flat against the tool. Several passes on each side of the edge should remove the burr.

Be careful not to press too hard when grinding; you'll not only risk burning the tool but the burr will be too big. This renders gouges, chisels and parting tools useless and scrapers almost so. For these occasions I keep a small softwood log or block of wood near the grinder—end grain up—into which I plunge the edge of the tool to remove the burr. This usually chips the edge slightly and I have to start the whole grinding process again, losing a bit more metal than I'd like.

Once I've achieved a good edge, it's fairly easy to maintain by passing the tool lightly across the 80-grit grinding wheel when absolute sharpness is lost. This leaves a small, even burr. With all but the lightest of cuts, the pressure of the wood being turned removes this burr in an instant, leaving a good edge. For delicate scraping, which requires a light touch, this fine burr remains and is ideal.

Slipstones

On the rare occasion when I use a slipstone it is usually to remove the burr that results from over-enthusiastic grinding, to soften a sharp shoulder on a hollow-ground bevel or to give a skew chisel or parting tool a razor edge for a super-fine cut. I tuck the tool handle under my left arm and move a fine stone across the tool with my right hand. I use a light machine oil to lubricate the stone and float away metal filings. If the bevel is hollow ground, the tool should contact the stone only at the bevel shoulder and the edge. If you lift the stone off the bevel shoulder, you'll round the edge or create a secondary bevel and the tool won't cut properly. To remove the burr from the inside of a gouge, keep the stone flat on the inside of the blade and avoid rounding the edge. The stone should rub only two or three times on each side of the tool.

Place the bevel of the chisel flat on the benchstone and push the chisel back and forth several times to remove the burr. Beware of lifting the bevel shoulder and rounding the cutting edge.

A bench stone can also be used to remove the burr on flat tools, such as chisels, parting tools and scrapers. Follow the same procedure as described for the slipstone except that the tool is moved over the stationary stone, which is held flat on a workbench.

A razor edge is relatively easy to recognize once you've got it. You can see it. No light flashes from flat spots on the edge and you won't feel the burr.

Afterword

Remember that turning tools remove a great deal of wood very quickly and consequently need attention more often than a joiner's chisel might. Don't worry if you seem to be going back to the grinder every five seconds. A fine edge can be lost quickly regardless of the steel. With very hard woods it is not unusual to regrind after every three or four cuts. In fact, I recall that I never even bothered to switch off the grinder when turning pieces of teak and elm that had silica or grit in the grain.

Too many of my students worry about their inability to achieve a so-called perfect bevel, when the shape of the edge (and the way it is presented to the wood) is usually much more important. You will note that some tools in the pictures throughout this book are ground less than perfectly—but they all cut well. I would like to dispel the myth of the ideal tool, steel, bevel, etc., that is so commonly held by woodturners around the world. I feel that I'm fairly typical of the professional brigade of turners who temper their quest for perfection in these matters with a need to earn a living. Sharpening, as I've described it above, is neither mysterious, lengthy nor difficult. It just takes practice.

Watch any master woodworker (joiner, carver, turner) producing magnificent shavings and you will find work suddenly stops while the edge receives a quick hone or grind. The master knows when to resharpen from experience gained during thousands of hours' work. In lieu of that experience, you would do well to find someone who will sharpen tools for you in the beginning, so that you can glimpse the joys of cutting with a good edge. You will then know what to aim for and should recognize it when you do it yourself.

Woodworking machines are dangerous, and the lathe is no exception.

If you doubt this, compare insurance quotes for woodturning against almost any other occupation. The machinery is fast-moving, and you are dealing with sharp tools (or, sometimes more hazardous, with dull ones). The risks are real and can't be overemphasized, plus it's easy to become complacent—and careless—when you think you have a machine under control. So, as you approach any machine, hesitate a second to remind yourself that it is potentially dangerous. Think about what you are about to do and advance with care from the right direction. Here are some specific safety precautions to keep in mind and incorporate into your routine.

Safety

Always wear eye protection. It is essential to prevent chips from flying into your eyes—secondhand eyes are still in short supply. If you wear spectacles, use shatterproof lenses. Less myopic turners can wear non-prescription safety spectacles. But the best protection is a Plexiglas face shield. With the shield in place, you are less likely to require cosmetic surgery if a block flies off the lathe and hits you in the face. I recently received four stitches across the bridge of my nose after a 7-in.- (180mm) diameter bowl came off the lathe and hit my spectacle frame. Shortly thereafter I acquired a face shield. My earlier suspicion that the shield would distort my vision proved groundless, and I wondered why I hadn't adopted this protection years ago.

Never wear loose clothing. Short sleeves are best or long sleeves with elastic cuffs.

Remove all rings or jewelry from your hands and bracelets from your wrists. These might catch or be worn away when you are sanding. Ties or chains and pendants around the neck must not hang free. Remove or tuck them away.

If your hair is long, tie it back. Or, even better, stick it under a hat and keep the dust off as well. If you do a lot of turning, you are gambling with the odds if you wear a long beard. (It has happened.)

In hot weather, wear shoes or strapped sandals rather than slip-on sandals.

Dust protection

Dust is a serious fire and health hazard. Fine dust and small shavings ignite easily. In particular, beware of sparks landing in the dust beneath your grinder. Keep the area swept clean.

Quantities of inhaled dust may lead to allergies or bronchial problems such as asthma. The dust of many tropical hardwoods, such as iroko and black bean, are particularly irritating. But while wood dust is a problem, recent research indicates that even more damage might be caused by the insidious dusts from the abrasive agents—silicon carbide and garnet—and the adhesives used to attach them to their backings. Because these substances break down to very fine particles, they can pass through most filtration systems. Also, the chemicals used to treat timber against insects or fungus are bound to be harmful if inhaled. I stopped turning pressure-treated wood years ago when I found it affected my breathing.

You can wear a pad mask, but the finer particles go through many of these, and if the mask is worn over a beard, the dust creeps around the sides and through the whiskers. A mask worn with an ordinary face shield can trap moisture, creating a misting problem (safety spectacles can be worn with a mask without misting). Various respirators are available, many of which are awkward to use in conjunction with eye and face shields. The Airstream helmet (made by Racal Safety Ltd. of England), which I am wearing in the photo at top right on the facing page, is comfortable, light and combines an effective air-filtration system with a face shield. It incorporates a small axial fan, which draws the dust-laden air through two filters. (The fan is powered by a battery pack worn at the waist.) The air then flows down across the face behind the visor and out at the bottom. A seal around the face prevents unfiltered air, shavings and dust from entering. Despite its apparent bulk, the helmet is comfortable to wear for extended periods. These helmets are not cheap, but are the most effective protection I have found.

An alternative is an extraction system that collects dust at its source, removes it from the workspace and deposits it either outdoors or in another room. For years I managed without one. I worked in a cloud of dust, with a ¾-in. (19mm) layer on every surface. I must have been mad, and I will never again work without it. There are a number of good small units that can be fixed to several machines simultaneously, but because I am between permanent workshops at the moment, I use only one, moving it to the tool I am using.

This dust extractor consists of a small fan, powered by a 1hp electric motor and connected to 5-in.- (125mm) diameter

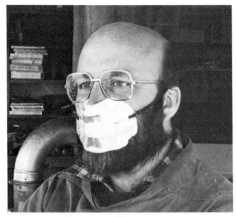

A pad mask, worn with safety spectacles will be sufficient for the beginner or occasional woodturner, though if you wear a beard, the dust will creep around through the whiskers.

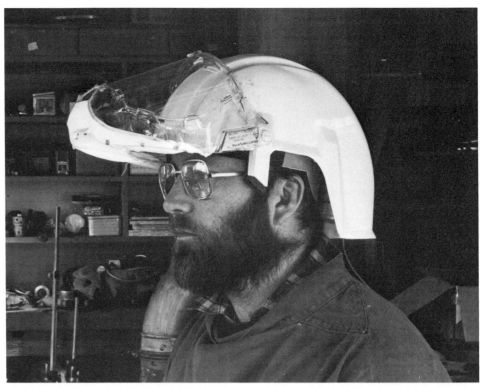

The face shield on the Airstream helmet flips up when out of use, and seals well against dust when in position (even with a beard).

flexible ducting. The duct is moved as close to the dust source as possible and attached to the lathe by twine. In a more permanent workspace, I would bolt the fan to the floor to reduce vibration and use fixed ducting, made from 3-in. (75mm) to 4-in. (100mm) plastic drainage pipe (available in most hardware stores), with rainwater funnels for suction heads at the machine. In designing your own extraction system, remember that air flows better if it doesn't have to negotiate right-angle bends. And try to locate the collecting and filter bags outside your workspace so that the finest dust particles won't pass through the system and back into the shop. This will obviously present problems with heat exchange in cold climates, so seek expert advice on how to keep your warm air while eliminating dust.

What is the best system? Big joinery factories can extract most dust at its source, but this may be too costly, noisy and impractical for a small workshop. Dust particles tend to be flung out, away from the work as it spins on the lathe. This means that even with an extractor you are sure to breathe in a fair amount of dust. So some form of mask is essential. My solution in recent years has been to use an extractor to remove most of the dust and to wear a mask to protect against the remaining fine particles. Today I wear the Airstream helmet, which provides clean air and protection against flying wood and chips, though I still use an extractor to collect the bulk of fine dust at its source. For the amateur, who won't constantly be working in a dust-laden atmosphere, safety spectacles worn with a soft, cotton pad mask should be sufficient. Breathe through your mouth with your lips pressed against the pad so the air passes through it, rather than around the sides.

Arrange the intake on your dust extractor as close as possible to the dust source.

A good, permanent extraction system uses rigid pipes with a minimum of bends. Dust particles are flung away from the rotating work, so a mask is added protection.

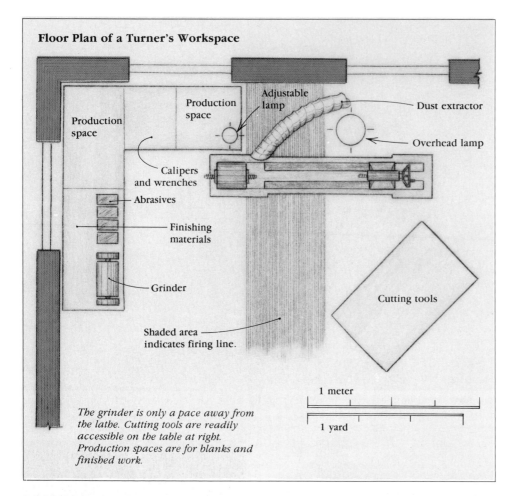

Floor Plan of a Turner's Workspace

Production space

Production space

Adjustable lamp

Dust extractor

Overhead lamp

Production space

Calipers and wrenches

Abrasives

Finishing materials

Grinder

Cutting tools

Shaded area indicates firing line.

1 meter

1 yard

The grinder is only a pace away from the lathe. Cutting tools are readily accessible on the table at right. Production spaces are for blanks and finished work.

Good lighting is important for safe lathe work. A 100-watt light, placed behind thin objects, such as the bowl wall above and at right, will help you judge thickness.

Workshop lighting & layout

Good general light, either from a window or a fluorescent tube, is an important safety consideration. In addition, it's essential to have one or two strong sources of light that can be easily arranged around the job at hand. I use two. I work with a 150-watt light to my right, which is on all the time to cast shadows on the surface being turned and highlight the ridges, curves, bumps and dips. A 100-watt light, placed behind a thin object, helps me judge thickness. I can determine how much wood to trim off by how much light shines through the wall of the object.

When placing your machinery, keep the following points in mind and refer to the drawings at left and on the facing page:
—Position your machines so that you can see anybody coming. If necessary, lock the door and install a bell and/or a light. It is dangerous to have anyone creeping up on a concentrating machinist.
—If you share your workshop with other workers, machine operators should be out of the line of fire of other machines to avoid off-cuts from a circular saw, oil from lathe polishing and shavings or wood from the lathe.
—Do not have a polished floor in machine areas. Floors should be non-slip.
—Position the lathe tools you are using so that you don't have to lean over the lathe to pick them up, inviting an accident.
—Mount the grinder near the lathe. You will regrind often and it should be only a pace away.
—Locate the lathe so that when you look up there's a view. Sanding is boring, and who wants to look at a brick wall?

Operating the lathe

—Always check the machine and work area before you begin. Check that speeds are set correctly, that all guards are in place and secure, that no wrenches or keys are left in shafts or chucks and that no tools or materials will interfere with its operation. A quick visual examination should become a regular work habit.
—Rotate the wood on the lathe by hand to see that it revolves freely. Check that the tool rest is immobile with all locking levers tightened. Stand clear of the firing line of the lathe when switching it on. Blocks are bound to come off now and then. When an object comes off the lathe, it is usually at 90° to the axis, as shown in the drawing on the facing page.
—After starting the lathe, never lean over the machine without first switching it off; you might easily catch your clothing.
—Never wrap a polishing cloth, sandpaper or steel wool around your hands or fingers.

Any of these can wrap around a rough spindle in a fraction of a second, and it's not worth being attached to the other end and risking a finger.

—Stop the lathe before adjusting the rest. If you move the rest carelessly and it makes contact with the rotating work, you are likely to damage the work or jar it from the lathe; delicate or fragile jobs will shatter. In any case, your hands will be perilously close to the action.

—Beware of sharp edges, corners and rims on the work. Razor-sharp edges can develop rapidly and are just as efficient as bacon slicers in cutting you to the bone—often without pain but with a lot of blood (and that stains the wood). Develop the habit of softening edges either with coarse abrasives or a tool.

These are the main dangers. There are others, such as pinched flesh or jammed fingers, that are common while learning. These are usually more tiresome than dangerous, though they can be painful.

Noise can be a problem if a lot of machinery is running at once. Worn bearings make more noise than new ones and three or four motors running at the same time will make it hard to hear the radio. But I've not found ear protection necessary unless using the tablesaw or hand drills for prolonged periods. Lathes and bandsaws run at slower speeds and their noise is less piercing.

Sounds from the lathe are actually among your best diagnostic tools. The turner with a well-tuned ear can judge the thickness of a bowl wall and hear loosely fixed blocks, splits or knots. Train yourself to listen and you'll be able to avoid most accidents before they happen. It is time-consuming at first, but you should stop the lathe every time a new sound comes along and investigate. You'll soon recognize all the basic noises. Turning sounds should be a series of crescendos and decrescendos resulting from smooth, flowing cuts. Students or apprentices frequently find it unnerving that skilled turners can tell exactly what they are doing by sounds alone. You can't get away with anything in a turner's workshop.

With experience comes an inevitable change in attitude toward safety. It no longer takes several minutes to approach your machine. What might appear to be shortcuts taken by an old pro should, hopefully, indicate an internalization—not a relaxation—of safety consciousness. There are procedures that simply should never be attempted by a novice, but would be absurd for an expert to avoid, such as adjusting the tool rest with the lathe running. As you become more competent

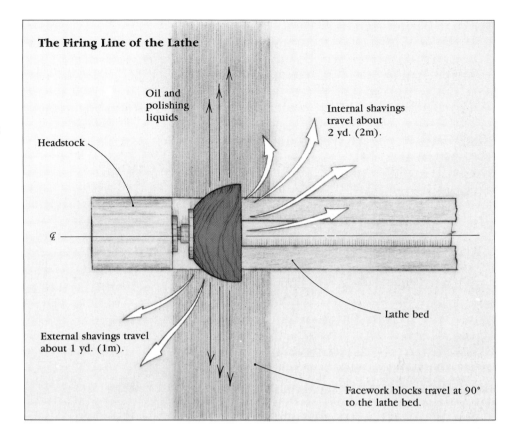

The Firing Line of the Lathe

Oil and polishing liquids

Headstock

Internal shavings travel about 2 yd. (2m).

℄

External shavings travel about 1 yd. (1m).

Lathe bed

Facework blocks travel at 90° to the lathe bed.

(and confident), try to remain aware of the limits of your skills and venture beyond only with extreme caution.

I consider myself lucky to have escaped serious injury over the 15 years since I began turning. But those years have not been without incident. Here are some of the blows inflicted by my trade. They serve as constant reminders not to be so careless in the future: On my left hand I have a scar across two fingers from the bandsaw and one on my thumb from jamming it between the lathe bed and a large platter. On my right hand are three broken knuckles from sanding a large platter (this happened twice). I have a broken nose from a shattering burr-elm bowl and a permanent lump from the time I headed a piece of flying teak back toward the lathe. A flying bowl smashed my shatterproof spectacle lens, leaving me with cuts and a black eye. In another incident, I only bent the spectacles, but received multiple cuts and stitches on my nose and around one eye from the frame.

These were the major accidents that stopped me working for a few days each time. All happened at the end of the day when I was tired and not concentrating fully, or showing off, and before I began wearing the Airstream helmet. You have been warned: Proceed with caution and remember that when anything happens on the lathe, or any other woodworking machinery, it happens fast.

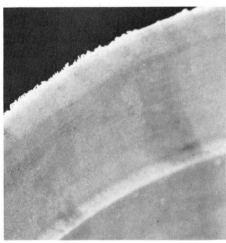

Sharp, serrated ridges like this can cut to the bone. Ease the edge with coarse sandpaper or a tool to avoid injury.

Lean your hip and stomach against the lathe for extra stability (above). Aim for a compact stance with your feet placed comfortably apart and elbows tucked into your side (right). Align the tool handle along your forearm for maximum support and control. Don't stand detached in front of the lathe with feet together, elbows out and the tool handle away from your body (far right). You'll never maintain control.

Tool Handling

There is more to woodturning than simply maintaining the correct angle of the cutting edge to the wood. The angle is important, but you must also be aware of what is happening behind the edge, how the tool is held and how to position your body to support it while still approaching the lathe safely. In this section I discuss general principles of tool handling. If these are not applied, it will be difficult to control the cutting edge; the wood will dictate the path of the tool. Beginners should read this section first before proceeding to the chapters on centerwork and facework.

Consider yourself apprenticed to the lathe. You can't just stand before it and produce excellence. As a musician practices scales, so the turner should practice routine exercises until mastered. When you begin turning, try to resist the temptation to make something; it is more important at this early stage to develop good form and work habits than it is to produce a functional object. Practice cutting wood away and enjoy the shavings that result as you develop basic tool-handling skills.

Stance

To move the cutting edge precisely where you want, you must get your weight behind the tool and guide it through space on a predetermined trajectory, regardless of the wood it meets on the way. On metal lathes, control is achieved by cutters that move in a rack-and-pinion system. In woodturning, the tools are hand-held, and support comes from the tool rest and the turner's body. Movement to manipulate the tools should come not so much from the hands, wrists and arms, as from the shoulders, hips and legs. Aim for a compact stance with your elbows tucked into your sides. Stand in a balanced position, with your feet placed comfortably apart, and the tool handle aligned along your forearm for maximum control, as shown in the photo at top center. Never stand in front of the lathe with your elbows waving about in space, as shown at top right. It's good practice to keep your upper hand on the rest, but try to maintain contact between other parts of your anatomy and the machine as well. Lean your hip against the bed or press a leg against the stand. This stance will not only give you extra support and stability, but also establish physical points of reference between yourself and the lathe.

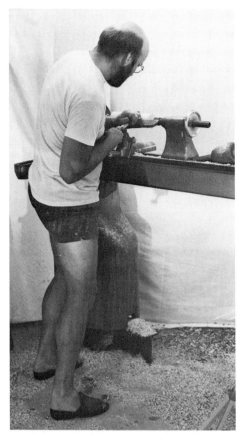

Begin a cut with your weight over one foot, transferring it gradually to the other as you move into the work with the tool. In these photos, the left foot is planted as the right heel rises off the ground, using body weight to support the tool.

Develop and enjoy the control gained from this approach by moving the cutting edge with a little squeeze or push, in conjunction with broader support movements from the rest of your body. As in steering a bicycle, control in woodturning is essentially a matter of shifting weight and coordination. If you want to move the tip of a tool slightly to the left, the movement should come from a nudge from your hip pushing the handle to the right. To move the tip to the right, draw your right elbow in close to your side, nudging the tool handle to the left. Your lower hand stays close to your side and you remain compact. If you want the tool edge to drop, extend your side by stretching upward, standing on tiptoe if necessary, to bring the handle up (and the tip down) with the weight of your entire torso and shoulders behind the tool. If the handle must leave your side, align it along your forearm for support.

Most beginners exhibit considerable inhibition when it comes to moving their bodies with a tool handle; it pays to overcome this self-consciousness. The photos above and on the following pages show the way your body can move to support and control your tools. Practice these movements a few times at the lathe to get the feel of it, even before you pick up a tool or turn the machine on.

Stance & Movement

The photo at left shows a good compact stance with the handle of the tool aligned along the forearm and feet placed comfortably apart. The sequence below and on the bottom of the facing page (from left to right) shows the typical movements necesary in turning a long cylinder. The weight begins over the right foot at the right end of the cylinder, shifting to the left as the cut moves along. The same motions are repeated farther down the cylinder.

Note: The strapless sandals worn in these photos are not recommended.

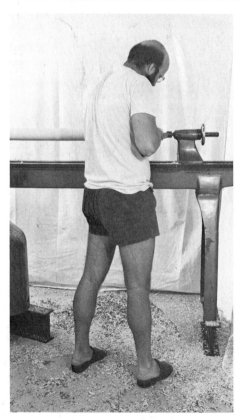 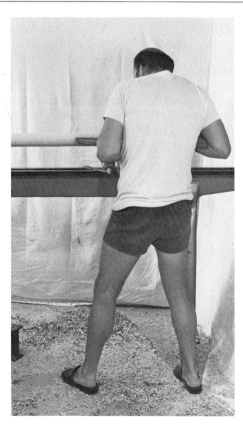 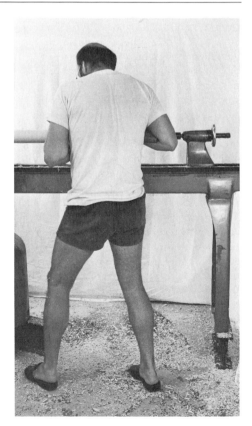

Richard Raffan
P.O. Box 9
Mittagong. NSW 2575
Australia

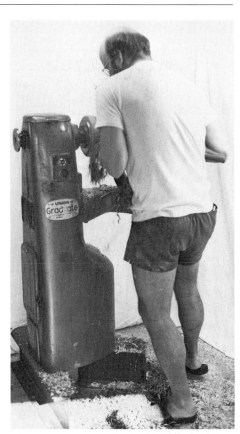

In shaping a bowl exterior (left to right), plant your feet and swing your body with the tool as the cut moves from the center to the rim.

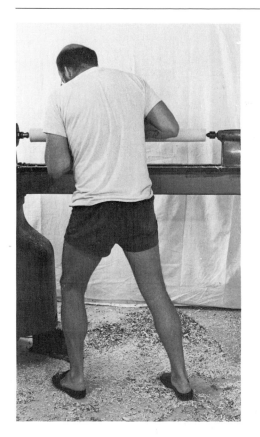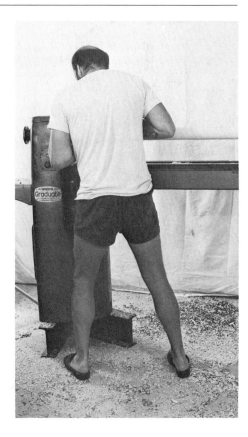

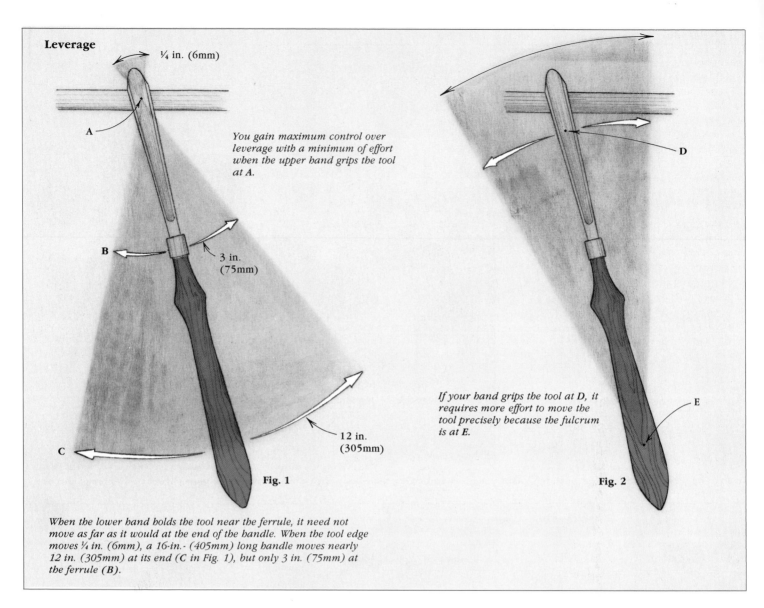

Leverage

¼ in. (6mm)

A

You gain maximum control over leverage with a minimum of effort when the upper hand grips the tool at A.

B

3 in. (75mm)

C

12 in. (305mm)

Fig. 1

When the lower hand holds the tool near the ferrule, it need not move as far as it would at the end of the handle. When the tool edge moves ¼ in. (6mm), a 16-in.- (405mm) long handle moves nearly 12 in. (305mm) at its end (C in Fig. 1), but only 3 in. (75mm) at the ferrule (B).

D

If your hand grips the tool at D, it requires more effort to move the tool precisely because the fulcrum is at E.

E

Fig. 2

Leverage

When a block of wood revolving on the lathe comes in contact with a tool, it exerts considerable downward pressure on the cutting edge of the tool. As force is applied to this end of the tool, there is an opposite reaction at the other end—your end. The farther the point of cut is away from the fulcrum (the tool rest), the more pressure the revolving wood exerts on the unsupported tip of the tool and the more difficult it will be to control. With the rest positioned about ½ in. (13mm) away from the work, for example, the tool is relatively easy to support. Move the rest about 4 in. (100mm) away from the work, however, and the force exerted on the edge of the tool acts like a heavy weight dropped on one end of a seesaw; you must grasp the handle with grim determination to control the cutting edge. Reduce leverage by keeping the rest as close to the point of cut as possible, and stop the lathe often to move the rest closer to the work.

The way you hold a tool will greatly affect your control over leverage. The tool should pivot on a fixed point on the rest, held there by a grip of your upper hand, as shown in the drawing above (*A* in Fig. 1). This gives you a great mechanical advantage with comparatively little effort. If you were to position your upper hand loosely behind the rest (*D* in Fig. 2), the fulcrum would effectively move to your lower hand at the end of the handle (*E*). To achieve lateral motion, you'd need to apply power with your upper hand near the cutting edge, which is much less efficient. To move the tool to the left, for example, your upper hand would have to pull the whole tool in that direction.

Tool grips

You can grip the tool from either above or below the rest. The former gives you less visibility but deflects shavings better than the latter, where you can actually watch the edge as it cuts. In either case, the object is the same—keep the tool in contact with the rest while controlling lateral movement along it.

The lower hand has more mobility and controls all broad movements and rotation of the tool while the upper hand provides fine control and helps deflect shavings. I grip the handle with my lower hand near the ferrule, because I find it more comfortable than at the end, and because it's easier to control the tool's movement. Also, gripping the tool near the ferrule means my hand need not move quite as far as it would at the end of a long handle. For example, if the point of a chisel moves through an arc of ¼ in. (6mm) with the tool rest ½ in. (13mm) away, a 16-in.-(405mm) long handle will move nearly 12 in. (305mm) at its end, as shown in the drawing on the facing page. At the ferrule this movement would be closer to 3 in. (75mm). I hold the handle against my side or along my forearm for additional stability whenever possible.

When a tool is to be rolled, anticipate the movement by reaching around the handle in the opposite direction (to the right if the tool will roll to the left). When the tool rolls into the cut, your lower hand and forearm can unwind and remain relaxed. In this way you will avoid straining, or having to stop and change grips in the middle of a cut.

Don't grip the tool as though you were clutching a wire stretched across the Grand Canyon—you'll never keep it up. A light, but firm grip is required. You should be relaxed but ready to tighten instantly if necessary. Your grip should act as a shock absorber so that when you have a catch it will be less disastrous. Catches are the bane of the novice turner's life. They are caused by the wood's grabbing at a tool held loosely or at the wrong angle. They happen suddenly, with a bang, and usually scar the wood's surface. The photo above shows the result of a classic heavy catch.

Following are four basic grips. These (and their variations) should enable you to maintain control in virtually every situation you will encounter at the lathe. You should try each with the lathe stopped to get the feel. Remember the importance of stance and let your body follow the handle as you move the tool around. Hold the tool with both hands, the upper hand on the rest near the cutting edge, the lower hand grasping the handle. For right-

A classic example of a catch made with a heavy skew chisel, the result of holding the tool at the wrong angle.

handers (and in my photographs), the left hand is uppermost, the right hand lower. Left-handers will use the reverse.

Lathes are designed with the right-handed in mind. Left-handed turners will have no trouble with long centerwork turnings or with any facework surface parallel to the lathe's axis. Problems arise when hollowing end grain in centerwork or working across a face in facework, unless the lathe has a short bed that allows you complete freedom of movement. Most left-handed turners I know have learned to use their right hands in these awkward situations. Another solution would be to stand on the other side of the bed, but this is dangerous because it is difficult to switch most machines on and off from this position. Some left-handed turners adapt their lathes so that everything happens to the left of the headstock, instead of the right. As a right-hander, I have trained myself to use either hand, and this is the best solution as it gives you the greatest flexibility in attacking awkward jobs.

There are no hard and fast rules to determine which grip is used when. In the photos throughout the book I hold the tools in a variety of ways—all variations on common themes. Which grip you use depends on the cutting situation—the need to deflect shavings versus the need to see what you're doing—or just general comfort. The main object of each grip is to control the centrifugal force generated by the revolving wood that wants to fling the tool away from the center. The power you use to grip the tool is more to prevent catches than to move the tool forward.

The normal hand-over grip is most commonly used for making broad movements of the tool along the rest. Keep your palm on the rest and your other fingers cupped to deflect shavings.

In this variation of the hand-over grip, the handle is nudged right while the fingers pull the edge left. The tool pivots on the thumb providing excellent control.

The secure hand-over grip provides a solid fulcrum. The thumb placed firmly on one side of the gouge prevents it from moving sideways in either direction, allowing precise control.

The hand-under grip allows a high degree of fine control and is best for making an initial entry into the wood or pushing forward to cut a groove. Grip the tool between your thumb on one side and your fingers on the other, and keep your forefinger hooked under the rest.

Normal hand-over grip—This is the most common method employed when the tool is moved laterally along the rest, as in roughing-down centerwork spindles. It is a good grip for broad movements and most roughing cuts. You can push or pull the tool along the rest but lack the precise control of the other grips, because your upper hand is not stationary on the rest. The tool lies beneath your curled hand, with your palm on the rest, and other fingers cupped to deflect shavings. You won't be able to see the edge cutting, but can watch the result of the cut on the top of the work, or opposite side if hollowing a bowl. (With practice, you'll be able to feel the cut without having to look at the shavings.) The photo at top right shows a variation of this grip, used to move the tool to the left. As the handle is nudged right, the fingers of my upper hand pull the edge left. The tool pivots on my thumb, which acts as a fulcrum. This provides more leverage than if the tool were merely pulled left by my upper hand with the fulcrum at the end of the handle.

Secure hand-over grip—This grip ensures a solid fulcrum on the tool rest by preventing the tool from moving sideways along the rest in either direction. It is a good, firm grip but it, too, can block your vision of the surface being cut. That part of your palm at the base of the little finger maintains firm contact with both the rest and the tool to prevent movement in one direction, aided by your thumb; your fingers curl over the top of the tool to prevent movement in the other. You should still retain a degree of fine control between your thumb on one side of the tool and forefinger and middle fingers on the other, pivoting the tool against your palm. The tool pivots from the same position on the tool rest, like an oar in a rowlock. I often use this grip when beginning a roughing cut.

Hand-under grip—This grip not only pulls the tool firmly down onto the rest, but allows you a high degree of fine control, especially when pushing forward to cut grooves, or for an initial entry into the wood. Grip both sides of the tool from below with your thumb and outer fingers and hook your forefinger under the rest. This grip allows you to push or pull the tool laterally along the rest, or you can ease the grip and push the tool forward with your lower hand.

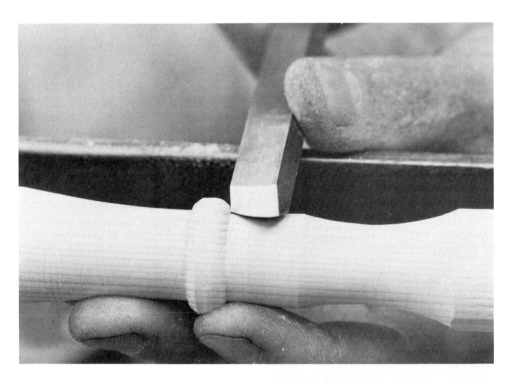

Stop grip—Frequently, you will want to stop the tool moving in one direction, especially when bringing the edge into the wood to begin a cut. In the event of a catch, you need your fingers on only one side of the tool to act as a stop. In the photo above, my thumb acts as a stop while still easing the chisel forward to clean the corner. At top right, two fingers act as a movable stop on top of the tool while the thumb serves as a lateral fulcrum. At right, my thumb acts as a stop to prevent a run-back (similar to a catch) and also as a lateral fulcrum while cutting a thin bowl wall. In the photo below, my little finger acts as both stop and fulcrum for lateral movements. A tool held with one of these stop-grip variations can still move, but under tight control over distances up to 2 in. (50mm). The fingers provide the forward power. This is the grip for cutting very precisely—flanges on box lids, grooves in jam-fit chucks or fine details such as beads or coves. You must be very alert and should guard against a catch by moving your fingers and the edge forward in one positive movement.

Remember that all of these grips should aim to prevent catches and run-backs and maintain control rather than promote forward thrust. As your skill develops you'll be able to adapt them in ways best suited to yourself.

The stop grip is more delicate than the others but allows you to move the tool straight ahead from a fixed point on the rest, carefully guided into the work by your fingers and thumb. The photos on this page show several stop-grip variations.

The photos above and at right show two different ways of providing extra support for thin stock. In both, the fingers of the left (upper) hand curl under the spindle and make contact with the work, the tool and the rest. The tool is held against the wood under tension between the thumb (pushing) and the lower hand (resisting).

Prevent vibration while hollowing end grain by cradling the work in your upper hand.

Extra support

As you become more adventurous and begin to turn slender pieces, it will not be sufficient to guide the cutting edge with one of the standard grips. When thin wood starts flexing, the cut becomes uneven, leaving spiral chatter marks. As this begins to happen you will hear it. The pitch becomes high, even screeching, if you're really overdoing it. If the wood is vibrating too much to allow you to remove the marks with a steady, gentle cut, then it must be suppported. There are all kinds of commercial gadgets to help you do this, but I use my upper hand because it's more flexible and sensitive than any mechanical steadying device.

Whether you are supporting centerwork or facework, the theory is the same: One part of your upper hand takes the bounce out of the wood while the rest of your hand maintains contact with the tool and rest. Your fingers or hand should support the wood behind the cutting area, with a pressure equal to that of the tool. (If you do have a catch, the tool will jump back away from your fingers, and you shouldn't get cut.) If your supporting hand gets too hot, your cut is too forceful. Your hand should be warm to hot, not burning, and provide just enough pressure to keep the wood rotating centrally.

In the photos at left, which show a 7-in. (180mm) by ¾-in. (19mm) spindle being turned and supported, you'll note that contact with tool, rest and wood is maintained by the upper hand. Hold the tool under tension against the wood between the thumb and fingers of your upper hand and move it forward with the thumb pushing, the lower hand resisting. Most of the pressure against the wood is absorbed by the upper hand and the wood is held on its true axis, resulting in ultrafine control. The same is true in the photo at bottom left, where the hand over the stock eliminates chatter while the end grain is hollowed. The thumb provides fine control of the tool edge.

The photos on this page show one hand supporting the wall of a thin holly bowl during a final shearing cut. The centrifugal force generated by the spinning bowl means only a stop grip is necessary on the rest, against which you can lever the tool. The wall thickness is only about ⅛ in. (3mm), and the wood is green and flexible. My palm contacts the end of the rest, my fingers are well behind the cut and able to reach further as the cut progresses. My thumb, used as a moving back stop, keeps the gouge securely in place, and the tool handle is tucked in along my forearm and against my side. The principle is similar to that of a thickness planer. The wood is shaved while being forced to pass between two fixed points; in this case, my fingers behind the bowl and the cutting tool in front. A smooth bowl wall is achieved by moving the gouge evenly and accurately along a predetermined parabola.

You'll find similar techniques constantly useful and will no doubt develop your own as the need arises.

You can provide extra support with your fingers while turning a thin bowl. The palm contacts the tool rest, the fingers are behind the cut and able to reach farther as the cut progresses (bottom). The thumb keeps the gouge securely in place and the tool handle is tucked in along the forearm and against the side for a maximum of control during this delicate operation (top). Note that the thumb creates a secure fulcrum on the rest—this is a variation of the stop grip.

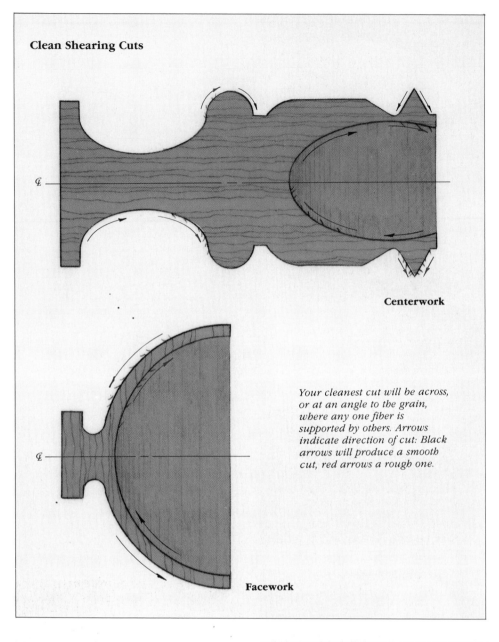

Clean Shearing Cuts

Centerwork

Facework

Your cleanest cut will be across, or at an angle to the grain, where any one fiber is supported by others. Arrows indicate direction of cut: Black arrows will produce a smooth cut, red arrows a rough one.

Cutting

There is absolutely no right or wrong way to turn. The correct way is that which feels comfortable and produces a clean surface. But there are several important rules to be aware of. You may find it useful to refer back to these after beginning the exercises in Chapters 6 and 7.

—Wood is essentially a bundle of long fibers lying generally in the same direction. Your cleanest cut will be across the bundle (the grain) where any one fiber is supported by others, as shown in the drawing above. Unsupported fibers will splinter away, as anyone who has cross-sawn a board will know. Plan your cuts in such a way that there is support for the area being cut by following the directional arrows in the drawing.

—The tool must contact the rest first, before moving forward to bring the bevel shoulder into contact with the wood, as shown in the drawing on the facing page. If the edge contacts the revolving wood first, the downward force will slap the tool onto the rest and you'll almost certainly have a catch. Such a catch will either leave a mess on the wood or, in extreme cases on lighter lathes, a broken tool rest. (I did this twice early on in my turning career.) Do not allow one side of a scraper or parting tool to rise off the rest.

—When the bevel shoulder is in contact with the wood, tilt the handle up about 10° to bring the edge down through an arc and into the cut. Do not simply move the tool horizontally across the rest into the wood. (This procedure applies to skew chisels and parting tools as well as to gouges, shown in Fig. 1. Scrapers are set flat on the rest and pushed into the cut, as shown in Fig. 2; the bevel is on the underside of the tool and cannot rub. Because only the cutting edge contacts the wood, scrapers should be eased forward with great care to make light cuts.) Rubbing the bevel is often impossible when you enter the wood, as there is no cut surface on which to rub, but do this whenever possible. The bevel shoulder can be used as a secondary fulcrum against which the tool pivots to bring the cutting edge into play.

The photos on the facing page show the bevel of a gouge rubbing on two different cuts: to begin a shearing cut down the outside curve of a bowl (left) and during a cut from the rim to the center of a bowl (right). To make a delicate cut, lever the edge back slightly against the bevel shoulder. For a heavier cut, change the angle of the tool so that it pivots on a fulcrum made by your palm and little finger on the tool rest. To continue the cut as it is, keep the bevel surface rubbing in the same position, so the tool is guided by the surface just cut; this will work as long as the bevel has a smooth surface to rub.

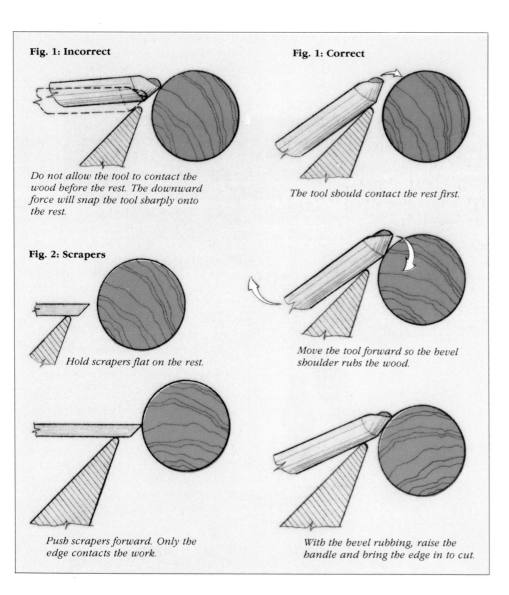

Fig. 1: Incorrect

Do not allow the tool to contact the wood before the rest. The downward force will snap the tool sharply onto the rest.

Fig. 1: Correct

The tool should contact the rest first.

Move the tool forward so the bevel shoulder rubs the wood.

Fig. 2: Scrapers

Hold scrapers flat on the rest.

Push scrapers forward. Only the edge contacts the work.

With the bevel rubbing, raise the handle and bring the edge in to cut.

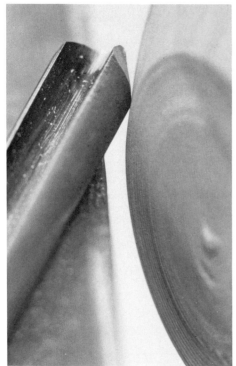

The bevel shoulder of a gouge or chisel should contact the wood before the edge is lowered to cut (left). Move the tool into the wood slowly under precise control, using the bevel to guide the edge into the cut (above). You can use the bevel shoulder as a secondary fulcrum for delicate cuts by levering the edge back slightly against it.

Supporting the Point of Cut

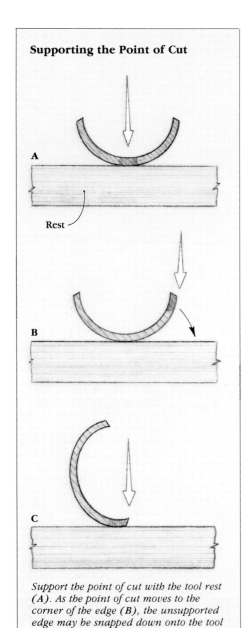

A

Rest

B

C

Support the point of cut with the tool rest (A). As the point of cut moves to the corner of the edge (B), the unsupported edge may be snapped down onto the tool rest. Roll the gouge so the rest remains beneath the cut (C).

Pressure on the unsupported edge of a gouge is the cause of many nasty catches. Roll the gouge in the direction of the cut so the part of the edge that is cutting is supported by the tool rest.

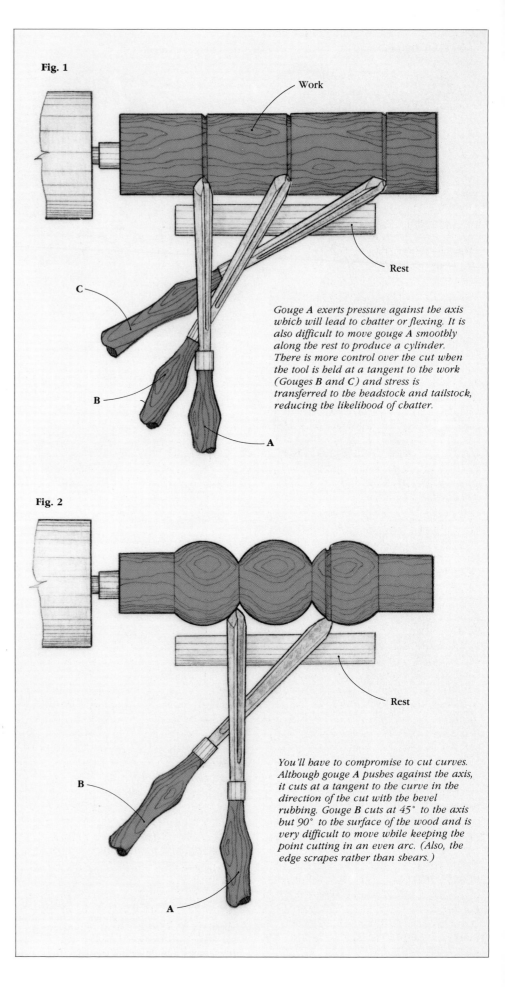

Fig. 1

Work

Rest

C

B

A

Gouge A exerts pressure against the axis which will lead to chatter or flexing. It is also difficult to move gouge A smoothly along the rest to produce a cylinder. There is more control over the cut when the tool is held at a tangent to the work (Gouges B and C) and stress is transferred to the headstock and tailstock, reducing the likelihood of chatter.

Fig. 2

Rest

B

A

You'll have to compromise to cut curves. Although gouge A pushes against the axis, it cuts at a tangent to the curve in the direction of the cut with the bevel rubbing. Gouge B cuts at 45° to the axis but 90° to the surface of the wood and is very difficult to move while keeping the point cutting in an even arc. (Also, the edge scrapes rather than shears.)

—Roll gouges in the direction of the cut, as shown in the drawing and photo at far left on the facing page. The pressure of the wood on the unsupported edge of a gouge is the source of many nasty catches. When the cut is made with the center (lower edge) of the gouge *(A)*, there should be no problem because the point of cut is directly supported by the tool rest. Problems arise when the point of cut moves up to the unsupported corner of the tool *(B)*. This can be corrected by rolling the tool so that it contacts the rest below the point of cut *(C)*. There is an exception to this rule when making a back-cut using a deep-fluted gouge (p. 106).

—Cut with the tool moving parallel or at a tangent to the axis on which the wood rotates, rather than against it, as shown in Fig. 1 of the drawing at right on the facing page. This will allow the force that is applied as the tool moves forward to be transferred to the headstock or tailstock. The idea is to put as little pressure against the axis as possible. Too much pressure can cause chattering, flexing or breaking of slender work, or it may even weaken a fixing. But cuts are rarely made parallel to the axis because you have to compromise and consider grain direction. In cutting the curved centerwork beads (Fig. 2), the tool will not cut cleanly when held at 90° to the surface of the wood.

—Always cut above a line from the top of the tool rest to the center, as shown in the drawing at right. If you cut below this line, the wood tends to grab at the tool. I raise the tool edge a maximum of 10° during a cut before bringing the edge down to finish at the center. As you cut into the center of the work, slow up and float the edge in gently, rolling the tool to maintain the most effective cut. Stop at the center; don't push and overshoot the center or the tool will meet wood travelling upward on the other side and you'll risk tearing or pulling out fibers.

—Initial cuts should be exploratory until you determine where the wood and the orbit of its extremities are. If the tool is pushed in too fast, too much wood will contact the edge at once, making the tool clear more wood than is advisable. That sudden force will lead to a catch. As you cut, you want to control the leverage and path of the edge rather than forcing the tool forward against the work. The tool should move forward only when the wood in its path has been removed. In the hands of an expert this is a rapid, flowing action. It's like a moving picture or animated cartoon where slightly different static images in each frame run in quick succession to produce a single, fluid

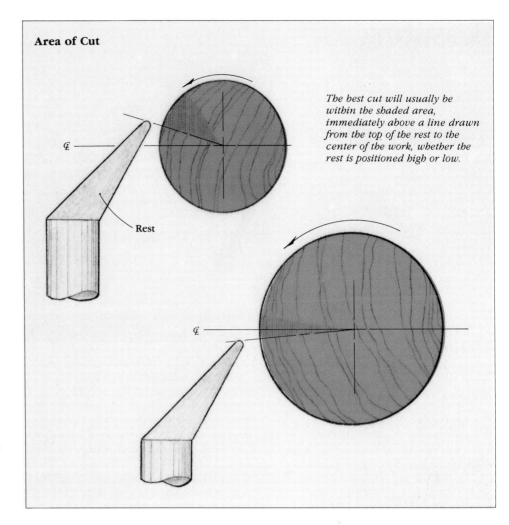

Area of Cut

The best cut will usually be within the shaded area, immediately above a line drawn from the top of the rest to the center of the work, whether the rest is positioned high or low.

Rest

movement. A sharp tool held in the optimum position will produce a large shaving with virtually no forward pressure. It is possible to use the tools effectively while holding them lightly between a finger and thumb. (I don't advise this because it won't give you much control, but it illustrates the importance of manipulating leverage without power.)

If a sharp tool begins to cut less efficiently or even stops cutting altogether, rather than pushing hard to find an edge, adjust the tool angle or roll it to a different position where it will cut. If you push hard at the wrong angle, the tool will often skate up and over the surface with little or no effect. The tool should never shoot forward and ride on the bevel if you lose an edge; this indicates lack of control and too much pressure against the wood. The aim is to move the tool precisely and evenly along a definite path, removing all that it encounters. Don't try to cut too much at one go.

Practice stopping in mid-cut by easing pressure so that the edge is barely in contact with the wood. In this position, the bevel still rubs while the edge produces light, fluffy shavings. Then

proceed and stop again. Soon you should be able to withdraw the tool and return it to exactly the same position. As you do this, practice bringing the bevel shoulder in contact with the wood first and letting it rub. Then gradually rotate and adjust the angle of the edge downward to pick up the cut. Move the tool into the wood slowly with precise control. Whenever you succeed in producing a good shaving and leaving a smooth surface, try to repeat the action. Do it over and over until you are confident you can make the same cut at will. Then build on your one basic cut.

Learning what the tools can and should do isn't easy. When is a tool not sharp enough? What is an acceptable finish from a tool? Such questions are best answered through experience, but when difficulties arise, ask yourself:

—Does the tool need sharpening?

—Is it the wood—difficult grain or a foreign particle (silica, wire or a nail)?

—Could the tool be used differently with better results?

—Would another tool be better?

—Is it me? In which case, keep practicing. Or go for a walk and try again later. Everyone has off days.

Measuring

5

It takes time to develop an accurate eye, so you'll need to measure at many stages in woodturning.

Finding centers, marking out spindles, and gauging outside and inside diameters, depths and wall thicknesses are the most common occasions. Whenever possible, I prefer to rely on my eye and sense of touch. This is quick and I feel lends spontaneity and vigor to my turnings; the work flows rather than proceeding in fits and starts. But it's a good idea to check yourself every now and then with instruments, especially in the beginning, to avoid drifting into patterns of error. Where precise measurements are essential, for example when turning chair spindles or fitting mirrors or lids to boxes, I look for quick, simple methods that limit my margin of error.

The photo at right shows a selection of basic measuring tools. I use an assortment of rulers and squares, inside and outside calipers, vernier calipers and dividers, plus a few small gouges or drill bits mounted in handles for establishing depths. You won't need all of these to begin with, just a couple pairs of dividers and inside and outside calipers, a vernier calipers and some rulers—and you needn't spend a lot of money on them.

Centering

It's important to center stock on the lathe carefully to reduce vibration and the amount of waste wood that will be removed. Where a square section will remain, as on the ends of a spindle, an accurate center is essential or the finished piece will be unbalanced. If large turnings are mounted off-center, they may loosen fixings or even fly off the lathe. Your first task, before mounting any object on the lathe, is to find its center.

Centerwork

On square-section stock, draw diagonals between opposite corners and center the piece on the lathe at the intersection of the lines, as shown in the photo at top left on the facing page. If the corners of a piece of wood are missing, draw lines parallel to and equidistant from the sides, as shown at top center. Then draw diagonals between the corners of the resulting interior square. If the sides of an equilateral polygon are the same length, you can also draw lines between opposite corners as described for square stock.

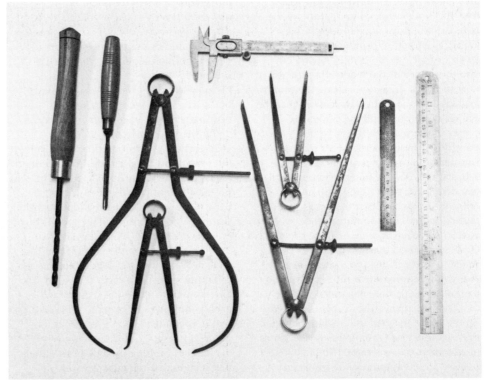

A few measuring tools are all you'll need to get started. A basic tool kit should include: (left to right) a ¼-in. (6mm) drill bit and ¼-in. gouge mounted in handles for drilling depth holes, spring-adjusted outside calipers, inside calipers, dividers, rulers and vernier calipers (top).

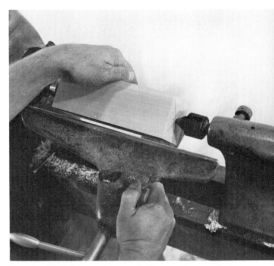

To locate the center of square-section stock, draw diagonal lines between opposite corners (left). If the corners are missing, draw lines parallel to and equidistant from the sides (right). Then draw diagonals between the corners of the interior square.

To check the accuracy of the center, move the tool rest in parallel to one corner of the stock. Rotate the stock by hand, checking that the gap between it and the tool rest is the same along each corner.

Once the work has been mounted between centers (p. 14), the accuracy of its center should be checked. There are several ways to do this. The quickest way is to move the tool rest in parallel and very close to one corner of the stock, and rotate the stock by hand, checking that the gap between the stock and the tool rest is the same along each corner (top right). Another way is to move the tool rest back so that there is no danger of its touching the stock. Start the lathe and make a nick with the long point of a skew chisel at each corner, keeping the tool in a fixed position on the rest. Stop the lathe and check that the nick at each corner is the same depth. A third method is to start the lathe and touch a fine, hard pencil against the end grain, marking as large a circle as possible on the wood, as shown in the photos at right. Stop the lathe and check that the circle is centered in the square.

If one of these checks reveals inaccurate mounting, it's easy to adjust the stock to the correct position by steadying your left hand on the tool rest while you move the work slightly in any direction, as the right hand adjusts the tail center tension.

On round-section or irregular stock, you can draw several approximate diameters on the end grain and take a mean center before adopting one of the procedures above to center the stock. But, if the stock is reasonably round, it's quicker and more accurate to mount the drive end in a three-jaw, spigot or collet chuck, which automatically centers it, leaving only the other end to be adjusted, in the same manner described for square-section stock. Chucks tend to grip better than spur drives, which can bore into end grain.

Here's another way to check your center. Mark a circle on the end grain with the lathe rotating (top). Then stop the lathe and check the circle. If it doesn't fall completely within the square (bottom), adjust the tail center and try again.

Faceplate Screw Holes

Fig. 1

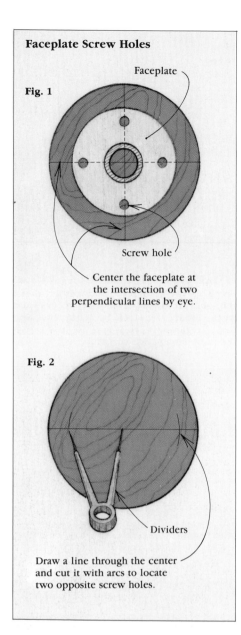

Center the faceplate at the intersection of two perpendicular lines by eye.

Fig. 2

Draw a line through the center and cut it with arcs to locate two opposite screw holes.

Use a pair of dividers to scribe a circle on the wood. After the circle has been cut out, the center point left by the dividers aids centering of a faceplate or locating a block between centers.

Locate the two screw holes by marking the work's center and the circumference of the faceplate. Then draw a diameter and drill where it intersects the circumference.

Facework

Locating the center of a disc should be easy, because dividers are commonly used to mark a circle on a block of wood before cutting it. The mark that the point of the dividers leaves at the center can serve to center the work on the lathe. To mount a disc on a center-screw faceplate, all you need is a pilot hole drilled at the center to accept the single screw. I mount small discs, about 5 in. (125mm) in diameter, in a jaw chuck (p. 19) for a more secure and speedy fixing.

It's best to mount large discs on a standard faceplate so that they can be attached with several screws for extra security. There are several ways of locating screw holes. One way is to draw two lines intersecting in the center at right angles and line them up in the screw holes, as shown in Fig. 1 at left (most faceplates have four symmetrical holes). My standard faceplates have hollow centers, so I can see the center mark. Instead of actually drawing the lines, it's quick and easy to align the faceplate by eye.

A second way is to scribe a circle the diameter of your faceplate when you mark out the disc. Align the faceplate within that circle and mark or drill the pilot holes with the faceplate in position.

A third way is to draw a line through the center of the disc and cut this with arcs to locate two opposite screw holes in the faceplate, as shown in Fig. 2. I frequently use this method when the external shape of a bowl has been turned on a faceplate and the piece is ready to be remounted at the base for hollowing: It's quick and I only need two screws to hold most work safely. You can mark the work while it's still on the lathe. With the lathe running, it will be easy to locate the center on all but very plain surfaces, as the grain patterns rotate around it. If you touch dead center with a pencil you will leave a dot; anywhere else the pencil will leave a circle on the wood. Mark the center of the work and measure out from it with a ruler to lay out the circumference on which the screw holes lie. Stop the lathe, draw a line through the center, crossing the circumference at two points, and drill pilot holes at the intersections. You can then sand and finish the base with the screw holes in the right position and all layout markings removed. If the wood is dry or will not be remounted, place the screws across the grain, otherwise along the grain as shown on p. 18.

One-hundred-percent accuracy when fixing or remounting a facework job is rare. Usually the piece will be slightly off-center—sometimes as much as $\frac{1}{32}$ in. (1.0mm). Frequently this won't matter, but for greater precision (as for parts that must be fitted together) the piece must be turned true. With practice, your eye should develop so that you can pinpoint the center of a disc with reasonable accuracy, without measuring.

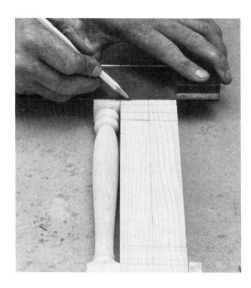

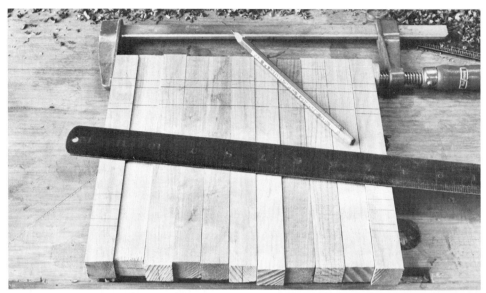

Marking Out Spindles

Where a square section is to remain on the spindle, it is easier to mark it out before mounting the stock on the lathe. Lay out a pattern or the spindle to be copied alongside the square piece of stock. Then, using a try square, mark or scribe the crucial points on one face of the stock. I mark corners, groove centers, cove sides and the bases of a bead. If a number of similar spindles are to be turned, clamp the squared blanks together and mark them in batches as shown in the photos above. When the stock is spinning on the lathe, a clear line drawn on one face will appear as a solid line around the spindle.

If the finished spindle is to be turned without leaving any square sections, the marking is easier to do with the rough-turned cylinder revolving on the lathe. If you are turning a quantity of similar spindles, a marking batten will speed this process. The batten has V-grooves for reference points, which I cut with a pocket knife. Place the batten on the tool rest so that it contacts the rotating stock lightly. Rest the point of a thin marking awl in the bottom of the V-groove. Push it forward, guided by the V, to scribe a line against the rotating stock. A scribed line is better than a pencil line (though I have used a pencil for clarity in the photos), which can disappear in the turning and fail to provide an accurate reference point.

A variation of this spindle-marking technique involves a batten with nails protruding in place of the V-grooves. This method requires an accurately roughed cylinder for all the nail points to touch the surface at the same time, so it works best for short lengths of up to 12 in. (305mm). The notched batten allows more margin for error and a less exacting approach.

For greater accuracy, when marking out several spindle blanks at once where a square section is to remain, clamp a marked blank on either side of the set and draw lines between them using a try square and a pencil.

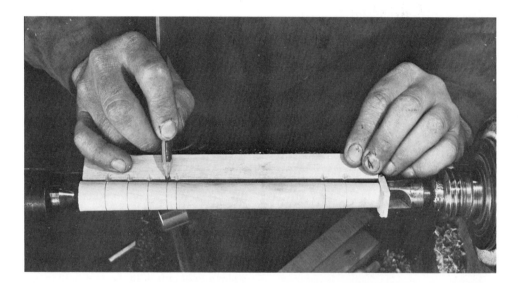

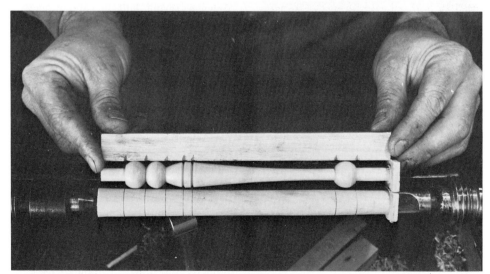

A marking batten is useful to speed up the process of marking cylindrical spindles after they are mounted on the lathe. The V-grooves in the batten at top are used to mark groove centers and the bases of the beads on a spindle. The photo at bottom shows the relationship of a finished spindle to the batten.

Screw-adjusted spring calipers can be used to measure an outside diameter while you turn the wood down to size. This is one of the few occasions when you do not keep your upper hand on the rest.

To measure an outside diameter, hold the calipers horizontally on the revolving wood (top). Never push the calipers vertically over the wood (bottom).

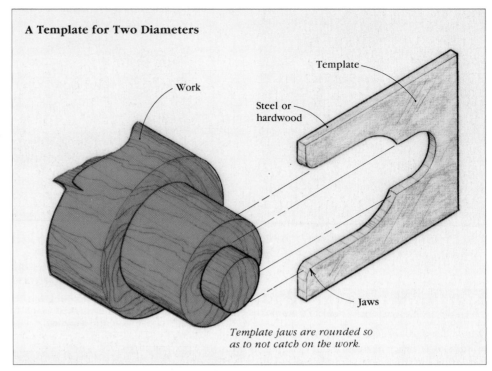

A Template for Two Diameters

Template

Steel or hardwood

Work

Jaws

Template jaws are rounded so as to not catch on the work.

Outside Diameters

Once the stock has been centered and mounted on the lathe, you are ready to begin turning. While turning, you will frequently need to determine outside and inside dimensions and thicknesses and this may be done with calipers, dividers, rulers and templates.

Outside calipers

For small jobs, hold the calipers around the rotating wood with your upper hand, as shown in the photos at top left, while making light cuts with the tool held in your lower hand. Pull the calipers gently against the cut surface until they pass over. The curved metal legs of the calipers are flexible, which will allow them to pass over a diameter fractionally larger than their setting (this provides a built-in margin of error).

When you simply want to measure an outside diameter, rest the calipers horizontally on top of the wood (while it's either stationary or revolving) and adjust the screw until the legs slip over the wood. Because the calipers are springy, never try to push them vertically over revolving wood, as shown at bottom left; the legs will catch and bend and possibly cause injury.

A good way to learn to use calipers properly is to rough-down hundreds of blanks to fit a cup chuck, or some other repetitive job, when the odd mistake doesn't matter too much.

Templates

Where absolute accuracy is essential (for example, when turning a spindle tenon to fit a drilled hole), use a template to avoid the possibility of the caliper jaws flexing or the adjustment screw coming loose. For production runs of hundreds or thousands of the same item, make a template from a hard material such as steel or hard plastic; wood or soft plastic will wear away too quickly. Round the corners of the template jaws to lessen the likelihood of a catch as you place it against the revolving wood. For short runs, you can make a template quickly by drilling a hole the size of the desired spindle in a scrap of ⅜-in.-(10mm) thick hardwood and cutting across the diameter of the hole. Hold this template against the wood as you turn until the spindle fits the semicircle, as shown at top left on the facing page.

An old turner's trick for cutting small centerwork to a precise diameter is to sharpen the top jaw of a wrench and round the bottom: The top jaw cuts like a parting tool, while the bottom rubs until the wood fits between the jaws. This is useful for cranking out large numbers of standard-sized dowels or tenons.

You can make a simple template by drilling a hole in a piece of hardwood. Cut the wood in half, bisecting the hole. Hold the template against the wood and turn the spindle until it fits.

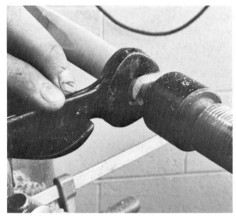

An old turner's trick is to sharpen the top jaw of a wrench so it will cut like a parting tool while the bottom jaw rubs until the wood fits between.

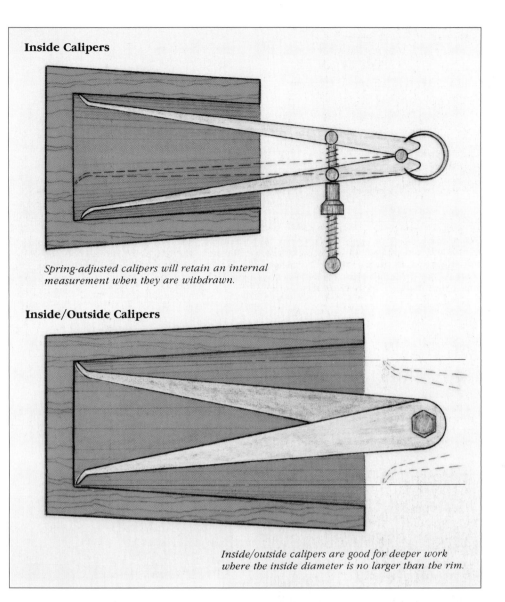

Inside Calipers

Spring-adjusted calipers will retain an internal measurement when they are withdrawn.

Inside/Outside Calipers

Inside/outside calipers are good for deeper work where the inside diameter is no larger than the rim.

Inside Diameters

Several different kinds of calipers may be used to take inside measurements, their selection being determined by the size and shape of the work and the degree of accuracy required. Turn the lathe off to measure inside diameters or the caliper points are certain to catch, spin around and snap together, possibly with flesh pinched between (very painful).

Inside calipers

The bent points on the screw-adjusted inside calipers, shown in the drawing above, can be inserted through a small opening to measure a wider space inside. The spring allows them to be squeezed together for withdrawal and then expanded for an exact measure of an internal diameter. I find them particularly useful for making box lids when parallel sides are essential for a good suction fit.

Inside/outside calipers

These are usually made from flat steel stock and are useful where the screw of the adjustable type interferes with the work. They are normally used to measure inside diameters but the points can also be crossed to measure outside diameters of small work. They are useless if the internal diameter is greater than the diameter of the rim, because they won't retain their measurement when they're withdrawn.

Vernier calipers

These are very useful for measuring inside and outside diameters of small work quickly and precisely. Their inside and outside jaws lie on opposite sides of a calibrated central shaft and move simultaneously. This makes vernier calipers ideal for jobs such as fitting a ferrule on a tool handle or a lid on a box. The inside jaws measure the inside diameter, while the outside jaws gauge the diameter of the flange that is being turned down to fit.

Vernier calipers are useful for measuring inside and outside diameters of small work quickly and precisely. One side of the calipers measures the inside of this ferrule while the other side transfers the same measurement to the work.

When marking a diameter on facework with dividers, both points are equidistant from the center when they line up in the same groove. But only the left point should contact the revolving wood. In the photo at left, the left point is too near the center, placing the right point wide of the line. Halve the distance between the right point and the line and move the left point that distance away from the center.

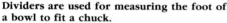

Dividers are used for measuring the foot of a bowl to fit a chuck.

You can mark out a diameter with a pencil and ruler.

Diameters on a Face

Dividers are the fastest and most accurate way to mark a diameter on a face. Keep the points sharp by touching them up on a grinder occasionally and set them to the exact diameter required. Position the rest slightly below center height and center the dividers by lightly touching the revolving wood with the left point so that the mark it makes lines up with the right point. In the photo at top, far left, the left point is too near the center, placing the right point wide of the line. Halve the distance between the right point and the line and move the left point that distance away from center. Both points are equidistant from the center when they line up in the same groove (top right) and a straight line drawn between them will pass through the center. With practice, you will be able to align the two points in a few seconds with only one or two adjustments, which makes this a valuable production technique. This is the best way to measure the fit of a box lid to its base or a bowl foot for a spigot chuck, as shown at center left. Be careful not to let the right-hand point touch the wood, because the upward rotation of the wood on the right-hand side can grab the point and carry it around to meet the left point, with a painful result if you have a finger in the way.

Where the diameter is greater than the maximum extension of your dividers, work from a radius instead of the diameter. Measure the diameter and halve it to get the radius. Set the dividers to the radius and place the right point at the center. (Remember that if the point makes a ring on the revolving wood, you are off-center.) Proceed slowly and take care not to touch the work to the right of center. Once the right point is centered, bring in the left point to mark the radius.

You can use a ruler to mark a diameter in much the same way as you would with the dividers, as shown at bottom left. Measuring with a ruler is based on a radius laid out from the center. In the photo at left I am laying out a 250mm diameter on the face of a disc. The ruler is held so that the 125mm mark is at the center and the pencil touches the revolving wood at zero. If my mark has been made correctly, the opposite side of the circle will align with the 250mm mark. To measure diameters larger than the length of your ruler, hold zero at the center and mark the appropriate radius. You can work more accurately from the diameter than from the radius; any error in measuring the radius will double when you mark the wood.

Make a small *V* in the center—as a guide for the gouge or drill—with the long point of a skew chisel.

Inside Depths

It is often important to know exactly what depth a hollow is or will be. Before I hollow, I use a ¼-in. (6mm) carver's gouge or a ¼-in. (6mm) drill bit mounted in a handle (see the tool photo on p. 58) to drill a hole to establish the desired depth and then work my cuts down to that point. I use the same technique for both but prefer the drill bit for any job over 6 in. (150mm) in diameter, and the gouge for anything smaller.

First, I make a small *V* in the center of the revolving wood, using either the gouge or the long point of a skew chisel. This acts as a guide for starting the tool. Next, with my thumb held as a stop along the top edge of the tool at the required depth (1½ in. in the photo at top right), I push the tool into the wood until my thumb contacts the surface. In the photos at bottom right I am using this technique to drill a hole into the end grain of a small light-pull knob. The gouge is presented to the wood with the tip tilted very slightly above horizontal and with the top of the gouge facing the center of the hole. Bring the lower part of the bevel into contact with the center *V*, then raise the tool handle until it is parallel to the axis and push it in firmly. Do not make your initial entry into the wood with the tool top-side-up; this is certain to catch on the left corner. You'll feel when the tool is centered and, once you've cut the first ⅛

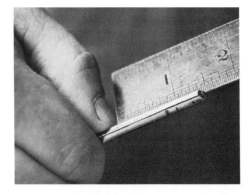

Position your thumb along the top edge of the gouge or drill. It will serve as a quick and reasonably accurate depth stop. Push the tool into the wood until your thumb contacts the surface.

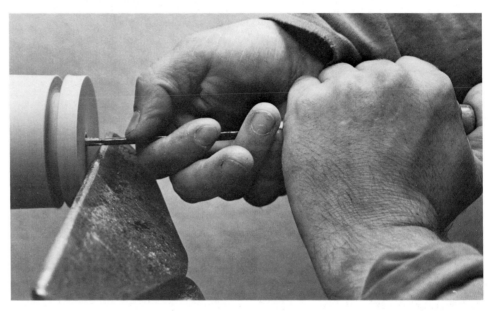

in. (3mm) parallel with the axis, it should go in easily, guided by the first part of the hole. The tool will now cut, whether the top faces up, down or sideways, but if it is not held parallel to the axis, you'll have problems; it won't penetrate the wood easily, if at all. And if it does, both wood and tool will jump all over. The tool doesn't touch the rest in this operation once the pilot hole has been cut.

This action is quicker and simpler than it sounds but if the depth is more than ¾ in. (19mm), complete the cut in a series of pushes, pulling the gouge or drill out most of the way after each thrust to clear the shavings. Don't push long or hard because the end of the tool and the shavings can get hot very quickly and it's easy to burn your fingers.

Rub the bevel with the tool tip angled slightly above horizontal. When the tool is centered, raise it parallel to the axis of the wood and push it in.

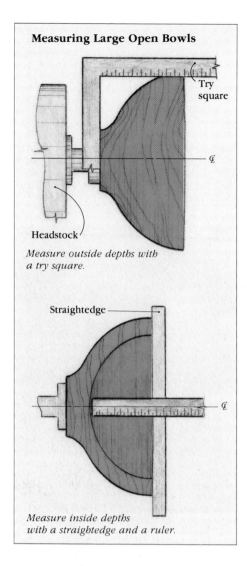

Measuring Large Open Bowls

Try square

Headstock

Measure outside depths with a try square.

Straightedge

Measure inside depths with a straightedge and a ruler.

Place a 150-watt bulb behind a very thin turning and gauge thickness by the amount of light that passes through the wood. The darker ring at the base indicates a thicker foot.

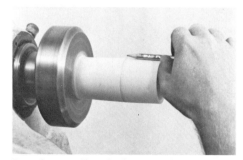

Rest the pencil at the bottom of the opening and position your thumb at the rim. Remove the pencil and, keeping your thumb in place, mark a line on the outside by rolling the pencil forward.

There are two ways of transferring the depth of a hole to the outside. The quickest method is to rest a pencil at the bottom of the opening while you position your thumb at the rim, as described for the depth gauge on the previous page. Keep your thumb rigidly in place, and lay the pencil along the outside of the work with your thumb at the top of the opening; roll the pencil forward to mark the work. This method is especially good on small centerwork, and can be used with the lathe in motion.

The second way, which is slower but more accurate, is to stop the lathe and measure the depth with a ruler. Whichever method you use, beware of a common trap. Many people are tempted not to mark the precise depths but to add a bit, especially when making boxes or goblets, which are hollowed before the outside is shaped. This is a bad practice. If you add a bit to ensure plenty of material, you lose track of exactly where the bottom of your hole is and you have no definite point to which to relate future cuts. Be precise.

To check the depth of large open bowls, measure the outside height with a try square and subtract the desired thickness of the bottom. To measure the inside depth, place a straightedge across the rim of the bowl and measure down from it to the bottom. Then you can decide if you need to hollow further or if you're already pushing your luck by having gone deeper than intended.

Wall Thickness

When turning very thin walls, usually less than ¼ in. (6mm), place a light behind the wood and gauge thickness by the amount that passes through it. This works well with most pale timbers, especially if still green, but not at all with dark woods.

With the lathe turned off, use outside calipers to measure wall thickness precisely. My larger ones are screw-adjusted and flexible enough to pass over a rim thicker than the rest of the wall, as shown at the top of the facing page.

Short-Cuts

It is possible to waste a lot of time and energy fiddling about with measuring. Working commercially, I try to save time by limiting the amount of measuring, particularly once an object has been mounted on the lathe. I prefer to gauge things by eye, touch, and by relating measurements to the tools I'm using. This is particularly important if you design an item for production.

Some time ago, it occurred to me that the spindles I was copying had certain common characteristics; beads were the same size and spaced in multiples of tool widths. Even if this was not the intent of the old chair bodgers, it is certainly mine now. If I design a spindle with grooves and beads turned out of square stock, I'll mark as few lines as possible on the stock. Only the square shoulders are actually laid out from a pattern. All other distances are a chisel-width, or portion thereof, apart.

But, won't the spindles vary? Yes, as will almost everything handmade, but that difference will be difficult to discern when they are eventually fixed in place. I am laying out grooves on the cylinder at right by eye—a chisel-width apart. I approach runs of small bowls in the same way. I cut the discs on the bandsaw and turn them to the largest possible diameter. This means there will be variations; 6-in.- (150mm) diameter bowls might vary by as much as ⅛ in. (3mm) in diameter, but they will still be quite similar and probably blend much better with a previous batch than if I had tried to make them exactly the same. If I want to make a set of six identically shaped bowls, they'll require more precision and individual measuring. I turn my kitchen scoops out of 2-in.- (50mm) square by 8-in.- (205mm) long blanks. I mount and turn them between centers to fit a 2-in. (50mm) cup chuck. These are rough-turned to fit the chuck by leaving the remnants of the flat sides of the blank along most of their length. I then turn a shallow taper on one end to a finished diameter slightly less than the 2-in.- (50mm) thick stock. They fit every time without my using calipers.

If you need to make thousands of tenons the same size, it would make sense to have a local machinist make a spur drive to match the diameter of the tenon. Simply turn the wood to the diameter of the drive—without using measuring tools at all. There are hundreds of ways of saving time and effort like this, and most of them develop when boredom sets in and you're forced to do something about it.

The flexible arms of the big spring calipers allow you to measure a thin bowl wall below a thicker rim, without losing the original measurement.

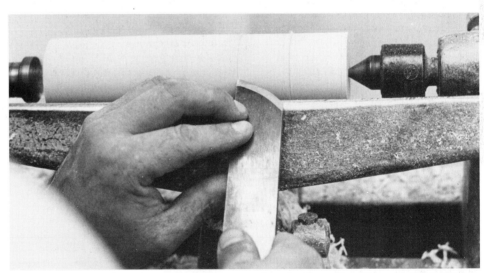

Plan ahead to allow for speedy production with a minimum of measuring. To save time, the grooves are being laid out on this cylinder by eye—a chisel width apart.

Scoop blanks can be rough-turned, leaving remnants of the original flat sides to make them easier to stack. Next, turn a shallow taper at one end to a diameter slightly less than the 2-in. (50mm) square stock. These will fit the cup chuck every time—without using calipers.

Centerwork

6

In centerwork, the grain of the wood is parallel to the rotational axis of the lathe.

The term can be misleading, however, because centerwork jobs are not necessarily turned between two centers. While work such as lace bobbins, rolling pins, bannister spindles and newel posts are turned between a drive and a tail center, items like boxes and eggcups must be held at the drive end only so the other end can be hollowed.

The straighter the grain, the easier the wood is to work and the smoother the surface you can obtain directly from the tool. Short grain, which runs at a tangent or right angle to the axis, is difficult to cut cleanly and accurately. It is especially awkward to cut with the skew chisel, which is the main centerwork tool. Because short grain is structurally very weak, you should avoid it for long or slender work.

Consider the nature of wood: a bundle of long fibers, all running in the same direction. The best, cleanest cut results from offering the tool to the work in such a way that each fiber being cut is supported by other fibers, as shown in the drawing on p. 54. This is often referred to as cutting with the grain. To cut in the opposite direction, or against the grain, results in a torn surface because each fiber being cut is unsupported by neighboring fibers. Further, it is best to keep the edge cutting at around 45° to the long grain, which results in a shearing cut. A scraping cut, with the edge parallel to the grain, will leave a torn surface, as the cutting edge levers the fibers off the bundle. If you proceed gently, you might get away with a scraping cut on fine-grained hardwoods, but it is better to learn the shearing cuts. By contrast, scrapers often produce the best surface on end grain, when each fiber is well-supported by others. Dense woods can finish like glass from a delicate scrape on end grain.

In this chapter I will explain the essential centerwork cuts and lead you through a series of exercises that demonstrate how you can achieve them. At the end of the chapter are three projects that will give you an opportunity to put these skills to work. I encourage you to practice the exercises seriously for they will enable you to develop your technique and give you the confidence you'll need to approach the projects. Don't think of your results as successes or failures. It is experience you are after, and everything you turn will be a step in the right direction. You may find it useful to refer forward or backward from the descriptions of tool usage to the exercises and the project photo strips as you turn your way through this chapter. Refer to Chapter 3 for further explanation of the types and shapes of tools available and how to grind their edges. If you still feel vaguely uncomfortable, review Chapter 4 for a better understanding of how to approach the lathe and control leverage. But in the end, there is no substitute for practice.

External Shaping

The cleanest cuts come from gouges and skew chisels shearing across the grain, and you can turn almost any spindle shape you want using these tools. I use gouges to rough-down square sections to round and to cut coves. Otherwise, I favor the skew chisel, which gives me a superior finish faster and with less effort. However, many turners use only gouges and still get satisfactory results, so there is an element of personal preference. Parting tools peel the wood like a rotary veneer knife and are used at a right angle to the grain to establish diameters or to cut finished work off the lathe. With a few exceptions, I feel that scrapers should be employed for external centerwork only when all else fails, usually on twisted grain or knots.

Gouges

Most gouges are useful at some point in centerwork, from the heavy 2-in. (50mm) gouges, used for roughing-down large square sections to round, to the ⅛-in. (3mm) ones used to cut tiny coves and areas of twisted grain that are difficult to work with a skew chisel.

Square-ground gouges (p. 29) are commonly used for roughing-down—their shape allows you to use all of the edge— and for fine cutting of smooth cylinders and tapers. To cut coves or beads you'll want a long, symmetrical fingernail edge as shown on p. 29, with no corners to catch the work. I use either deep-fluted or shallow tools for roughing-down and for long curves, but for coves or corners, shallow gouges are better than deep-fluted; the longer curve of the edge provides a good angle for a shearing cut while the narrow radius of the tip can reach into

External Shapes and Tools

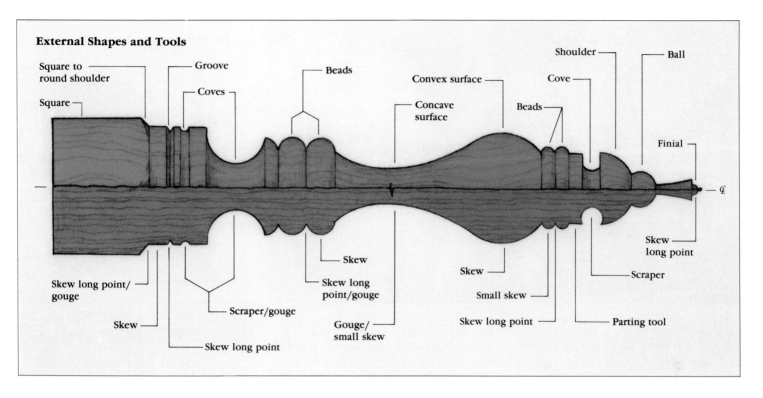

tight corners. If your tool budget is limited, I recommend the shallow fingernail gouges. As a guide, I suggest the following tools for roughing-down squares to round:

—For work less than 1 in. (25mm) in diameter: ½-in. (13mm) to ¾-in. (19mm) standard gouge or skew chisel.

—1 in. (25mm) to 2 in. (50mm) in diameter: 1-in. (25mm) to 1⅜-in. (35mm) standard gouge or 1-in. (25mm) to 1½-in. (38mm) skew chisel.

—2 in. (50mm) to 4 in. (100mm) in diameter: 1-in. (25mm) to 1⅜-in. (35mm) standard gouge.

—Above 4 in. (100mm) in diameter: 2-in. (50mm) long-and-strong gouge.

Refer to the speed chart at right for all centerwork projects.

When turning the cylinders, coves and beads in the following exercises, always ensure that your upper hand contacts the rest. If the wood starts to chatter as it becomes thinner, hold your hand behind it to remove the flexing and cut with less pressure. Set the rest parallel to the work and about ¼ in. (6mm) above center height. By holding the tool rigidly on the rest with your upper hand as you move it along the rest to make your cut, you can keep the cutting edge in the same plane; the rest acts as a reference point, or jig, for the tool edge.

Centerwork Speeds

Diameters	Lengths					
	6 in. (150mm)	12 in. (305mm)	18 in. (460mm)	24 in. (610mm)	36 in. (915mm)	48 in. (1220mm)
½ in. (13mm)	3000	2500	1250	900	700	700
2 in. (50mm)	2500	2500	1750	1250	700	700
3 in. (75mm)	1750	1250	1250	900	700	700
4 in. (100mm)	1250	900	700	700	700	700
5 in. (125mm)	1250	900	700	700	700	700
6 in. (150mm)	900	700	700	700	700	700

Note: *The figures in the chart above are expressed in rpm.*

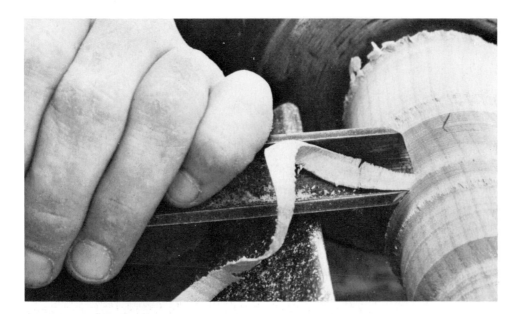

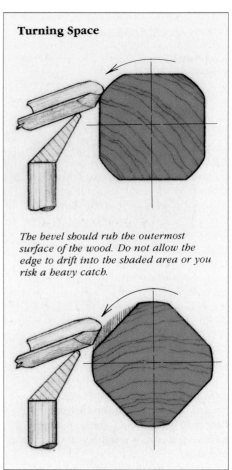

The bevel should rub the outermost surface of the wood. Do not allow the edge to drift into the shaded area or you risk a heavy catch.

Use the hand-over grip to rough-down with a gouge. Ensure that the bevel rubs the wood when cutting in either direction.

Step 1: First make a smooth cylinder, without bumps and dips. Select a piece of wood between 6 in. (150mm) and 8 in. (205mm) long and about 2 in. (50mm) to 3 in. (75mm) square. Ensure that the grain is straight, without knots or splits, and runs the length of the piece. Mount and center the blank between a drive and tail center (pp. 14 and 58-59), and check that it rotates without obstruction. Be sure that the tailstock is wound in tightly. If you have a tablesaw, bandsaw or hand plane, you can reduce the weight of the blank by removing the corners of the square to produce an octagon, but this is not essential; a block properly centered on the lathe should not vibrate. Adjust the lathe speed to no more than 900 rpm.

Use a 1-in. (25mm) shallow gouge. The angle of the tool to the wood is dictated by a combination of personal preference, the precise shape of the gouge and the angle of the gouge bevel. I generally use the tool at about 15° off a right angle to the axis and angled up about 10°. Place the tool on the rest using the hand-over grip (p. 50). Initial passes must be very light, to establish precisely where the edge of the wood is, after which progressively heavier cuts can be taken.

Make the first cut with that part of the edge just below the center of the curve. If the point of cut on the gouge is allowed to drift to the upper side of the cutting edge, the tool has little support under the cutting area and will snap down on the rest unless firmly controlled (p. 56). This type of catch usually leaves a spiral mark or a hole. Roll the tool slightly with your lower hand, so the top of the gouge faces the direction of the cut, as shown in the photos above. Move the tool into the cut by pushing or pulling with your upper

hand, depending on whether you are working to the left or to the right. Keep the bevel rubbing whenever possible. This is difficult to do before your square block becomes a cylinder, so you must hold the tool firmly on the rest to resist its normal tendency to chatter.

This is the stage at which to learn not to press the tool against the wood; the bevel should rub the wood but not be forced against it. Apply your power to controlling leverage. As you start to remove the corners of the blank, you'll develop portions of a cylinder. When there is no wood to cut, the tool must be moved cautiously in the same plane so that as the next corner comes around, the edge takes a fine shaving as the bevel rubs the cylinder surface again. If your upper hand fails to keep the edge an even distance from the axis, but allows the tool to move forward into the space, a catch is probable and the tool will jump about on the rest and be difficult to control. As the corners are reduced and the shape approaches cylindrical, this becomes less of a problem. When you turn a spindle with a square section left at both ends, you'll have to be able to move the tool along a definite path, turning space as well as wood. This is where you develop that skill.

Rough-down the cylinder in two stages. First reduce the cylinder from one end in a series of short, scooping movements. This is probably the quickest way to remove waste; the tool travels rapidly along the rest. In the photos at right the scooping movements are made to the right, and after each one the tool moves down the rest to the left about 2 in. (50mm) to begin the next cut. The final scooping cut is made to the left, off the other end of the cylinder. Do not try to start a cut by coming into the end of the piece, but work off the end, as shown at top right. Because the grain runs parallel to the axis there is a tendency for the wood to split if you cut into the end grain, and it is difficult to know exactly where the surface of the wood is in relation to the rest and the tool. Where a cut has to be made from space into the end of a cylinder, make a trial pass just above the surface of the wood before easing the tool forward fractionally to make the cut, rather like a golfer taking a preliminary swing before hitting the ball. Try this when you feel more confident.

As the wood becomes thinner, move the rest closer to the work and drop it slightly so that the tool can still be used at the same angle. Move the tool along the rest, keeping the handle against your body, elbows in and shifting your weight. Once you reach the end of the cylinder, swing the tool handle around to align the tool in the opposite direction and begin another series of cuts just in from the end.

Once most of the flat surfaces have been eliminated, as shown at bottom left, use the tool in long flowing movements along the rest to true the cylinder. Begin just inside either end of the cylinder and make two long smoothing cuts (one in each direction), working off the ends.

To check if your cylinder is even, place a straightedge on the surface and be satisfied only when little or no light comes between it and your cylinder. Or you can line up the top of your cylinder by eye with the lathe bed. This is a fairly accurate way of judging a cylinder without using measuring tools. Initially, it is more important to get straight, smooth surfaces than a true cylinder, so if your cylinder tapers slightly from one end to the other, don't worry.

Make scooping cuts to the right, working off the end of the cylinder. After each one, move the tool down the rest to the left about 2 in. (50mm) to begin the next cut.

Continue the scooping cuts until most of the flat surfaces have been removed.

Once the cylinder has been rough-shaped, true it with long flowing movements in both directions until it looks like this.

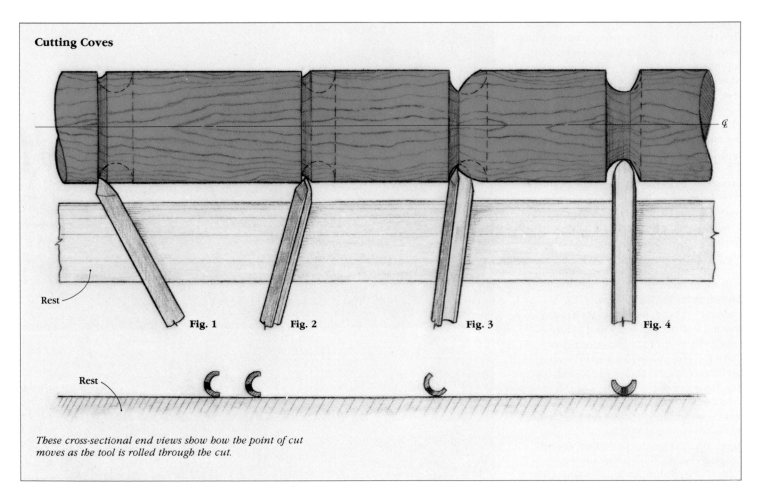

Cutting Coves

Rest

Fig. 1 Fig. 2 Fig. 3 Fig. 4

Rest

These cross-sectional end views show how the point of cut moves as the tool is rolled through the cut.

To make coves, control the tool with a stop-grip. As the cut progresses, you will have to ease your grip and allow the tool to roll.

Step 2: Once you've turned a smooth cylinder, cut coves into its surface. Try to keep the shoulders of the coves well defined, not rounded over. I suggest using a ½-in. (13mm) shallow gouge, and spacing the shoulders of the coves about ¾ in. (19mm) apart. (If you use a different size gouge, make the coves proportionally larger or smaller.) You can mark out the coves with a pencil and a ruler.

When you start to cut a cove, you won't be able to rub the bevel before you bring the edge in to cut, so catches are likely if the tool is not properly controlled. Use a secure grip, with the tool angled up about 10°. By squeezing, pushing and pulling with the fingers and palm of the upper hand, very fine control of the edge is possible while still maintaining control of the fulcrum.

In starting the cut, the gouge should be on its side with the top of the gouge facing the center of the cove and the bevel aligned in the direction of your proposed cut, as shown at Fig. 1 in the drawing above. Raise the handle to bring the edge down into the wood. As usual, keep the point of cut just below the center of the tool's edge. The moment entry is made there will be a shoulder against which the bevel can rub. As you move the tool into

the wood, it will want to snap back. Control this by holding the tool with a firm but movable stop-grip (p. 51), as shown in the photo at left. As the cut progresses, ease the grip of the upper hand slightly, allowing the lower hand to roll the tool evenly (Fig. 2 and Fig. 3). The gouge starts on its side at the top of the cove and finishes with the top facing up at the bottom of the cove (Fig. 4). At the same time, push the tool across the rest into the wood, keeping the bevel rubbing on the newly cut surface.

Cut the cove in from both shoulders. Don't attempt to go down one side and back up the other in the same cut. That would splinter the wood away at the top because the grain is unsupported, but you'd have a catch well before then. When you cut in from both shoulders, the cuts resist the centrifugal force of the revolving wood, which tends to fling the tool away from center.

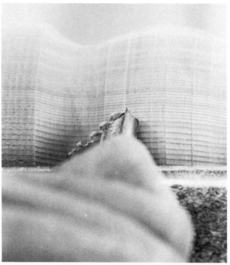

Turn the coves into a series of undulating curves by cutting down from the top of the cove shoulder (left). Begin with the tool facing up and rotate the gouge about 45° to pick up a shaving (above). Roll the gouge so that it faces up at the bottom of the curve.

Step 3: Once you've achieved a cylinder with a series of coves equally spaced along its length, you can round over the flat areas to produce an even, undulating surface. With the top of the gouge facing up, let the bevel rub the top of the cove. Then roll the tool in the direction of the cut until the edge produces a shaving, as shown at top right. Again, the point of cut is just below the center of the edge. Either a hand-over or hand-under grip will do. The power you apply to the tool should aim to prevent kick-backs more than to force the edge into the wood. Keep your upper hand steady on the rest. It acts as a stop that moves forward with the tool as wood is removed. The tool cuts down to the bottom of the curve, rolling again to end up facing upward.

You can vary this procedure to make beads. Instead of rolling the tool so that it faces upward at the bottom of the cut, keep the gouge rolling so that it completes the cut on its side, as shown at right. At the bottom of the curve, the point of the cut moves from the lower part of the edge to the center. It is held there momentarily to define the *V* between two beads. Resist the common temptation to push the tool point into the *V*. When you have finished a row of beads, use the same tool to flatten them, eventually producing a slimmer, smooth cylinder and repeat the process. Continue making beads and removing them until the wood snaps. You'll soon discover your limitations, which will give you something to build on.

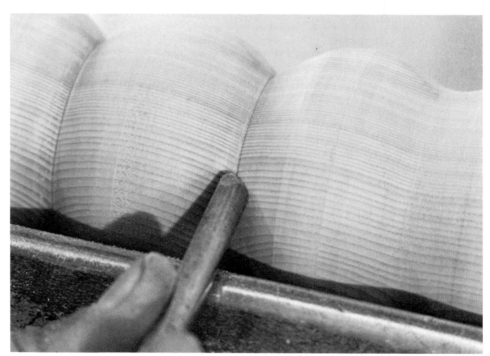

Define the *V* between two beads by finishing the cut with the gouge rolled on its side.

The tool will cut well when held in a variety of positions. Here, the skew is used long point up to produce an ideal shaving. Experiment with tool angles to see what you can produce.

Skew chisels

The skew chisel is the ideal tool for working along the grain. It functions best on absolutely straight-grained, knot-free wood. Deft wrist movements can flick the tool from one side to another, from the long, sharp point to the heel, shearing to a near-perfect finish. To make best use of this tool, however, a great deal of practice is needed. It's all worthwhile, because once mastered, the skew chisel can provide tremendous satisfaction.

The edge of the skew chisel is ground with a bevel on both sides and it angles to a long point. I grind all my chisels with a curved cutting edge, as shown on p. 31, because it allows a wider range of use. (The shearing cut, used to make grooves on p. 77, cannot be made with a straight-edged skew.) The bevel can be ground either concave or convex, depending upon the shape of the work. A concave, or hollow-ground, edge is ideal for the convex curves I usually cut, though it has a hard shoulder that can easily mark the wood. For this reason, the smoother convex-ground chisel is often preferred by traditional spindle turners for cutting shallow coves and other concave shapes. In either case, the burr should be removed in order to produce shavings in long continuous spirals. I recommend using the following chisels:

—For work less than ¼ in. (6mm) in diameter: ¼-in. (6mm) to ½-in. (13mm) skew chisel.
—¼ in. (6mm) to ½ in. (13mm) in diameter: ½-in. (13mm) skew chisel.
—½ in. (13mm) to 2 in. (50mm) in diameter: ½-in. (13mm) to 1-in. (25mm) skew chisel.
—Above 1½ in. (38mm) in diameter: 1-in. (25mm) to 2-in. (50mm) skew chisel.

It is not possible to define an ideal rest height or cutting edge, except to say that the rest should be slightly above center height. The precise angle of the tool will depend on a number of variables: the height of the lathe relative to your own height, the diameter of the wood and how the tool is ground. The tool will cut well when held in a variety of positions, and you'll have to determine what is best on each occasion. Your problem is in knowing what to strive for, and the shaving illustrated in the photo at left will give you a good idea. It was made as the lathe slowed to a stop, with the wood revolving against a tool held in the optimal position. Experiment with tool angles and see what you can produce.

I have two basic rules for the skew chisel. First, adjust the rest so that the tool cuts high on the wood when it is angled up only a few degrees. Maintain contact between the rest and your upper hand, pulling or pushing the tool depending on the direction of the cut. Second, keep the bevel rubbing at all times, except when the point first enters the wood to cut a groove (when the bevel cannot rub). The rubbing bevel provides a triangular base for the chisel—composed of the shoulder of the bevel, the cutting edge and the tool rest—and your upper hand should ensure that the tool stays in this position. There is a tendency, especially among students, to allow the bevel shoulder to rise, leaving only the edge in contact with the wood. This results in tool chatter, kick-backs and a rough surface on the wood. The bevel shoulder acts as a secondary fulcrum (besides the rest) and helps to control these kick-backs, so if the tool begins to chatter, in all likelihood the bevel is not making contact with the wood.

Step 1: Begin by reducing an 8-in.- (205mm) long by 2-in.- (50mm) square blank to round with a gouge, as described on pp. 70-71. Set the rest just above center height and the speed to about 900 rpm. Now smooth the cylinder using a ¾-in. (19mm) to 1-in. (25mm) hollow-ground skew chisel, held in a hand-over grip. You can hold the skew two different ways to turn a cylinder, long point up or long point down. Try it both ways.

First use the skew with the long point up and just off 90° to the stock, as shown at top right. Do not place the tool flat on the rest; it contacts the rest only on the corner of the tool between the side and the flat. (This is an exception to the general rule that square-section tools lie flat on the rest.) The cut must be made with the lower half of the cutting edge, but not the bottom corner (the heel). Ideally, the cut should be made about one-third of the way up the edge of the tool from the heel. If you use the heel, the action is not so much a shearing as a levering-up of the wood fibers (p. 81). This splinters the wood away, so the surface is rarely as good as that left by a shearing cut. If the point of cut drifts to the top of the tool, the unsupported edge is likely to snap down on the rest, making a nasty mess of the wood. The farther away from the heel the point of cut, the greater the leverage and the greater the likelihood of a catch. An imaginary line drawn through the point of cut and the fulcrum on the rest should be at 90° to the axis; any centrifugal force will then be well opposed by the position of the tool. The problem with using the long point up is that it's difficult to prevent the tool's rocking as you move it along the rest. This will create an undulating surface as the edge moves into or away from the wood. If you rock the tool with the long point down, you are much less likely to create an irregular surface because the tool is held at a tangent to the wood.

When you feel comfortable cutting with the long point up, try roughing-down a cylinder using the long point down and leading the cut, as shown at bottom right. In this position, the cut must be made between the point and the center of the edge and the handle will move much farther around, approaching 45° to the wood surface. With the tool held at such a tangent the centrifugal force can be difficult to control, so I hold my lower hand on the ferrule and align the handle under my forearm. The tool should be held horizontally, or with the edge tilted up 10° to 15°. When the tool is horizontal, the edge is in an ideal position for a shearing cut and it produces a particularly clean surface. But, if the tool is tilted up slightly, it opposes the downward force better and is easier to manipulate.

This is an excellent thrusting cut for rapid waste removal. I prefer to use the tool this way even though the point of cut is farther away from the fulcrum on the rest than if the tool were held with the long point up. Any forward pressure exerted against the work will be absorbed by the supporting centers and will be less likely to cause flexing and chattering than if the tool is held long point up. Because the force is behind the chisel, it is easier to direct, especially along a cylinder. The slender lengths of the spillikins on p. 138 were turned using this technique. I use the skew with the long point down to rough-down most centerwork less than 2 in. (50mm) in diameter and for smoothing any long curve.

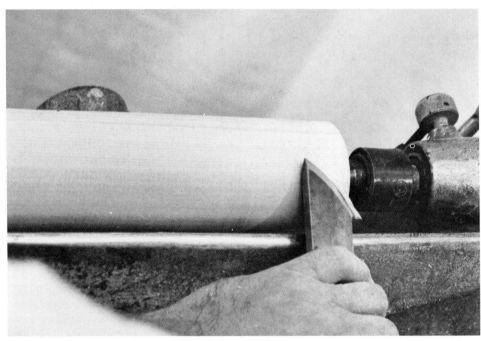

When cutting with the long point up, hold the skew just off a 90° angle to the work and angled up about 10° so it cuts high on the wood. The cut should be made between the heel and center of the edge.

When the skew is used with its long point down, leading the cut, the tool lies at about 45° to the wood surface, depending on the angle of the bevel. The cut is made between the point and the center of the edge, with the tool held horizontally or angled up 10° to 15°.

Only the bevel side should contact the wood (top). Don't lever the point of the skew out of the cut (center) or allow the bevel to lift off the surface of the wood (bottom).

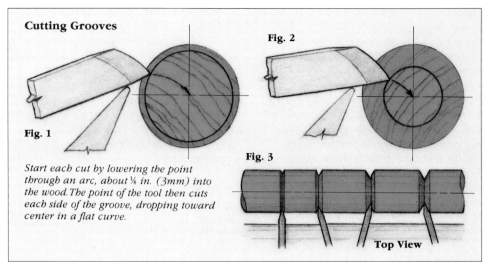

Cutting Grooves

Fig. 1

Fig. 2

Fig. 3

Start each cut by lowering the point through an arc, about ⅛ in. (3mm) into the wood. The point of the tool then cuts each side of the groove, dropping toward center in a flat curve.

Top View

Step 2: Having successfully smoothed a cylinder, cut a row of grooves in it. Mark the centers of the grooves about ¾ in. (19mm) to 1 in. (25mm) apart (depending on the width of your chisel). Gauge the distance quickly with your tool by placing it flat on the rest at 90° to the cylinder (p. 67). Move the tool forward far enough for the long point to score the surface of the revolving wood. Then move the chisel along the rest and repeat the action with the heel of the bevel aligned with the mark you've just made. In cutting the grooves, aim to achieve a straight-sided V, about ⅜ in. (10mm) deep. A straight side will give you a definite goal, one that is easily defined and measurable.

You can cut grooves in two ways, both of them using the long point down. In the first method, the point is tilted up about 20° and brought down through an arc. The second technique calls for shearing cuts made with the leading part of the edge, just above the point as the tool is pushed straight into the wood. You can cut end grain exceptionally cleanly by the latter method, but problems arise as you begin the cut that make the tool more difficult to control. Make several grooved cylinders bringing the point down through an arc before trying the shearing cut. This should teach you much about fine control.

Make the first cut with the long point of the skew on the center mark of the groove and the tool held at 90° to the work. The point travels through an arc—about ⅛ in. (3mm) into the wood. (Don't push it straight in. The skew cuts with a softer sound and with less effort if brought through an arc.) This marks the bottom of the groove to which the side cuts will be made. The first side cut goes to the bottom of the center mark and should leave you with a clean half-V. (Remember to bring the tool through an arc to enter the wood

when you make the side cuts, too.) The next cut from the other side completes the V. Then cut in from either side, keeping the bottom of the V centered between the shoulders. Alternate cuts from each side, widening the V as you go (Fig. 3 above). These cuts are made by the point of the tool and only the bevel side—from the point to the shoulder—should contact the wood, rubbing the newly cut surface. The angle of the bevel dictates the angle at which the tool lies to the wood, about 30° in the photo at top left. Keep the cutting edge away from the surface of the wood to prevent a catch, as shown in the photo.

Making a straight cut requires the tool to be manipulated precisely. The tool point must be moved through the arc positively. As you cut in from either side to deepen the groove, move the tool forward (after you've made the initial entry cut through an arc) by easing it over the rest with the thumb and fingers of your upper hand. The point cuts on a trajectory similar to that of a ball thrown for distance: It goes out in a flat curve and drops steeply, as shown in Fig. 1 and Fig. 2 above. Do not allow the point to drop below a line from the rest to the center (p. 57).

In cutting grooves, as with all cuts, it is critical to keep the bevel rubbing. (The bevel can't rub until the point has entered the wood.) If the sides of your groove are uneven or bumpy it will be for one of two reasons. You are either levering the point out of the cut, as shown in the photo at center left, or you are lifting the bevel side by moving the tool in the opposite direction (bottom left). This leaves you with only the long point contacting the wood, without the stabilizing contact of the bevel. With practice, you will sense when the bevel is rubbing and will be able to align it properly each time without having to look or even think about it.

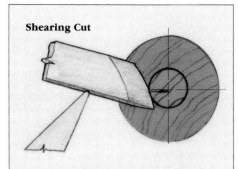

Shearing Cut

Position the rest at center height (or slightly below) and about ⅜ in. (10mm) away from the wood. Then drop the point below a line from the center to the rest. The edge cuts (above the point) on a straight line toward center.

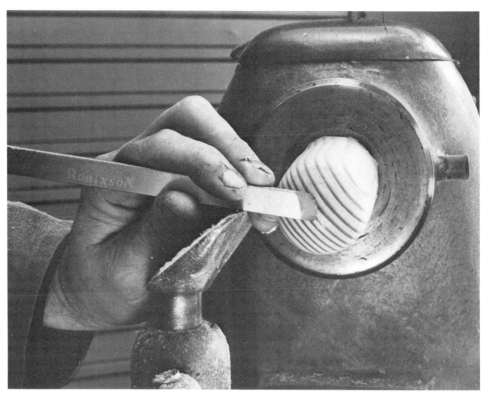

For the shearing cut, move the tool as you would cue a pool shot. Angle the chisel so that when it is pushed straight into the wood the point will be just below the line from the rest to the center while the edge cuts right on it.

This finished row of grooves shows a typical surface from the skew chisel. The crisp shoulders indicate a good shearing cut.

Once you feel comfortable cutting grooves with the point, try shearing side cuts. (Make a central cut first, as shown in the drawing on the facing page, to locate the bottom of the *V*.) Place the tool on the rest and raise the handle slightly so the point falls below the line from the rest to the center. Move the tool forward so the curve of the edge (just above the point) enters the wood first on the line between rest and center. As you push the edge against the wood, it tends to kick sideways, so your upper hand must prevent all lateral movement. Your lower hand moves the tool forward. The action is similar to cuing a pool shot. Once the edge has entered the wood, you have a surface against which the bevel can rub, and the cut should proceed without problems.

Because the entry to these side cuts is so difficult, my solution is to take the point about ⅛ in. (3mm) into the wood through the normal arc (Fig. 1 on the facing page) before raising the handle to drop the point below the line between the rest and the center. The edge then cuts just above the point and can be pushed straight into the center, as shown in the drawing above.

If you find yourself having difficulties with either of these techniques, forget about grooves and simply make cuts in one direction across the grain. When you achieve a satisfactory cut that feels easy and produces a good surface, repeat the action in the same place again and again. Do nothing else for ten minutes or longer until you can do it every time. When you've mastered one action try it in the other direction. Then go back to the grooves. Don't be intimidated by the fact that there's a whole row to do. Just take each groove one at a time, forgetting what's to come and what's gone.

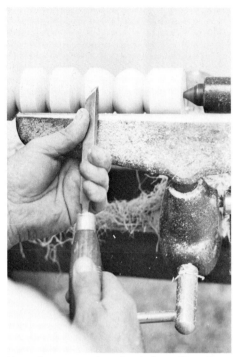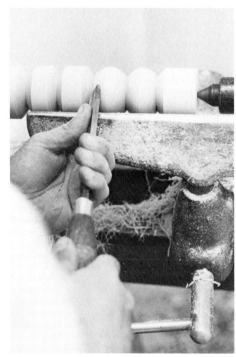

Turn the grooves into beads by rolling the tool in the direction of the cut in one smooth, flowing action. Your lower hand should reach around the handle in the opposite direction of the cut about to be made so you can complete the motion with your wrist and forearm relaxed.

Step 3: Now that you have turned a cylinder with a series of even grooves, use the same skew chisel to turn the grooves into beads. Think positively. Don't say: "I'm sure I can't do this." It's very difficult to start cutting a bead with the long point down, as the angle of the tool to the wood places the fulcrum on the rest too far away from the point of cut. So begin the cut holding the skew with the long point up. This is a more economical movement than using the tool long point down where the handle would move through a much wider arc as it rounds the curve of the bead.

Rest the bevel on what will be the fullness of the bead and roll the tool very firmly in the direction of the cut until the edge picks up a shaving. Then move the tool forward. This requires good coordination of both hands. Your lower hand rotates the tool while your upper hand moves the edge forward into the wood. (Other than rotating the tool and moving it forward, the cutting action is the same as when smoothing the cylinder.) Your lower wrist should move in a smooth, flowing motion; the upper hand acts as a moving backstop to prevent kick-back and provide fine control, while easing the tool forward with gentle pressure from the thumb and middle fingers. Small beads can be turned with a flick of the lower wrist. Smooth, flowing curves come from smooth, flowing actions. Decide what you want to do and try to do it. Don't dither in the middle of a cut.

Keep the tool cutting just below the center of the edge. The handle lies at about 90° to the axis of the wood and it will swing through about 10° during the cut. The tool will start near flat and will roll as it moves forward to end up on its side. To round one-half of a bead should take only a second or two. The tool should feel almost spongy on the wood, encountering little resistance and cutting cleanly—all yours when you get it right.

Often you'll be left with a thin frill of wood at the bottom of a bead, especially where a pair of beads meet. To remove this, it is easier to see what's happening if you turn the chisel over and use the long point as if cutting a groove. Turn the tool over and bring the bevel in to rub the surface just cut. Then bring the edge in to continue the cut to the bottom of the bead. When making this cut, the tool will lie close to 90° to the axis, so the fulcrum moves nearer the point of cut, reducing the leverage (even as the edge moves farther away from the rest). Don't use force to remove the frill; a delicate touch is all you need.

The finish on this row of beads is straight off the skew chisel.

Having achieved a row of beads, use the same tool to reduce the spindle to a smaller cylinder. To do this, begin cutting at the top of the bead at one end of the cylinder with the long point down. Move the tool along the rest evenly through space and wood. Don't allow the edge to jump forward into the spaces between the beads. This is a good opportunity to practice moving the tool on a predetermined course, and it will become easier as the beads are reduced in size. Once the cylinder has been smoothed, repeat the process, making a row of grooves first and then beads. No matter what size chisel you use, the same rules apply. The cut is always made with that portion of the edge just below the center and, whenever possible, the bevel should rub the wood before you bring the edge in to cut. The smaller the tool, the more precise your technique will need to be. I use a 5/16-in. (8mm) skew for my salt scoops, but generally you can do almost any small spindle with a 1/2-in. (13mm) tool. When each cycle is completed, do it again until the spindle breaks.

Once you have reduced a number of spindles to the breaking point using this cylinder-grooves-beads-cylinder process, it is sensible to move on to making something useful. I developed my skew chisel technique by making rolling pins, meat bashers, honey dippers and knobs for window blinds or light-pull cords. The advantage of such objects is that they need not be identical. That's just as well, because catches and general lack of tool control will probably demand an alteration to your initial concept. At first, keep your shapes simple and develop your repertoire of cuts gradually. When you make a clean cut, do the same thing again and again

until you can do it every time as you want (and not as the wood or lathe dictates). As you master each cut, go on to others. I recall that my early spindles had few rounded beads but plenty of long curves and V-shaped grooves. The rolling pins had square or conical ends that were easier to duplicate until my skill and confidence grew and I could make them rounded with buttons. Keep the lathe speed down to 900 rpm to start. As your confidence grows and catches become less frequent and the finish from the tool improves, raise the speed as high as 1200 rpm. When you find it reasonably easy to smooth a cylinder and to cut grooves and beads, it's time to examine several other useful functions of the skew chisel.

Reduce a cylinder rapidly by using the skew in a rotary-peeling action. Keep the cutting edge just below the surface of the wood. As the edge peels, push the tool forward and raise the handle to maintain the same relationship between the cutting edge and the top of the wood.

The skew can be used to rotary-peel on an angle by pivoting the tool down into the wood diagonally. Be sure to lift the edge away from the wood quickly at the end of the cut to avoid a catch.

Skew as rotary peeler—By holding the tool flat on the rest with the edge parallel to the axis, you can reduce a diameter drastically in an instant. This technique is especially useful when turning a goblet stem, scoop handle or other spindle where a great deal of waste has to go quickly. The angle at which the cutting edge is presented to the revolving wood is crucial. Get this right and your problem may be in removing too much too quickly, with virtually no effort. Get it wrong and you can lever the wood off the lathe just as quickly. To peel effectively, the cutting edge must be kept just below the surface of the wood. Should it drop, the action becomes a slow, heavy scrape that badly tears the grain.

To begin this cut, the bevel should ride the wood first, as usual. But as you bring the cutting edge down by raising the handle, you must slide the blade back across the rest slightly until the edge is just beneath the surface of the wood and producing a very fine shaving. The moment the edge starts peeling, push the tool forward, maintaining the edge position relative to the top surface of the wood. Deftness is required to keep the cutting edge peeling toward the center accurately. All the movement is controlled by your lower hand; your upper hand simply holds the tool on the rest. Shavings should come off the wood in paper-thin ribbons that break up as they leave the tool. The surface will need to be cleaned up with a final shearing cut.

This is not a technique for general use on square-section wood, because the edges are likely to splinter. (Although I frequently rough-down blanks for the cup chuck this way, and the occasional splintered corner is no problem because the wood will be turned down later.)

Using this cut very delicately is often the best way to deal with twisted grain or to clean up the base of a bead or box flange when fitting a lid. This is where the curved edge of the skew really comes into its own. It is possible to move the point of the skew sideways into a corner without touching the surface just cut (top left on facing page). A sharp tool has three effective cutting edges that form the point. Two can be used simultaneously—the normal cutting edge and the upper bevel side—so long grain can be cut and end grain scraped at the same time. The tool must be moved in very gently to avoid tearing the grain (a vibration-free lathe is essential for such an operation). The bevel doesn't get a chance to rub and the edge only lightly strokes the surface. There should be no shavings—only fluff. Control the movement with your upper hand while your lower hand provides stability. Stand well balanced. (You might want to hold your breath for this cut as well.)

Skew peeling on an angle—This is a variation of the previous cut and is a quick, effective way to rough-out deep V-grooves, but again you will need a final shearing cut to smooth the surface. Hold the tool as if for a conventional shearing cut, with the long point leading. Raise the handle diagonally while pivoting the tool on the rest. The long point of the tool moves through an arc deep into the wood and the edge peels a thin ribbon, as shown below (much the same as if the tool were held flat, as in the previous exercise). Having reached the required depth, pivot the tool on its point so that the edge of the tool is moved out of the cut. Otherwise, there will be too much wood in contact with the edge, causing a catch. As with the previous cut, deftness is required; you cannot make this cut slowly. The main

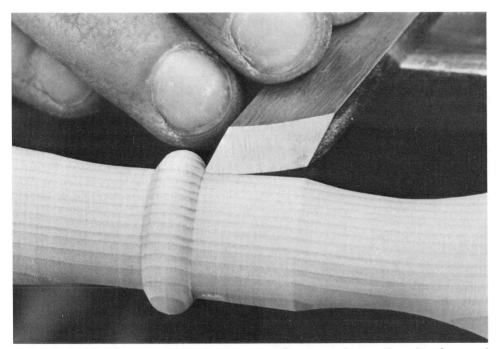

A curved-edge skew is much more useful than a straight-edge tool. Here, the point of a curved skew is moved sideways to clean a corner without touching the rest of the surface.

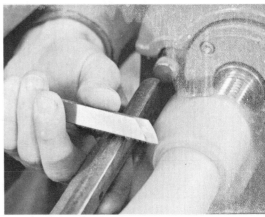

When cutting from square to round, pivot the tool so the point drops in an arc, as for cutting a groove (p. 76).

power comes from the lower hand, but the upper hand adds firmness to eliminate possible catches. Because the tool contacts the rest on only one side, care must be taken to keep the cut near the point on the cutting edge. This cut is also similar to the one used to cut grooves using the point (p. 76), but with an important difference. When you cut grooves, you were at pains to use only the point and to keep the cutting edge clear of your newly cut surface. Now you are cutting with the point and adjacent portion of the edge. You should be doing (rapidly and under control) what you avoided before. What is disastrous in one situation can be used to great effect in another.

You'll find that the skew requires many hours (months or years) of practice, but it is all worthwhile. In the hands of an expert, wood is removed and shaped even faster than clay on a potter's wheel. A 2-in.- (50mm) diameter scoop handle, for instance, will take no more than 10 seconds to shape, while the whole external shape might take only 20 to 30 seconds. With the right straight-grained wood, the cut is clean. One movement and type of cut will flow into another and the wood will curl off the tool with a rushing sound. It's a great feeling.

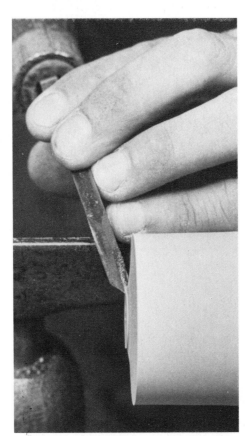

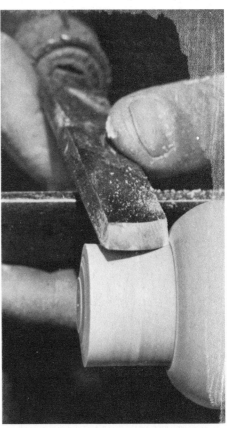

When trueing an end-grain face using the long point (left), ensure that only the leading point and bevel, not the cutting edge, contact the wood. This cut keeps the work pressured against the headstock, which is useful in turning the box on pp. 92-97. The heel of the skew should only be used when precise definition is required, as in turning the base of this bead (right).

A fishtail parting tool cuts in the same manner as a rotary-peeling skew chisel. Don't let the edge drop too far into the wood or it will begin scraping.

Parting tools

Parting off is the process of cutting across the grain to remove a turned piece from the lathe while it still rotates. Parting tools are also used in confined spaces where a skew or a gouge cannot operate effectively, or to establish diameters in spindle work (p. 62). The tool edge is kept just below the surface of the wood, where it peels off a ribbon-like shaving in exactly the same way as the peeling skew chisel. The edge is held at 90° to the work and cuts from the outside surface of the wood to the center, dropping in an arc as the wood is reduced. Don't let the edge drop too far into the wood too quickly, or it will begin scraping rather than peeling.

When parting off small jobs, the last part has to be done with the tool held in your lower hand while your upper hand catches the piece, as shown in the photos at center and bottom left. The lathe keeps running and the work spins off into your waiting hand. If a large or long job is parted off while the lathe is still running, there is always the risk that you'll fail to catch it properly and it will bounce off the rest and be damaged. If you can stop the lathe just as you've finished cutting, this won't happen. (I can lean against or step on the stop button on my lathes, so it's possible to stop the machine at the last moment.) Try not to touch the piece until it is actually parted. The least pressure can cause the last bit of grain to spin and pull out of your finished piece. Another way to remove a job is to cut in with the parting tool, leaving a slender portion between the waste and the spindle that can be sawn off. I keep a small hacksaw for this purpose.

While parting tools are often used to remove work from the lathe, it is common practice to use the long point of the skew. I am using the skew to part off the tool handle on p. 156. The thumb and fingers of my upper hand prevent the tool's kicking sideways. This action is the same as the cut used to make grooves on p. 76.

When parting off small jobs, try not to touch the piece or you can cause the last bit of grain to spin and pull out.

Scrapers

Scrapers are not generally suitable for roughing-down, especially on external centerwork surfaces. The surface obtained by using a scraper along the grain bears no comparison to what you can achieve with a good shearing cut from a skew chisel or gouge. The scraping action tears off the wood fibers, so the finish scrapers leave when used forcefully is poor. Scrapers are best used very gently to produce a fine finish; the slightest pressure and the grain will be torn. They can also be useful in small spaces or, with specially ground edges, they can be used to produce complicated shapes in one pass, as on a chess piece.

The scraper must have a burr on the edge in order to cut effectively. I find the best edge comes straight from a light touch on the 60-grit grinding wheel. The best way to tell an appropriate burr is to touch the tool lightly to the surface of the work. If fluff results then it is sharp. If not, don't push the tool in, which will give you a monumental catch, but return to the grinder. If the burr is too big, remove it with a slipstone and start again.

When using scrapers, let the tool trail slightly below the line from the rest to center so that in the event of a catch the edge will travel away from the wood into space. If the tool catches when it is tilted above this line, it will try to travel down in an arc through the wood; all kinds of exciting things can happen. Damage of some sort is certain; definitely to the wood, possibly to yourself.

Occasionally, the skew chisel or gouge will have little effect on a particularly twisted or difficult section of grain. If a firm but light shearing cut fails to pare cleanly, try using a skew chisel as a scraper. Grind one bevel of the chisel lightly on the 60-grit wheel to produce a small burr. Hold the skew flat on the rest with the edge at center height and the burr on the top. Make a series of very light sideways cuts, using the entire edge to stroke the surface of the wood. If that fails to work, try moving the sharp point of the chisel into the wood slowly and steadily. Failing that, resort to abrasives.

Scrapers can be used with better results on end grain. Many of the dense or oily woods, such as ebony, sandalwood, cocobolo, African blackwood, mulga or gidgee definitely prefer end-grain scraping. On these, a very, very light touch can produce a glass-like surface, superior to the shearing cut of a skew chisel or gouge. The slightest excess pressure spells disaster, however, as the tool will pull lumps of wood from the end grain.

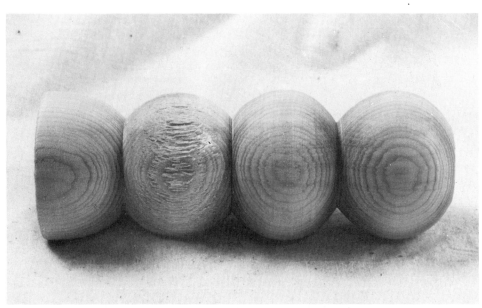

The cleanest cut shears across the grain. If you cut against the grain, the tool will lift the fibers and leave a rough surface. These celery-top-pine beads show a variety of finishes. Left to right: Sanded, scraped, gouge-cut and skew-cut.

On the end grain of dense or oily woods, such as this piece of cocobolo, you can produce a very smooth surface using a scraper. The two inner rings have been shear-cut using a skew chisel. The outer ring has been scraped using a skew chisel held flat on the rest with a slight burr ground on the top.

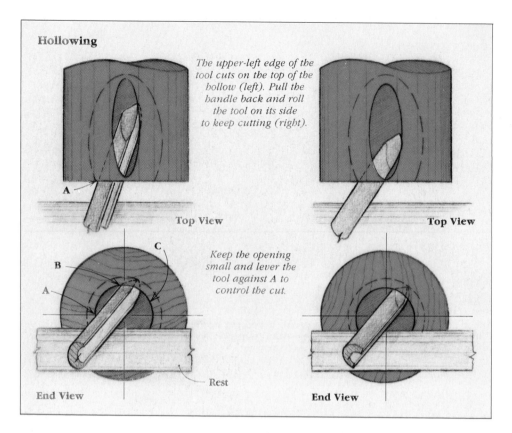

The upper-left edge of the tool cuts on the top of the hollow (left). Pull the handle back and roll the tool on its side to keep cutting (right).

Top View

Top View

Keep the opening small and lever the tool against A to control the cut.

C

B

A

Rest

End View

End View

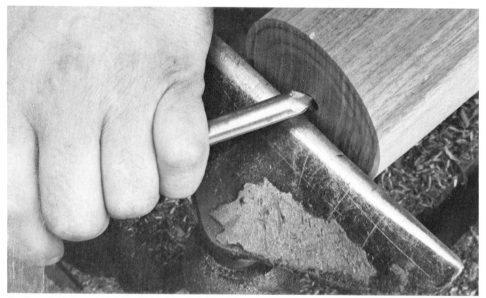

Begin with the gouge facing the center of the hole, tilted up about 5° (above). Pull the handle back to engage the upper-left part of the cutting edge (right).

Hollowing

You can use a drill bit mounted in the tailstock to sink a hole into end grain when making boxes, scoops, eggcups or goblets, but you will always get a poor surface (especially in the bottom) and the straight sides are uninteresting. Moreover, the spur of the bit will often leave a mark. There is a faster, more appealing way of hollowing end grain, and it is done in two steps. In the first step you use a gouge to make the opening; in the second step you use a scraper to finish it.

You cannot hollow end grain with the work held between centers. It must be held by one end only, preferably in a cup chuck or spigot chuck, either of which hold the work more securely than a jaw chuck. For practice, I suggest using blanks about 6 in. (150mm) long and 2 in. (50mm) to 3 in. (75mm) square. Choose a close-grained timber; green (freshly felled) wood will be easier to turn. A small, straight branch is ideal.

Gouges

First true the end-grain face using either a gouge or chisel (p. 81). (A gouge is easier, but this is a good opportunity to practice clean cuts across end grain using the skew.) Then rough-out the hollow with a gouge. I use a technique where the tool cuts on the far side of center and almost upside down—against all normal rules and expectations. I've used this method thousands of times to make scoops or small boxes. Select a long-and-strong ½-in. (13mm) gouge with a long bevel (about 30°) and ground well back on the left side. The edge should be a full curve, without any flat sections. Adjust the rest so that the center of the edge is at center height when tilted up about 5°. To shear cleanly, you'll be cutting from the center outward. Place the tool on its side on the rest with the top facing the center, just left of center, and with the bevel rubbing against the end grain, as shown in the photo at top left. Use a hand-over grip to provide a firm back-stop and fulcrum while preventing a run-back. Push the tool into the center of the wood, cutting in about ⅛ in. (3mm). (Any presure you apply here will be absorbed by the headstock.) Then pull your lower hand back toward your body so that the tool starts cutting on its upper left edge, moving away from center between points B and C in the drawing above, removing wood as it revolves upward. As you pull the handle back, roll the tool slightly to the right to maintain the optimal cutting

Hollowing Patterns

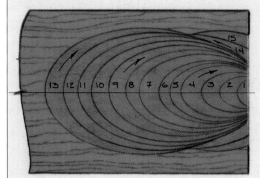

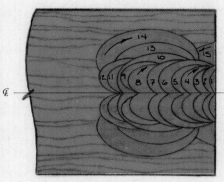

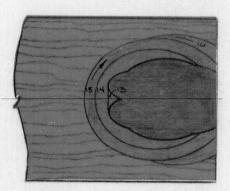

Fig. 1: *Cuts should sweep away from the center in the direction of the arrows and following the numbered sequence. Keep the opening narrow for use as a fulcrum.*

Fig. 2: *This common hollowing pattern produces problems. The gouge starts cutting at center, but a central cone is created by pushing the tool forward while the edge sweeps sideways.*

Fig. 3: *This is what the hollow will look like after cuts 1-12 in Fig. 2. Eliminate the central cone using either the gouge or a round-nose scraper. Then proceed to enlarge the opening with cuts 13-16.*

angle. (Remember to keep the bevel rubbing as the tool is rolled throughout the cut.) The photo at top right shows the tool early in the cut, just to the right of center. As the cut approaches the far side of the opening (bottom right), take the edge away from the wood and back to the center and repeat the process. From the position at the end of the cut you can perform the action in reverse (like running a film backward), bringing the edge back to the center and removing more waste as it goes. As the hollow develops, you can achieve a clean shearing cut where the form expands behind the rim. The surface will not be as smooth near the bottom of the opening, where the curve sweeps back toward the center, because the tool will be cutting into end grain.

Maintenance of a good fulcrum is important. Unless the tool is held down, the upward-moving wood (between *C* and *B*) will lift it. The entry hole *(A)* provides an additional fulcrum. The tool is supported on the rest, but it is also levered against the rim of the hole. This involves a fine sense of balance because the pressure put on the cutting edge must be offset precisely. Failure to do this can hook the block from the chuck, split the wood, or at least knock the block off-center. Keep the mouth of the opening small until the internal space has been hollowed. This will give you better leverage than if the hole were larger and will help you keep the tool cutting nearer to parallel to the axis, where it is easier to control. As the tool begins cutting on the far side of the hollow, it will unavoidably move away from parallel. If the entry hole is wide, the tool will be cutting closer to 90° to the axis as it approaches the rim and will be likely to catch or kick back.

If the rim becomes damaged and uneven, turn it true or you'll have an eccentric secondary fulcrum and cutting will be difficult. It is not possible to see what is happening most of the time while using the gouge this way, especially when starting a cut at the bottom of the hole; so don't even try. You have to feel it.

If you push the edge too far forward as it swings beyond the center you will form a central cone, as shown in Fig. 2 in the drawing above. On subsequent cuts this can enlarge if you fail to locate the point of the cone accurately and instead allow the bevel to rub down the side of the cone before the edge contacts the wood. When beginning a cut, feel for the center at the bottom of the hole, then locate the cutting edge by rolling the tool. Pull back on the handle only when you feel the edge actually cutting. I suggest practicing this technique in solid end grain. (In making the box on pp. 92-97, I've drilled a depth hole first. The bevel is then rested on the rim of the hole to begin the cut.)

This is not an easy technique to learn—mainly because you have to feel, rather than see, what is happening—but once mastered, this is a very rapid method of making holes. The bulk of a 2-in.- (50mm) diameter box or scoop can be removed in 3 to 4 seconds. But it is not particularly smooth. The job is finished with scrapers.

The tool will remove wood, cutting on the top as it rolls to the right. With practice you can reverse this process at the end of the cut, rolling the tool back to center.

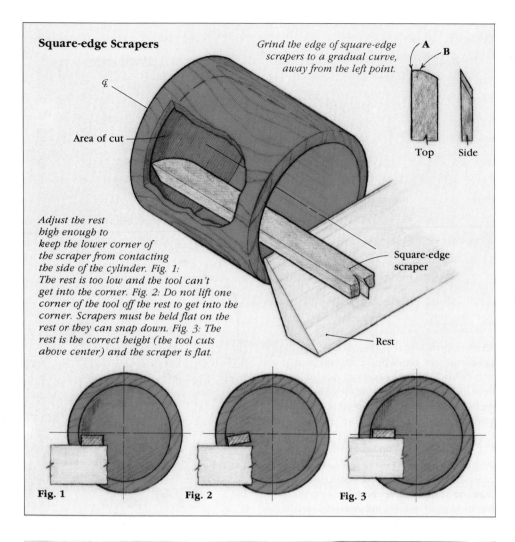

Square-edge Scrapers

Grind the edge of square-edge scrapers to a gradual curve, away from the left point.

A B

Top   Side

₵

Area of cut

Adjust the rest high enough to keep the lower corner of the scraper from contacting the side of the cylinder. Fig. 1: The rest is too low and the tool can't get into the corner. Fig. 2: Do not lift one corner of the tool off the rest to get into the corner. Scrapers must be held flat on the rest or they can snap down. Fig. 3: The rest is the correct height (the tool cuts above center) and the scraper is flat.

Square-edge scraper

Rest

Fig. 1   Fig. 2   Fig. 3

Scrapers

Having removed the bulk of your hole with a gouge, scrapers are used conventionally (on the left side of center) to finish the hollow. I use two different scraper shapes (in various sizes, depending on the opening) for this process. Square-edge scrapers (at left) are for the sides and bottoms of cylinders. Scrapers ground with a long, curved left edge (in the drawing on the facing page) are for the sides and bottoms of curved hollows. For practice, make two different forms: a flat-bottom cylinder and a round-bottom hollow.

Step 1: First make an internal cylinder using a square-ground tool with a long bevel. As is usual with any of my square-ground tools, the edge in fact curves slightly, in this case back from the left corner. This is to avoid presenting the whole edge at once to the wood, especially 2 in. (50mm) or more away from the rest, when a heavy, damaging catch would be almost inevitable. Use about a quarter of the cutting edge (the area between *A* and *B*, in the drawing at left). Whenever you use a scraper to cut the long, straight wall of a deep cylinder, it is vital to keep the tool horizontal in order to maintain an accurate side. The rest must be high enough to keep the lower corner of the tool (between the bottom and the side) from riding against the portion just cut by the top edge. If the rest is too low and the lower corner of the tool rubs, it will force the cutting edge toward the center. Push the tool in firmly, but not too fast. Too much pressure and the slightly brittle, hollow sound will be replaced by a vibrating, high-pitched noise, and torn end grain will result. It is important that your first scraping cut be accurate because the tool will be guided into the hollow by the upper cylinder wall. (Ensure accuracy by cutting in about 1 in. [25mm] with the scraper and measuring the opening with internal calipers.) The farther away from the rest the point of the cut, the less wood should be removed at one time. The leverage is tremendous and a catch at the bottom of a deep hole is usually disastrous. (While you should escape injury, you will probably tear the end grain or split the work.) Align the tool handle along and under your forearm to counteract its tendency to catch. Don't tilt the edge above horizontal on the end grain in the bottom of the hollow.

Finish the straight side of a cylinder using a square-edge scraper. Hold the tool horizontally and push it in firmly. The initial cut is important because the tool is guided into the hollow by the upper cylinder wall. Cut in 1 in. (25mm) and measure the opening to ensure accuracy.

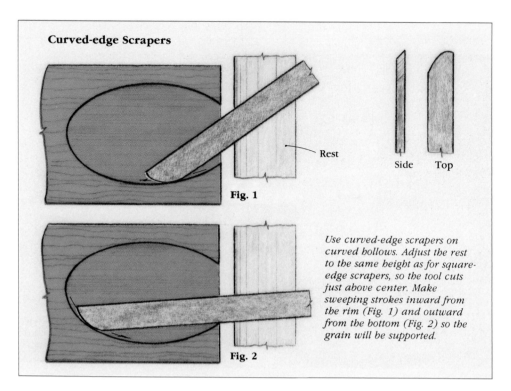

Curved-edge Scrapers

Rest

Side Top

Fig. 1

Fig. 2

Use curved-edge scrapers on curved hollows. Adjust the rest to the same height as for square-edge scrapers, so the tool cuts just above center. Make sweeping strokes inward from the rim (Fig. 1) and outward from the bottom (Fig. 2) so the grain will be supported.

Angle the scraper up when cutting the long grain on the side (top). To cut end grain, raise the handle so that the edge is angled down to cut at center height (bottom).

Step 2: Now try finishing an internal curve using a curved scraper. Because I always work on the inboard side of the headstock, all my curved scrapers have long left-hand edges, as shown above. Any tool I select will have a slightly tighter radius than that of the curve it is meant to cut. The tool makes a series of sweeping cuts, moving outward from the bottom of the hollow and inward from the rim. (In this way, the grain is supported as much as possible, as described on p. 54.) If the shape flows outward only, as in an open cup, then the cuts are made entirely from the bottom out. Initial shaping can be forceful, but the final cuts must be light, producing only fluff. When using curved scrapers internally, I find the best cut on the long grain of the side of the hollow is made with the tool angled upward, as shown in the photo at top right; if it does catch, there will be space below. As the scraper moves around to cut the end grain in the bottom of the hollow (left of center), you'll have to tilt the tool edge down so that it cuts slightly below horizontal, as shown in the photo at center right.

Remember when scraping internal curves, as in turning anything else, that flowing shapes come from flowing movements. To obtain a good internal line, don't jab at the wood with a blunt round-nose scraper. Use a sharp tool and sweeping, light cuts, and you'll end up with a reasonably clean surface without bumps or ridges. Otherwise, coarse abrasives (50 grit) will be required to get a really smooth surface.

Frequently, you'll be left with a small bump at the center, as shown at right in the photo below. If you simply push the edge of the scraper straight in against this, you'll create a dip. Instead, rest the bevel of the tool on top of the bump to locate its position. Then, move the edge around the bump to cut up from below and the left of it. This should give you a curve that sweeps cleanly and evenly through the bottom of your hollow.

These cross-sectioned internal curves show the stages of hollowing. Right to left: Roughed-out with gouge, scraped and ready for sanding, sanded and ready for oiling.

Make a Light-Pull Knob

1 Knock a ⅞-in. (22mm) by 3-in. (75mm) piece of wood into a No. 3 morse-taper drive shaft. (If your lathe takes a smaller taper, rough the blank between centers.) Peel-cut a groove at the drive end using a ½-in. (13mm) skew. The groove makes it possible to cut the grain cleanly at the base of the knob when you rough the square to round.

2 Rough-down the cylinder using the skew.

5 Complete the shaping with the skew.

6 Sand, oil and polish the knob.

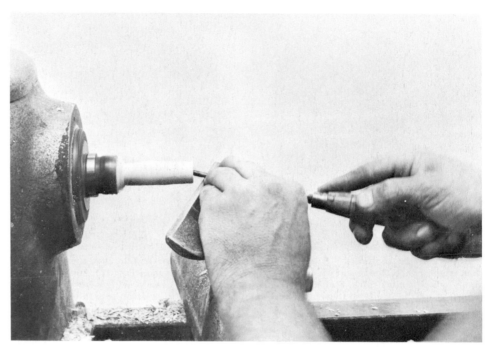

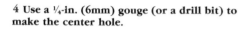

3 Make a ¼-in.- (6mm) deep recess, using the long point of the skew. This will guide the drill bit in the next step and later hide the knot at the end of the pull cord.

4 Use a ¼-in. (6mm) gouge (or a drill bit) to make the center hole.

7 Part-off the knob using the long point of the skew gently. If you use little forward pressure, the end should require minimal hand-finishing.

Make a Scoop

1 Mount a 2½-in. (65mm) by 5-in. (125mm) blank in a cup chuck. True it to a cylinder and then true the face. Rough-out the hollow using a ½-in. (13mm) gouge (above), until the wall is about ⅜-in. (10mm) thick. Finish the inside using a scraper ground with a curved left edge (right). Sand the inside so that you can develop the outside in relation to a fixed surface.

3 Turn the bead between the bowl and the handle (left). Finish turning the handle with the skew, using the tool either way up (center). Round over the end of the handle and make a parting cut, leaving about ⅜ in. (10mm) of wood to hold the scoop for finishing (right).

2 Mark the internal depth on the outside of the cylinder with a pencil and part in about ½ in. (13mm). It's important to hold the right corner of the parting tool on the depth mark (above left) if you are to obtain an even wall when you shape the bowl of the scoop. Cut the external curve using a skew chisel (above right). Then use the skew as a rotary peeler to rough-down the handle (right).

4 Sand the exterior (top); beware of developing a razor-sharp rim. Part off the scoop using the long point of the skew (above).

5 Remove part of the bowl with a bandsaw or coping saw and smooth the curve on a sander. Hand sand the top of the bowl and the end of the handle to finish the scoop.

Make a Box

1 Mount a 6-in.- (150mm) by 3-in.- (75mm) long blank between centers and true it to a cylinder. Then turn a ⅛-in.- (3mm) long flange on both ends to fit the 2-in. (50mm) spigot chuck. (If you use a three-jaw chuck, make a longer flange, about ½ in. [13mm], and cut a groove at its base to prevent pulled-out end grain [p. 20]).

2 After the flanges have been turned, make a pencil line about ⅓ of the distance from one end. Then cut the blank in two pieces on the line; the larger piece will be the base of the box, the smaller one will be the lid, and should result in near matching grain in the finished box.

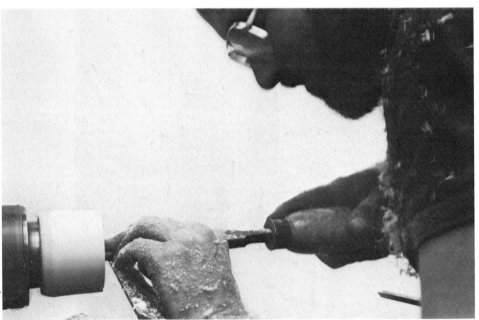

5 Rough-out the hollow with a ½-in. (13mm) shallow gouge until the walls are about ⅜ in. (10mm) thick.

6 Finish the interior of the lid. Make the flange at least ½ in. (13mm) long, using a ½-in. (13mm) square-edge scraper. Use a round-nose scraper for the rest of the sides and bottom.

3 Mount the lid section in the spigot chuck and true the sides with a skew chisel.

4 True the face of the lid with the skew. Cut the first ¼ in. (6mm) cleanly to reduce sanding. Parts should be sanded as little as possible for the best fit.

7 Sand the inside of the lid and finish with oil and wax. Mark the depth on the exterior and make a parting cut about ⅛ in. (3mm) from the line to allow sufficient wood in the top. Don't part the lid off—leave about ½ in. (13mm) of wood at the center.

8 Shape as much of the lid as possible with the skew chisel, cutting down to the bottom of the parting cut.

9 Mount the base section in the spigot chuck and true the face with the skew.

10 Turn a tapered flange on the end of the cylinder so the lid fits roughly on the first ¼ in. (6mm). (Do not spend a lot of time fitting the lid at this stage, in case you knock the base off-center during hollowing.)

13 Turn the flange down, using the long point of the skew, so that the lid fits tightly. The flange on the base should be about ⅛ in. (3mm) shorter than the lid flange. If you overcut the flange so the lid is loose, you can cut farther into the base. If the fit is good but fails to grip, try holding wax against the flange until it builds up in a viscous pile. Stop the lathe and push the lid on quickly, before the wax cools. When the wax hardens it should grip the lid enough to allow you to turn and sand it.

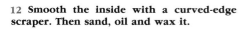

11 **Rough-out the inside of the base using the ½-in. (13mm) shallow gouge.**

12 **Smooth the inside with a curved-edge scraper. Then sand, oil and wax it.**

14 **With the lid in place, finish the external surface and turn a finial on top.**

15 **Smooth the external wall. Then, remove the lid and cut and chamfer the shoulder, from the side of the base to the flange, using the long point of the skew.**

Make a Box (continued)

16 Cut a decorative groove in the cylinder with the skew (above). A horizontal line will break up the expanse of the side. Mark the depth of the box on the outside of the cylinder with a pencil. Make a ¼-in.- (6mm) deep parting cut about ⅛ in. (3mm) below the mark. Then cut a slight chamfer down to the parting cut (right). The chamfer makes for a better transition between the side and the base than would a sharp corner.

19 Turn a slightly concave surface on the bottom of the box using the skew. Sand and finish the base.

18 Turn a tapered flange on the end of the stub left in the spigot chuck after the base has been parted off. Reverse the base of the box so that it jam-fits over the flange.

17 Sand the exterior and finish with oil and wax. Adjust the fit of the lid by sanding the flange lightly. Complete the parting cut using a diamond-shaped parting tool (above).

20 Cut the finished box in half and examine the profile. Here the inside curve of the lid could be fuller. Likewise, the bottom curve in the base could reach farther into the corners. The suction fit of the flanges is excellent.

Design Points: The interior has been rounded, which is more interesting than a cylindrical shape. More wood could be removed from the interior to lighten the base. Because wood moves with changes in humidity, an undetailed exterior that feels smooth at completion will soon show an obvious joint. The chamfered shoulder where the lid and base meet reduces the impact of the wood's movement. In the spillikin box (pp. 138-139), this is achieved with grooves.

Facework

7

Facework is mounted with the grain running at a right angle to the axis on which the wood rotates.

The end grain faces outward, rather than toward the headstock and tailstock. Work is usually set this way for any job where the diameter exceeds the height (such as bowls and platters). Generally the work is attached to the lathe by one face, though often there is no good reason why it cannot be mounted between centers. In fact, there are several advantages to employing tail-center support with facework, as described on p. 15.

The range of tools used for facework is greater than for centerwork because of the problems involved in cutting twisted or end grain. You encounter end grain twice on any external form, and twice more internally if the form is hollowed; difficulties most often arise in these areas. Once you learn to cut end grain cleanly, you're almost there. I use gouges to remove the bulk of the waste with a variety of shearing and scraping techniques and finish the surface with scrapers before sanding. On external surfaces, I often use gouges on their sides to make the scraping cuts, instead of flat-section scrapers, which are usually reserved for internal surfaces. I use skew chisels and gouges to cut grooves, coves and beads.

When cutting end grain, always aim to cut across the fibers (across the grain), where they are supported by others, as shown in the drawing on p. 54. In general, this means working from a smaller to larger diameter externally, and from larger to smaller diameters internally. When cutting a corner between a face and the side of a disc, always cut in from the face, as shown below. Never cut from the side to the face, where the grain is unsupported, because this will splinter the edge. Whenever possible, cut in a direction parallel to the axis, so that any pressure will be absorbed by the headstock (pp. 56-57). If the form is curved (as in a bowl), it's not necessary to true the disc to a cylinder before developing the shape. Develop the external form first, with the blank held by what will be the top of the bowl. It is safer and quicker to ignore the rough sides and start by removing the corner and shaping the base, which will reduce the bulk (and the vibration) more rapidly. An accurately cut disc should not vibrate too much if mounted properly.

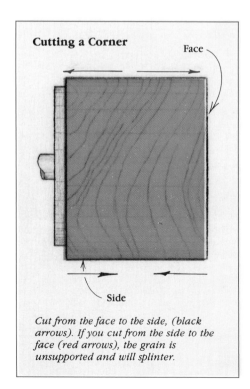

Cutting a Corner

Face

Side

Cut from the face to the side, (black arrows). If you cut from the side to the face (red arrows), the grain is unsupported and will splinter.

External Shaping

Because I frequently use gouges as scrapers, I rarely use the flat-section tools to shape outside curves. When I do use conventional scrapers, I often grind them to bizarre shapes for getting into odd corners or turning beads and grooves. On the odd occasion when I use a straight-edged scraper externally, it's usually a heavy scraper, ground at a skew angle so that it lies at a tangent to the surface of the wood. This allows me to make the light stroking cuts from a smaller to larger diameter, as shown in the drawing on p. 112. A square-edge tool in such a situation would lie at 90° to the surface, and would be more difficult to move accurately and smoothly along the surface of the wood. Always use scrapers so that there is no wood directly below the cutting edge, as shown on p. 113. If the tool catches, it will be ejected into space.

Gouges
Gouge techniques are similar for cutting both internal and external surfaces, but there are fewer problems with the latter, mainly because the wood is easier to reach and the edge of the tool can be supported close to the point of cut. It's best to learn what gouges can do on external surfaces before moving on to cutting internal shapes. Familiarize yourself with the steps in the exercises on pp. 100-107 before attempting to hollow a bowl or cut at any great distance from the rest, where the leverage will be difficult to control.

I have found most of my gouges useful and effective for external shaping, with the exception of the shallow tools in excess of 1 in. (25mm) wide. Gouges can be ground from straight across to a long fingernail shape, as described on p. 29. Whatever way you grind them, ensure that the bottom of the cutting edge is even with, or proud of, the sides. This will enable you to obtain a good, wide shaving, which is desirable for roughing-down. It is easy to grind the center of the edge back from the sides, severely limiting the tool's cutting capability. However, as with most rules, there is an exception; I often find the best shearing cut comes from a slight spur ground on the point, or on the vertical portion of the edge, of a normal fingernail-ground gouge, as shown at top right.

Five of my gouges are in almost constant use and I recommend these for the exercises in this chapter. Three are deep-fluted: ¼ in. (6mm), ½ in. (13mm) and 1 in. (25mm). Two are shallow: ¼ in. (6mm) and ½ in. (13mm). All are ground to a long fingernail edge and can be used for two types of shearing cut as well as on edge as a scraper. This gives the tools more versatility than if they were ground straight across. All the gouges I use are made from round-section, high-speed steel, but you could substitute any good-quality carbon-steel tool.

Mount a 6-in.- (150mm) to 7-in.- (180mm) diameter by 3-in.- (75mm) to 4-in.- (100mm) thick disc on a center-screw or standard faceplate (pp. 16-18). Do not mount the block between centers while you are learning how to use the gouges because you will cramp yourself and limit the use of the tool. Remember to choose a wood that is easy to work and preferably green, which will be much easier to cut. Hardwood should present fewer problems than softwood on end grain. Set the speed of the lathe no higher than 850 rpm. Although discs of this size can be rotated safely at 1250 rpm, speed is not necessary at this stage and the slower speed will demand correct use of the tool and give you a better view of what is happening. And the inevitable catches, when they occur, will be less frightening. Refer to the speed chart at right for guidance in tackling discs of different sizes.

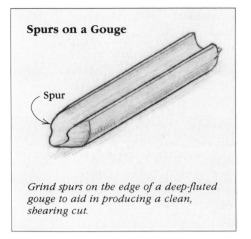

Spurs on a Gouge

Spur

Grind spurs on the edge of a deep-fluted gouge to aid in producing a clean, shearing cut.

Facework Speeds

Diameters	Lengths		
	2 in. (50mm)	3 in. (75mm)	4 in. (100mm)
8 in. (205mm)	1250	1250	1000
10 in. (255mm)	1250	1000	900
12 in. (305mm)	1250	1000	900
14 in. (355mm)	1000	900	850
16 in. (405mm)	750	650	600
18 in. (460mm)	650	500	400

Note: *The figures in the chart above are expressed in rpm. Reduce speeds when turning larger or longer work.*

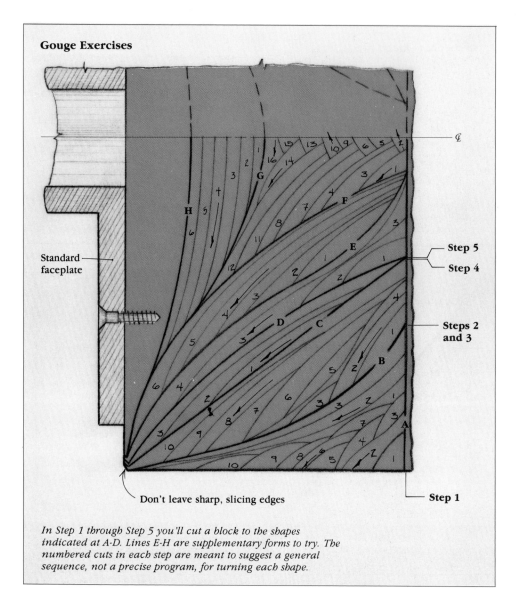

Gouge Exercises

Standard faceplate

Don't leave sharp, slicing edges

Step 5
Step 4

Steps 2 and 3

Step 1

In Step 1 through Step 5 you'll cut a block to the shapes indicated at A-D. Lines E-H are supplementary forms to try. The numbered cuts in each step are meant to suggest a general sequence, not a precise program, for turning each shape.

Begin by turning a series of curved and flat shapes, following Steps 1 through 5. First, true the face of the disc (Step 1), then turn a smooth convex curve (Steps 2 and 3). Next, reduce the form to a straight line (Step 4), followed by a shallow concave curve (Step 5). Practice each technique until the block is turned away (and watch out for the faceplate screws). Do this to several blocks before proceeding to turn a cylinder, which will be more difficult (particularly on the end grain).

In all the steps be sure to make your cuts as near parallel to the axis as possible (toward the fixing) and keep the tool horizontal or tilted up no more than 10°. Stop the lathe frequently to examine the surface and the quality of your cut. Listen to the sounds as you cut and relate them to the quality of the surface. You'll find that the most effective cut can vary from disc to disc, even when the discs are from the same plank. File all this information away in your mind for later reference.

Step 1: First true the face of the disc. This is the easiest place to begin because there is no end grain to contend with. You are confronted by the full length of the fibers running at 90° to the axis. As you cut, these fibers will be lifted off the surface. It is difficult to achieve a smooth surface when trueing a face because the fibers lie at the wrong angle for a shearing cut.

To achieve a flat face, adjust the rest parallel to the eventual finished surface so that the tool can be held in a constant position relative to the rest. (Later on, if you want a flat or slightly dished surface at the bottom of a hollow, such as the curve at the bottom of a 4-in.- [100mm] to 6-in.- [150mm] deep bowl, it is unlikely that you will be able to use any gouge satisfactorily unless it is ground with a very steep bevel. You'll have to use heavy scrapers instead.)

To obtain a flat surface when trueing up, or facing, a disc or platter, I usually employ a shallow gouge as a scraper, pulling it from the center out to the rim. When I reach the rim I make a shearing cut back toward the center. By starting with the scraping cut and working out from the center, the rotating wood is less likely to spring surprises. For example, when you true up a warped disc there will be no erratic undulation at the center. But the moment you leave the center, you'll begin to experience the irregular surface of the face that becomes more pronounced toward the rim of the disc. If you start at the rim, a catch is more likely because the irregularities make it difficult to know exactly where the surface of the wood is. It will help you start the shearing cut into the center if the rim has a smooth surface for the bevel to ride on. If the surface is very rough, make several scraping cuts from the center outward before attempting the inward shearing cut.

To make the scraping cut, place the gouge at the center of the disc, with the tool rolled at least 45° and the top facing in the direction of the cut, as shown in the drawing on the facing page. If the top of the tool faces up, the pressure of the revolving wood on the tool's unsupported left edge will cause a catch (p. 56). The effect is the same as if you stepped on the gunwale of an empty dinghy. Both the dinghy and the gouge will roll with disastrous consequences unless held firmly or counterbalanced. As the tool is rolled in the direction of the cut, the edge is supported close to the point of cut and you'll be able to take light shavings. Squeeze the edge into the wood with the upper hand. Move the tool along the rest to the rim. On an irregular face, the same

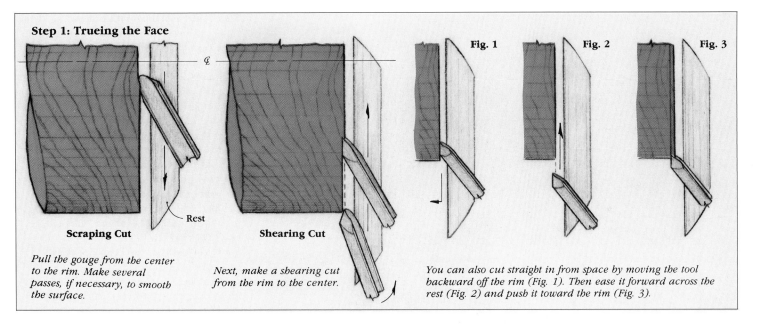

Step 1: Trueing the Face

Scraping Cut

Pull the gouge from the center to the rim. Make several passes, if necessary, to smooth the surface.

Shearing Cut

Next, make a shearing cut from the rim to the center.

You can also cut straight in from space by moving the tool backward off the rim (Fig. 1). Then ease it forward across the rest (Fig. 2) and push it toward the rim (Fig. 3).

Fig. 1   Fig. 2   Fig. 3

centerwork (p. 81), so be careful not to let the tool move across the rest into the gap. Keep the edge moving steadily on a path a constant distance from the rest, using your upper hand as a jig on the rest. You'll be able to tell when the surface is smooth because the sound will change from a knocking to an even tick-tick as the irregularities in the surface are removed. (Don't forget to round the sharp edges between the face and side of the disc, or risk getting cut if you slip.)

When the face is relatively flat, ensure that the outer edge of the face is true by making a final scraping cut about ¼ in. (6mm) in from the rim. This will provide a smooth surface on which to rub the bevel. Then roll the tool over so that the top of the gouge faces toward the center of the disc at about 45°, as shown at right. Beginning at the rim, bring the bevel shoulder in to rub before pivoting the edge forward to pick up the shearing cut to the center. When making this cut you need to control the possible catches caused by centrifugal force. Your upper hand must take the form of a firm stop-grip to prevent the tool's running back. I use my palm to provide a back stop.

When you gain experience, you can attempt to cut into the rim from space. To begin the cut this way, tee it up like you would a golf shot. Hold the tool in the shearing cut position, with the bevel rubbing, and move it backward off the rim, away from the direction it will cut. Then ease the tool slightly forward across the rest before pushing it in to the rim, keeping the edge moving at 90° to the axis. The motion toward center must be firm and the edge tightly controlled to prevent a kick-back.

Make the shearing cut to true a face by rolling the gouge so it faces in the direction of the cut at about 45°. The bevel rubs the wood and the tool cuts just below the center of the edge.

Step 2: Turn an external curve to the shape shown at line *B* in the drawing on p. 100 by scraping with the lower edge. This is a good technique for speed, to be used during the early stages of rough-turning an external shape. The finished surface will not be particularly smooth because the tool lies at 90° to the wood surface, but there should be a minimum of torn end grain. Shallow gouges are generally better than deep-fluted for this because the upper edge of the deep-fluted gouges can get in the way and limit the size of the shaving. In either case, the edge must be ground to a fingernail shape. This cut employs a relatively safe pulling action, always made from the center outward so each fiber is supported by others.

Place the gouge on the rest, rolled over on its side so that the top faces in the direction of cut at a 45° angle. Hold the tool at about 45° to the axis of the wood and horizontal, or with the edge tilted up slightly, as shown in the photo at left. Your upper hand must maintain firm contact with the rest, with your fingers gripping over and around the tool. Your lower hand controls the angle of the cut. Move the edge into the cut by squeezing the tool toward the wood as you move the handle around with your body so that it approaches parallel to the axis. This will cause the edge to swing through an arc as it enters the wood, as shown in the drawing at left. (Remember that when the edge moves ³/₁₆ in. [5mm], the handle moves 4 in. [100mm] to 4¾ in. [120mm] at the ferrule.) After the initial cut, the tool swings back to its original angle at the same time that your upper hand pulls it about 1 in. (25mm) along the rest to begin the next cut farther down the curve. Keep your elbows tucked in and the tool handle aligned against your body or along your forearm (preferably both). You must ensure a balanced stance so that you can place your weight behind the tool as you pivot back and forth with the handle (p. 47). A common fault that leads to a hefty catch is to hold the tool flat, with the top facing up, instead of rolled over. As long as only the side of the tool contacts the rest, the edge cannot snap down because it's already there.

At first you'll need to adjust the rest after every few cuts, especially when removing a corner. (Position the rest post so that you can simply swivel the rest to make your initial adjustments without having to move the entire assembly.) As each cut becomes longer, you will need to move the tool along the rest by pulling with the upper hand while maintaining the optimum cutting angle by swinging the handle

To make the scraping cut using the lower edge of the gouge, roll the tool so the top faces in the direction of the cut at about 45°. Use a firm hand-over grip and move the tool around the curve with good body support. The handle will be pivoted to the right as it moves through the cut, ending up almost parallel to the axis of the wood.

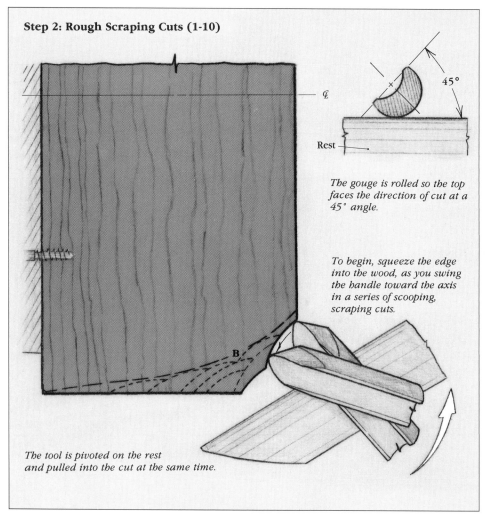

Step 2: Rough Scraping Cuts (1-10)

Rest

The gouge is rolled so the top faces the direction of cut at a 45° angle.

To begin, squeeze the edge into the wood, as you swing the handle toward the axis in a series of scooping, scraping cuts.

B

The tool is pivoted on the rest and pulled into the cut at the same time.

around. You should be able to feel when the tool is cutting well. If you think the shaving could be larger, don't exert more force but adjust the cutting angle by rotating the tool slightly with your lower hand. Remember not to cut off the side of the disc into space, which will splinter the corner, but cut in from the face, as shown in the photo at right and at far left in the drawing below.

Because the bevel doesn't contact the wood when you use the gouge as a scraper, take care not to exert pressure against the axis, which would tear the end grain and increase the chance of a catch. Where the angle of cut approaches 45° to the axis, a fair amount of force can be applied because it is absorbed by the faceplate. But remember that as the pressure is increased, so is the likelihood of torn grain (though this won't matter during initial cuts, when speed may be more desirable than the quality of the finished surface). Using this cut, you should achieve a smooth curve with little torn end grain but often slight grooves, or steps, left by the tool. This surface can now be smoothed using the same tool in a different way.

Always cut in from the face, rather than off the end, to avoid splintering the corner. This shows a scraping cut, using the lower edge.

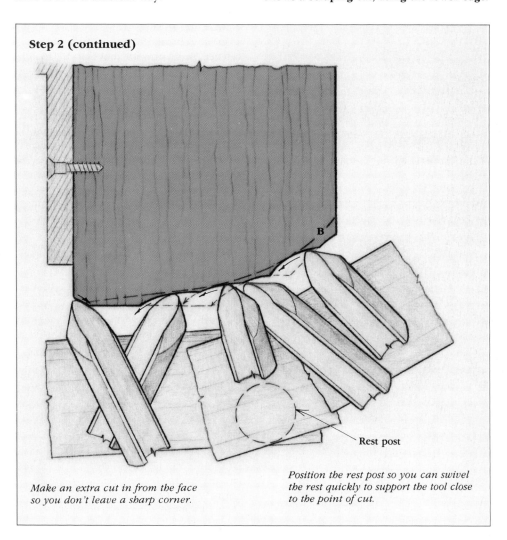

Step 2 (continued)

B

Rest post

Make an extra cut in from the face so you don't leave a sharp corner.

Position the rest post so you can swivel the rest quickly to support the tool close to the point of cut.

Step 3: Finish-scrape an even curve using the lower edge of the gouge, as shown at line *B* in the drawing on p. 100 and in the photo at left. You can get a very smooth surface by using a gouge on its side as a scraper. The shallow gouges are easier to use this way, and my favorite is ½ in. (13mm). As with all scrapers, the burr is important and I find the best edge comes from a light touch on the 60-grit wheel.

Place the tool almost on its side on the rest, as shown in the drawing below. Keep the gouge horizontal, with the lower portion of the edge cutting at center height. The tool must be held so that a catch will carry the edge into space. The edge should only stroke the surface (without pressure) in a series of sweeping cuts moving away from the center around the curve. If the edge fails to produce fluff, or very fine, curly shavings, don't exert more pressure on the cut but go back to the grinder. Any pressure can cause the tool to catch and pull out tufts of end grain. (If this happens, you'll hear a slight tick-tick sound as you cut.)

This is often the safest and simplest way to produce a smooth, flowing surface suitable for sanding, but such a fine, delicate cut requires that you have absolute control of the tool. To avoid catches, make sure the tool rests on its side and not with the top facing up. Keep the handle tucked firmly into your side and move with it. Your upper hand makes the fine adjustments needed to ensure that the edge sweeps through a series of flowing arcs. I generally prefer the hand-over grip, which allows my hand more movement along the rest.

Take a finish-scraping cut using the lower edge of the gouge. Keep the tool horizontal with the edge cutting at center height.

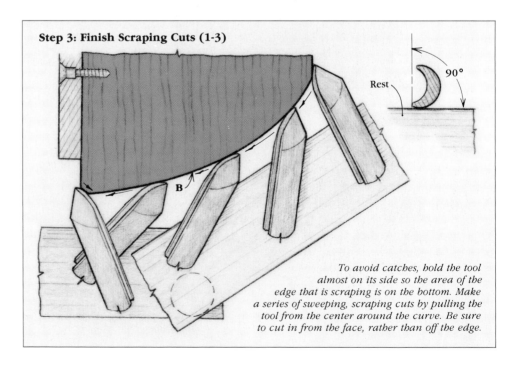

Step 3: Finish Scraping Cuts (1-3)

Rest

90°

B

To avoid catches, hold the tool almost on its side so the area of the edge that is scraping is on the bottom. Make a series of sweeping, scraping cuts by pulling the tool from the center around the curve. Be sure to cut in from the face, rather than off the edge.

Step 4: Remove the curve to produce a straight profile, as shown at line *C* on p. 100, using a shearing cut with the lower edge of the gouge. This is the best roughing cut and is a thrusting action made with the tool aligned in the direction of the cut. It should give you an even smoother surface than the smoothest of scraping cuts. Either deep-fluted or shallow gouges can be used. The best cut comes from a gouge ground to a full fingernail curve.

Place the tool on the rest, rolled over about 45°, as shown at right. Hold the tool horizontally, or with the edge tilted up slightly, and pointed in the direction of the cut. The bevel should rub against the newly cut surface at all times. If you fail to do this, only the edge will be in contact with the wood and the cut surface will be uneven as the tool chatters. You should be able to watch the bevel rub until you learn the feel of it. The angle and movement of the tool is controlled by the lower hand while the upper hand keeps it on the rest with the bevel rubbing and deflects shavings. With the gouge in this position, the center of the cutting edge is nearly vertical and cuts across the grain, while the lower portion of the edge is almost horizontal and removes the bulk of the waste with a scraping action, resulting in spiral shavings and a smoothly cut surface. This action is similar to that of a plow that cuts and turns soil at the same time.

The most difficult part of this cut is starting it before you have a surface for the bevel to contact. So to make the initial cut, you must pivot the tool through an arc into the wood or ease the tool straight in with a firm grip. The bevel can be guided effectively on as little as ⅛ in. (3mm) of wood. Once the bevel is rubbing, you have a secondary fulcrum that gives you very fine control over the edge. Keep the rest close to reduce the leverage.

Cut a curve by making a shearing cut using the lower edge of the gouge. This should produce an even smoother surface than the best scraping cut.

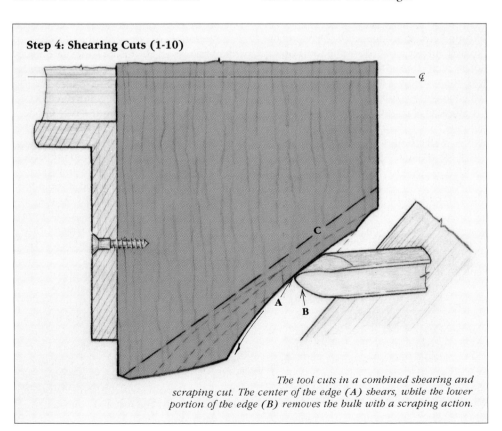

Step 4: Shearing Cuts (1-10)

The tool cuts in a combined shearing and scraping cut. The center of the edge (A) shears, while the lower portion of the edge (B) removes the bulk with a scraping action.

Step 5: Finishing Back-Cut (1-3)

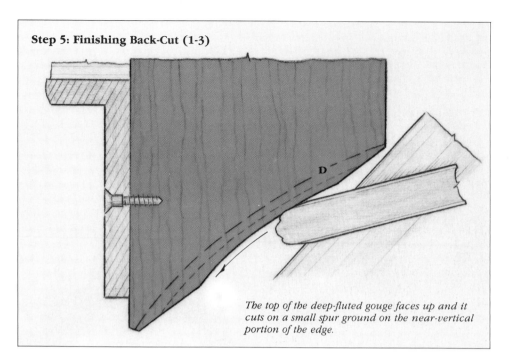

The top of the deep-fluted gouge faces up and it cuts on a small spur ground on the near-vertical portion of the edge.

The shearing back-cut requires a spur to be ground on the edge. The tool cuts on the almost vertical wing and produces a smooth, finished surface. Note the rubbing bevel.

Step 5: Use a back-cut with the deep-fluted gouge to produce a shallow, concave curve, as shown at line *D* in the drawing on p. 100. This is a thrusting and shearing cut similar to the previous one, but the top of the tool faces upward, as shown at left, instead of being rolled in the direction of the cut. The tool cuts on its upper edge. Never use a shallow gouge (you cannot present a vertical cutting edge to the wood) or a deep-fluted gouge in excess of ½ in. (13mm) wide (the risk of a catch is too great). This is strictly a finishing cut. It produces fine shavings and the best surface of all from the tool. Do not attempt to produce a heavy shaving, as with the previous cut.

The quality of this cut is determined by the shape of the cutting edge. I find the best cut comes from a small spur ground on the normally full curve of the deep-fluted gouge, as shown on p. 99. The exact position of the spur will depend on how you use the tool and the situation. It is likely to be slightly different for cutting a convex, as opposed to a concave, surface. (Usually the spur is quite pronounced, contradicting an earlier-stated rule that the sides should not be ground proud of the center.) It's easy to put on this small spur as you grind the tool—I discovered this cut because I couldn't grind the tool with an even edge—so it is chiefly a matter of placing the spur where you want it. If you use a firm hand-under grip as you rotate the tool against the grinding wheel, you'll find it easy to move the position of the spur down the edge a fraction. I grind a spur on the edge of any deep-fluted gouge when I need it, and remove it afterward

with a quick pass on the grinding wheel. I admit this sounds a bit like wasting expensive metal, but very little is actually removed and the cut produced is far superior to most others.

I use this cut to follow the shearing cut made with the lower edge (Step 4). The shearing cut removes the bulk of the waste and leaves you with a good surface. Rotate the tool so that the top faces up and take a delicate final pass, bringing the spur in to cut. The tool is held horizontally (or with the edge tilted up slightly) and the cut is made with the almost vertical portion of the edge, with the bevel rubbing against the surface just cut. Because the cut is made near the top edge of the tool and the maximum possible distance from the fulcrum, the tool has a tendency to roll over toward the wood, which can make for a hefty catch; it is even more important than usual to hold the tool firmly and move with it. As is often the case with anything really good, disaster is lurking close by, so the narrower the tool you use, the better.

By now, you will have experienced much that gouges have to offer. When you've achieved a nice smooth cut at *D,* go through all the cuts again, varying the lines of the curves. I realize it will be difficult to resist the temptation to proceed straight to hollowing, but I urge you to reduce several blocks to shavings while you practice the cuts. The drawing on p. 100 suggests further curves to attempt at *E, F, G* and *H.*

In practice, of course, you will use a combination of all the above techniques, and your own quirks in tool grinding and handling will lead you to develop your own style. In the roughing-down stages particularly, I find I move the tool in one fluid motion, alternating from one technique to another, cutting all the while. You should be able to do the same with practice. Pay attention to and learn the sounds of your cutting and if the pitch changes, stop and find out why. As the wood becomes thin, the last 1 in. (25mm) or so at the rim will begin to sound brittle. And a tick-tick sound might mean you've nicked a screw point.

When cutting around a long curve, be prepared to move your body quite a distance while you sway with the tool handle. It's always a good feeling to cut a curve in one pass, but to achieve it your feet will have to be well apart with your weight balanced over one foot. Follow the tool as it cuts the curve, transferring your weight to the other foot. Alternatively, you can stop, adjust the rest and your stance and carry on.

When the shearing cut reaches the top of the foot, pivot the tool around to bring the lower edge in to scrape the bottom of the curve and the corner.

Shoulders—Before you can move on to hollowing, you will have to learn to cut a shoulder, or foot, so that the bowl can be reversed and held in a chuck. I normally use a shallow gouge for this job, because the point gets into the corner more easily than that of a deep-fluted tool. The cut is the same as any other made from space into the wood: The edge is either lowered through an arc or pushed straight in, under tight control, until the bevel can rub. Hold the tool on its side on the rest, with the top facing toward the direction of cut. Tilt the tool edge up about 10° and move it in a direction almost parallel to the axis. Make the initial cut using the point and the area just below it. At the bottom of the foot, pivot the tool to bring the lower edge in to scrape the curve and the corner, as shown above. Alternatively (contradicting another previously stated rule), you can cut gently against the grain to fair the curve into the corner, as shown in the photo at bottom right on p. 120. Cuts made against the grain will rarely be as smooth as those made with the grain, so try to make most of your cuts from the smaller to larger diameter (from as close to the foot as possible) before cleaning up the last bit in the corner from the other direction. I also cut against the grain when roughing-down forms between centers if the tailstock prevents an approach from the other direction. The surface is acceptable for a rough cut. I watch the top of the form take shape as I cut, which helps me develop a flowing line that will be cut more cleanly at a later stage.

Cylinders—Cylinders present you not only with the obvious difficulty of how to get a smooth, straight cut, but also with the nastiness of two encounters with a maximum of end grain with every revolution. Practice cutting them when you are familiar with the tools. It's much more difficult to cut at 90° across end grain than to make the curved shearing cuts in the previous exercises. Use the rest as a guide for your hand by setting it parallel to the surface you want. Use a shearing back-cut, as shown in the photo on the facing page, with a narrow, deep-fluted gouge (¼ in. [6mm] to ½ in. [13mm]) for the best results. Keep the tool horizontal and at a tangent to the wood surface. It is particularly important to keep the pressure toward the headstock and not against the axis. Don't rush the cut, but try to proceed steadily along the rest.

Once you have reduced a few blocks to shavings and feel comfortable turning outside curves, it is time to turn a form for hollowing. Try an open-shaped bowl. Avoid curved-over rims for now, which present all sorts of control and cutting problems. Do not be deceived by the simplicity of the form. It is very difficult to produce a really good-looking, flowing line. The inside curve is as important as the outside one, and how the two relate to each other is just as critical. A common fault in bowls is that the outside looks fine and the inside looks fine, but the whole feels terrible. There's too much material left in the wrong places. The word "wooden" is partly defined in my dictionary as: "dull, insensible, heavy; lacking animation or grace of manner or execution." It's a common enough adjective in this sense, and I assume it derives, in part, from the millions of dull, heavy objects that have been and are still being produced by woodturners. I would like to see this trend reversed. As you make your bowl, aim for a shape that lifts itself visually off a surface rather than squats—turgid, menacing, immobile.

As your confidence grows, increase the size of the bowl you attempt. But it is wise to learn on blocks less than 4 in. (100mm) thick by 8 in. (205mm) in diameter because they present few technical problems and are less of a financial loss if things go wrong. I still have my first large project—a 3-in.- (75mm) thick by 12-in.- (305mm) diameter European ripple-ash bowl that took a long morning to make after my initial six weeks of turning. I tote it around now when I conduct workshops to illustrate what I consider to be almost every undesirable aspect of bowl design. Structurally, it was well enough made, but the shape is dumpy and the result is unbalanced, both visually and in the handling. It is not a joy forever.

You'll soon discover (as I did) that as the diameter increases, so do the problems of controlling leverage. There is more weight in the wood, which leads to heavier catches. You'll need to hold and use the tools in much the same ways as for the smaller exercise bowls, only with greater firmness. On external shapes you'll be able to arrange the rest close to the work, so there shouldn't be too much leverage to cope with after the blank has been trued. Inside shapes are a different story. The tool will often be cutting as much as 5 in. (125mm) away from the fulcrum. Proceed with caution.

Gouges

In hollowing, my basic rule is to cut toward the drive shaft (and faceplate or chuck). I never work from the center back up a curve to the rim because there are too many problems in controlling the tool and the cut is against the grain. Often the main concern with hollowing is how to remove waste material as quickly and efficiently as possible, while still leaving a relatively smooth surface. Always drill a depth hole in the center first (p. 65). Not only will this give you one less thing to worry about (you won't need to stop frequently to measure depth), but by removing the center you can be much freer in using the tool at the end of a cut, though it should still ease in. Try to keep the cut moving as close to parallel to the axis as possible so that any force is directed toward the drive shaft. When your cut is within the diameter of the faceplate a certain amount of forward pressure can be used, though if this is too great and you have a catch, the wood is likely to come loose on the faceplate screws or to be pulled out of the chuck. Only practice and experience can tell you what the limitations are. Wood mounted on loose screws will rattle as you cut. As always, stop if something sounds unusual and find out why.

I rough-out the hollow with gouges and then finish the form with scrapers. By far the best way of learning how to use a gouge is by rough-turning a large quantity of bowls. I used to hollow 6-in. (150mm) bowls with the ¼-in. (6mm) deep-fluted gouge. Because this tool takes less of a shaving than would a larger gouge, it requires more cuts to achieve the desired surface, providing more practice on each bowl. Try to make each cut as clean as possible. Use every opportunity to improve your technique.

Because the cuts are made toward the drive shaft, it is difficult to use the tool without having the bevel rub. The deep-fluted gouges are better than the shallow here. If you use shallow gouges, they should be long-and-strong. All the techniques are basically the same as for the external curved cuts, except that it is unwise to use the gouge as a scraper because of the centrifugal force. Use only shearing cuts to hollow.

Make the bowl in two stages. First, attach the disc to a faceplate by what will be the top surface of the bowl and turn an external shape and base, using the techniques described previously. The shape should resemble one of the forms shown below. Then, reverse the half-finished bowl so that it is held by its base in a jaw, spigot or collet chuck, or on a faceplate, and hollow the inside. Make the walls of your first few bowls about ⅜ in. (10mm) thick. Later, when the inside has been finished, you can reverse the bowl in a jam-fit chuck to refine the shape of the foot and lower curve (p. 115).

Adjust the rest across the face to be hollowed so that the gouge cuts just above center when the edge is angled up a few degrees above horizontal. Remember that the more you angle the tool upward, the farther the point of cut will be from the rest and the greater the leverage you'll have to control. A tool angle of 5° is ideal; a much steeper angle will create problems and dangers. Avoid using a gouge at a right angle to the surface of the wood. If you tilt the tool up less than 5° and keep the bevel rubbing on the surface just cut, this should be impossible. The handle should lie between 30° and 45° to the surface being cut (the precise angle depends on the angle of the bevel). I have seen a number of students hold the tool with the bevel

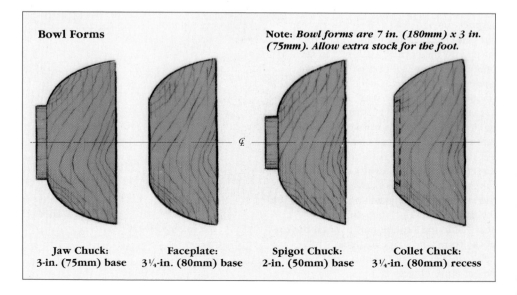

Bowl Forms

Note: *Bowl forms are 7 in. (180mm) x 3 in. (75mm). Allow extra stock for the foot.*

| Jaw Chuck: 3-in. (75mm) base | Faceplate: 3¼-in. (80mm) base | Spigot Chuck: 2-in. (50mm) base | Collet Chuck: 3¼-in. (80mm) recess |

rubbing (good), but angled up over 45° (bad) and at a right angle to the wood (worse). This places the point of cut much too far from the fulcrum and provides very little force behind the cut, which reduces your control of the path of the edge. Remember to make your first cuts light to establish the orbit of the disc's extremities and true up the face before you proceed to hollow, roughly following one of the sequences indicated below.

Making an entry presents two problems. First, there is no surface for the bevel to rub. Second, the centrifugal force wants to kick the tool away from center. To cut in cleanly without a run-back, use a secure stop-grip, with the gouge held on its side and its top facing the center (the direction of the cut). Your upper hand maintains a fixed fulcrum at the rim of the opening, as shown at right. Line up the bevel in the direction of the cut and tilt the edge of the tool up 15° to 20° so that you can bring it down through an arc into the wood. Once you have cut about ⅛ in. (3mm) so the bevel can rub, roll the tool so the top approaches 45° for a better cutting angle, as shown at top far right, and proceed. Aim for a single, fluid movement. When you feel more confident, try keeping the tool horizontal and easing it forward firmly until the bevel can rub.

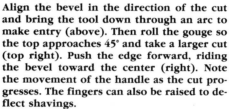

Align the bevel in the direction of the cut and bring the tool down through an arc to make entry (above). Then roll the gouge so the top approaches 45° and take a larger cut (top right). Push the edge forward, riding the bevel toward the center (right). Note the movement of the handle as the cut progresses. The fingers can also be raised to deflect shavings.

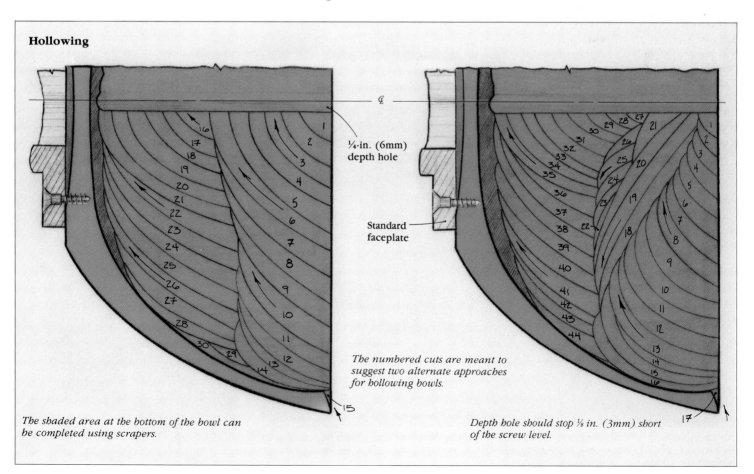

Hollowing

¼-in. (6mm) depth hole

Standard faceplate

The numbered cuts are meant to suggest two alternate approaches for hollowing bowls.

The shaded area at the bottom of the bowl can be completed using scrapers.

Depth hole should stop ⅛ in. (3mm) short of the screw level.

You can control the run-back by cutting a groove with the long point of the skew chisel (above). Rest the bevel of the gouge against the groove to make the entry and then push the tool forward to pick up the cut (right).

Another way to control the run-back during an entry cut is to make a groove against which you can rest the gouge bevel. Use the long point of a skew chisel, as shown at left. Push the point in gently but firmly, easing off for a gentle scrape.

If I cut away from the center, as shown below, my fingers will be over the tool while my palm provides a very firm back-stop to control the chatter. When working from the rim into the center, as shown in the photos at the top of the facing page, the forward motion of the tool opposes the centrifugal force. All you need do is provide a stop. This allows you to provide support with your upper hand when turning thin walls.

The most effective roughing-out cut (as for external shaping) is made with the lower edge of the gouge. The tool will cut when it is rolled at almost any angle, from a fine shaving back-cut, where the possibility of a catch is omnipresent, to a heavy scrape as the tool is rolled on its side. As you move it forward, rotate it slightly to find the biggest shaving with the least effort, somewhere between the two extremes. Again, don't push if the tool is not cutting, but adjust the angle or regrind, or both. If the tool is cutting well, force won't be needed to move it forward. Your attention should be directed toward moving the edge in the direction you want without its wavering. I find I can cut the first 2 in. (50mm) cleanly enough to sand. After that there are often small ridges or undulations from tool chatter, best eliminated with a scraper.

An alternate way of hollowing is to cut away from center. Hold the tool with a firm stop-grip to prevent chatter. Make cuts as close to parallel to the axis as possible to keep pressure against the fixing.

When working from the rim to the center, the forward motion of the tool opposes the centrifugal force, so all you need is a light back-stop to prevent a run-back. This is an advantage when turning thin bowls that require extra support from your upper hand.

As the depth of your hollow increases, the gouge will be cutting farther away from the rest. You'll need to get more weight behind the tool to maintain control. In these situations, long-and-strong tools are essential, because their bulk of metal will keep flexing to a minimum. There are curved rests, designed for internal shaping, but I have never found them very satisfactory for use with gouges and I don't have any. They tend to be flat-topped (p. 10) and are more suitable for flat-section scrapers. When hollowing, I use the gouges as far as possible around a curve, usually until the bevel ceases to rub or the leverage becomes too much to control. Then I use scrapers.

As you work farther into a bowl, it is possible to use a gouge with a steeper bevel instead of a scraper. In that way, bevel contact can be maintained and the shearing cut can be used—even across the bottom of a deep bowl—at 90° to the axis. Many turners have gouges with near-vertical bevels for this, but I tend not to use them because of the problems involved in cutting a precise line using a tool held at a right angle to the surface. I find the heavy scrapers much easier to control. Used delicately, they will leave an excellent surface. It is likely to take a while before you acquire enough skill to cut a smooth internal shape of your choice using gouges, so you'll need scrapers to finish and even out your curve.

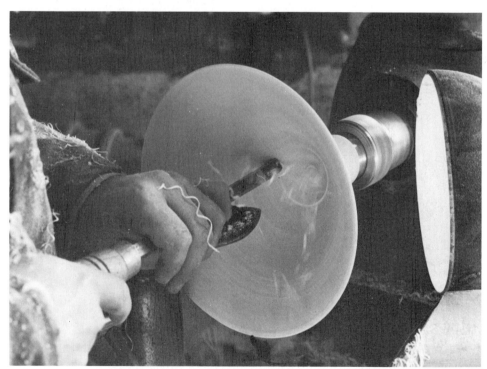

Use a long-and-strong gouge when cutting deep hollows well away from the rest. Use the gouge as far as possible around a curve, until the bevel can no longer rub. Then use a scraper.

Scrapers

I regard scrapers primarily as tools for fine finishing. To use them effectively requires a smooth, flowing and very delicate touch that removes only fluff and small, curly shavings, as shown at left. The bowl in the photo is being turned from green holly and the shavings are typical.

I grind my scrapers with a curved left edge for finishing hollows and use them to make sweeping cuts toward the center *(A, A-1* and *A-2* in the drawing below). Use a scraper with a slightly tighter radius than that of the surface of the wood. The bottom can be cut with a square-edge scraper ground back from the center of the edge *(B)*. It's easier to swing these flatter, curved tools around to use more of the edge than a tight-radius round-nose scraper. I use a scraper with a straight skew edge *(C)* to cut convex curves (such as a bowl exterior). The scrapers below are the basic ones I use for hollowing and they will cope with just about any bowl.

Scrapers are often the best tools to use far away from the rest, where the bevel of the gouge can't be kept rubbing. They must be used with a smooth and delicate touch to produce fine, curly shavings, as on this green holly bowl.

A 1½-in. (38mm) scraper with a curved edge is used for the final shaping of this green applewood bowl. The cut sweeps from the rim toward the center.

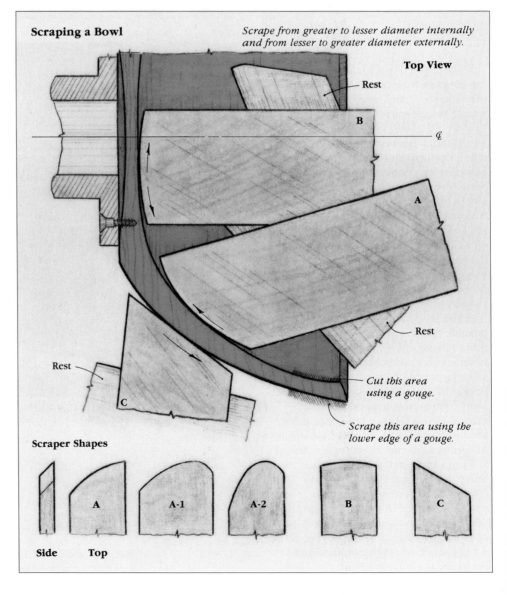

Scraping a Bowl

Scrape from greater to lesser diameter internally and from lesser to greater diameter externally.

Top View

Rest

B

₵

A

Rest

Rest

C

Cut this area using a gouge.

Scrape this area using the lower edge of a gouge.

Scraper Shapes

A   A-1   A-2   B   C

Side   Top

When there is only a small opening through which to hollow, narrow round-nose scrapers (¼ in. [6mm] to ½ in. [13mm]) are usually best, although a square-edge scraper with a sharp corner would be equally effective (though the finish it leaves is appalling). Square-end scrapers should be used for roughing only. My scrapers are all ground at about 45° and all are used in the same manner. I find the best edge comes from a light pass against the 60-grit grinding wheel. As with the other tools (only even more so), don't use forward pressure if the scraper is not cutting. Go back to the grinder.

I don't use scrapers to rough-out hollows if I can avoid it. But sometimes they're the best tool to use for heavy internal cuts made far away from the rest, where gouges cannot operate at their best. The scrapers I use for this are about ⅜ in. (10mm) thick and 1⅜ in. (35mm) wide (occasionally as large as 2 in. [50mm] wide). You need this width for weight and strength, but if you present such a wide edge, or even a ⅝-in.- (15mm) wide edge to the wood at once, the catch will be larger than you can control. So never use more than a small portion (about ⅜ in. [10mm]) of the edge at one time. Scrapers must be moved into the wood gently because the bevel can't rub. The normal technique of lowering the tool through an arc and rubbing the bevel to begin a cut applies to all gouges and chisels, but not to scrapers. As the wood and the scraper edge meet, the tool is always liable to catch under the sudden pressure.

The golden rule with flat-section scrapers is to keep them flat on the rest (p. 86). There is a tendency to lift one side, which can easily catch and snap down. This is bad for the work and often just as bad for the fingers. It is good practice to keep pressure on top of the tool to ensure full contact with the rest. As for external shaping, always use scrapers so that there is no wood directly below the cutting edge, as shown at right; just above center height on an internal surface.

Use the scrapers to even out the curves you've cut with the gouge. Hold the tool firmly and keep the handle against your side or forearm and move your body with it. The upper hand ensures that the flat section remains fully on the rest and provides the fine adjustments for the cut. Move the edge cautiously so that the wood brushes past, barely touching. Any real pressure will lead to a catch or a possible tick-tick sound, which indicates torn grain (often pulled from end grain). If the job is thin and vibrates, it will need support and an even lighter cut. The biggest problem

with scraping techniques is that often, especially on internal shapes, the point of cut will be well away from the fulcrum—perhaps as far as 8 in. (205mm). The greater the distance, the greater the leverage to control. Most of my scrapers have handles between 14 in. (355mm) and 18 in. (460mm) long and these are aligned under my forearm for greater support and control. The farther from the rest you cut, the more cautious you must be in moving the edge and the less of it should contact the wood.

Aside from controlling the leverage, you will have to keep the edge moving to produce flowing curves. On a regular curve you'll be able to swing the edge through an arc by pivoting the tool on the rest, but this is rarely possible. It is more common to encounter a parabolic curve, so the tool will have to move along and across the rest at the same time that it sweeps around. You'll need to develop good coordination for such complex movements. As you swing the tool (using the lower hand), the upper hand provides a movable stop, firmly maintaining the path of the edge to remove the ridges.

I learned to use scrapers by making hundreds of breadboards, platters and shallow dishes, and you might try the same. I suggest 1¼-in. (32mm) by 12-in. (305mm) blanks for breadboards, 1⅛-in. (28mm) by 10-in. (255mm) blanks for platters and 2-in. (50mm) by 10-in. (255mm) blanks for dishes. Discs of these sizes will present fewer cutting problems than larger ones, when weight and peripheral speed combine against you. Discs should be flattened and sanded on one side, which will be the base. They are then mounted to the fixing (usually a center-screw faceplate) by the base and turned completely without being transferred to another fixing.

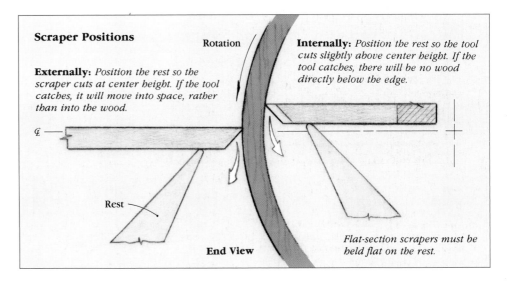

Scraper Positions

Rotation

Externally: *Position the rest so the scraper cuts at center height. If the tool catches, it will move into space, rather than into the wood.*

Internally: *Position the rest so the tool cuts slightly above center height. If the tool catches, there will be no wood directly below the edge.*

℄

Rest

End View

Flat-section scrapers must be held flat on the rest.

Cutting Internal Cylinders

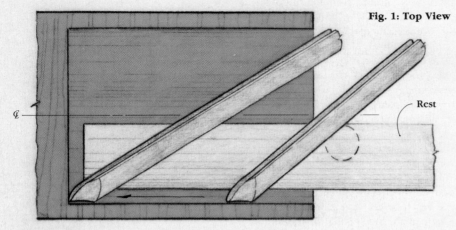

Fig. 1: Top View

Rest

If you can get the rest in, you can cut the sides using a gouge. The gouge cuts at center height (or slightly below) and is tilted up about 2° to 3°.

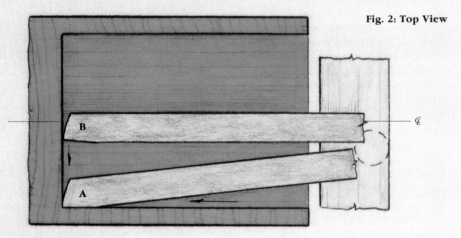

Fig. 2: Top View

B

A

The scraper should be ground back about 1 in. (25mm) on the left side so that it cuts on its side as well as its edge.

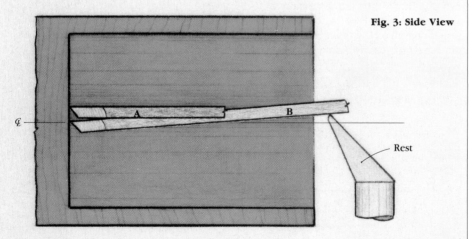

Fig. 3: Side View

A   B

Rest

The corner cut at A is made above center height, while the cuts on the bottom (B) are made at center height.

Note: *The area ground back 1 in. (25mm) from the left corner of the scrapers in Fig. 2 and Fig. 3 has been exaggerated for clarity.*

Cylinders—The inside bottom of a deep cylinder always presents the worst problems. Catches are easy. If you can get the rest in, the inside wall of a cylinder can be cut using a gouge, as shown in Fig. 1 at left; if not, I prefer to use the sharp left corner of a 1-in. (25mm) long-and-strong scraper. I move the corner across the bottom face into the wood, as shown in Fig. 2. The edge curves away from the left corner to avoid too much contact with the wood. The scraper is ground on the left side (about 1 in. [25mm] up from the corner of the tool) so that it cuts on the side as well as the edge, as shown in Fig. 2 and Fig. 3. Internal corners on a cylinder are awkward to work and should be approached gingerly. If the tool is moving outward from the center, it is likely to catch the side. If it proceeds down the cylinder wall to the base, the edge is likely to catch on the bottom. In either case, ease in the tool, taking care not to allow too much of the edge or the sharpened side to contact the wood at once.

At one time I had a small production run of teak kitchen-storage containers 8 in. (205mm) wide by 6 in. (150mm) deep. These cylinders proved too time-consuming and expensive to produce. Catches were frequent when working so far off the rest, especially when finishing the bottom of the hollow. If I were to produce these now, I would eliminate the awkward hollowing by gluing up staves to reduce the turning. (I might even leave the inside faceted and turn only the outside.) This would also overcome the considerable problem of warping.

Refining the Form

When you feel comfortable and reasonably confident turning the exterior of a bowl and hollowing it with gouges and scrapers, you can try remounting the bowl in a jam-fit chuck, so that the foot and base can be refined. The photos on this page show the process for turning a jam-fit chuck to accept the rim of an English ash bowl. (Refer to pp. 24-25 for more information about jam-fit chucks.)

First, measure the outside diameter of the bowl rim with dividers and transfer this to the face of a flat disc, mounted on a faceplate. Cut a 1° to 2° tapered groove, about ½ in. (13mm) deep, on the divider line. You can use the skew chisel as a scraper for this, but try using a ¼-in. (6mm) gouge, as shown in the photo at center. This is a good opportunity to practice bringing the tool from space into the wood precisely. Ensure that your upper hand provides a good back-stop on the rest. Hold the gouge on its side (with its top facing the center) and take it either through an arc into the wood or straight ahead, under tight control.

When the bowl has been fitted to the chuck, use very gentle cuts to shape the base. Any catches with such a fixing can easily flip the bowl out of the chuck. I try to keep my upper hand against the center of the bowl as a flexible tailstock, as shown at far right, while my thumb stays on the rest and maintains contact with the tool. I use a ¼-in. (6mm) fingernail-ground shallow gouge for all jobs of this type. I move the edge in through a series of small arcs to scrape-cut with the lower

To make a jam-fit chuck, first transfer the diameter of the bowl to the face of the chuck (top left and above). Then cut a 1° to 2° tapered groove inside the line using either a skew chisel as a scraper or a ¼-in. (6mm) gouge (left). Tap the bowl into the groove and rotate the chuck by hand to ensure that it runs true.

After the bowl is mounted in the chuck, turn the foot using a ¼-in. (6mm) fingernail-ground gouge. You can use your upper hand to provide extra support.

edge. My lower hand pivots the tool (against the thumb of my upper hand) and grips the handle firmly to ensure that the tool is kept rolled to the same angle. Beware of the upper edge contacting the work and rolling back into a catch. While a shearing cut is best for the final surface, I frequently prefer the less hazardous finish-scraping cut here, because the tool is used on its side where a catch is least likely. This is a good technique for removing the holes left by faceplate screws or the bruises left by a jaw chuck.

Once you've made several open-shaped bowls with a ⅜-in.- (10mm) thick wall and you feel ready for a greater challenge, try a thinner version of the same form, taking the wall down to ⅛ in. (3mm) or ¼ in. (6mm). This will demand a more precise and controlled use of the same techniques and, if you are successful, will show what you can achieve. I can cajole most students into producing an ultra-thin bowl and I do so as a confidence-builder. After that, a thicker (usually more practical) wall will be easy to achieve. I see no point in making ultra-thin bowls because they present technical problems. I feel there should be reasons other than pure exhibitionism. Do one or two to boost your confidence and then return to reality.

As the wall of a bowl becomes thinner, you will also encounter problems with chatter. This is caused by excessive pressure of the tool against the wood, which will flex and vibrate, developing characteristic parallel-angled ridges (this effect can be controlled for surface decoration when you get the hang of it). But you'll hear the chatter long before you see it. If you cut too forcefully, the pitch will rise to a shrill screech. The thinner the wall, the worse the noise. Eliminate this by using less tool pressure and by holding your fingers around the rim to support the wood behind the point of cut of the gouge or scraper.

When you feel comfortable turning an open, outward-flowing bowl shape, move on to one with upper walls that curve inward to form a narrower opening. The standard tools are more awkward to handle on this sort of shape because of the restricted angle of approach. (My short-bed lathes, with the tailstock removed, are ideal for this kind of job, because I can move freely around the face, working from any angle.) The angle of the bevel becomes more critical and it will need to be longer the more you undercut the rim. I use a narrow gouge, ground with a very long bevel on the left side with a pronounced leading spur on the shoulder, to make a back-cut from the rim outward to the point where the wall begins to curve back toward the base. Then I use scrapers or a gouge with a steeper bevel. Try to keep the rest at 90° to the tool for best support. If the rest lies at an angle to the scraper and the tool is tilted, the edge will cut at an angle to the wood. The tool will shear in this position, but it is more difficult to control.

It is most important at this stage, while you are acquiring basic skills, to refine the profile of your wall. You can keep one or two early bowls—as points of reference for later—but I strongly recommend that some of your first efforts be cut down the middle, as shown in the photo at left. In this way you'll be able to examine what you actually did in relation to what you think you did or tried to do. Plane or sand the profile smooth and trace the outline on paper if it helps. You'll see clearly how your lines flow (or don't flow), how inside and outside curves relate, and where more wood could have been left or removed to improve the balance and tactile quality of the whole. Even now, I still cut bowls in half from time to time. Bowls of marginal quality serve you far better if cut and learned from than if they are left to damage your reputation when placed on public display.

It's a good idea to cut bowls in half to examine their cross section. You'll be able to see clearly how the inside and outside lines of the form relate to each other, and where you might improve your technique.

Decoration

There will be occasions when you feel some decorative grooves, coves or continuous beads are required. Grooves or coves are simple to make because they are cut into a finished surface. Beads are different. I feel that beads should look as though they were applied on top of a finished surface. The shape on which they sit should flow beneath them unless the bead is used at a point where the profile changes direction dramatically. If the basic form looks as though it should flow beneath a bead or other raised area but doesn't, the whole thing will look uncomfortable. In commercial terms, grooves and coves can be used to good effect in breaking the surface visually, while being easier to cut than beads.

Grooves & coves

Although it is easiest to push a flat scraper straight in to create a groove or cove, the finished surface will rarely be even remotely equal to that which is shear-cut, no matter how delicate your touch. But because a shearing cut must be made at right angles to the surface, many normal tools cannot be used on internal curves. Where you have to cut a groove into an internal curved shape, it will probably be necessary to grind a special tool, and I keep all my old skew chisels, parting tools and scrapers for this purpose. Fortunately, though, most decoration is applied to external shapes that are easy to get at.

To cut coves, use a gouge in the same manner as for centerwork (p. 72). Grooves can be cut into convex or flat surfaces using a diamond-point scraper or a skew chisel held on its side. The long point of the skew chisel is better if used precisely in the same way as for cutting grooves on a centerwork spindle (p. 76). Because of the grain direction on the outside of a bowl, there is an increased possibility of a run-back, so be sure to keep a firm grip on the tool, preventing it from kicking sideways in either direction. When turning a groove or cove on the flat face of a platter, your grip needs to be just as secure to control the centrifugal force that tends to throw the tool outward. Certainly it is much less risky to cut grooves using scrapers, but you can obtain such a clean surface using the skew that it's worth persevering.

Use the skew chisel, held on its side, as a scraper to cut small grooves.

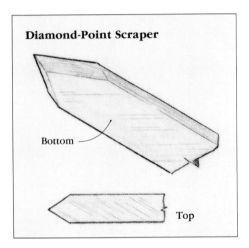

Diamond-Point Scraper

Bottom

Top

Beads

I leave these roughed square, as shown at left, while the surface on which they sit is finished. Shear-cutting beads can be difficult, because they are usually small and have no surface on which the gouge bevel can ride satisfactorily. Begin by cutting beads at least ⅜ in. (10mm) wide.

Where two or more beads adjoin, I define their sides using the long point of the skew chisel, as shown in the photo at center left, before rounding off the corners with a gouge. If the beads are very small, I use only the skew chisel, cutting the sides with the long point before flicking the tool over to act as a scraper to round the corners, as shown at bottom left.

You can cut larger beads using a gouge, as shown in the drawing below. You'll need to employ a solid hand-over grip so that you can swing the edge through an arc when beginning the cut. The procedure is the same as for cutting centerwork beads using a gouge (p. 73). Have the top of the tool facing up at the beginning of the cut, then rotate the tool so that it is on its side at the end of the cut. If the tool does not finish on its side, you will have problems getting good definition at the base of the bead. As the side of the bead takes shape, not only must the tool move forward across the rest, but it must rotate as well. As always, you should slow down toward the end of the cut and ease the edge forward to achieve a sharp corner where the bead meets the surface.

More often than not I will cut a bead in a series of arcs (either sideways or downward), with the fulcrum in a fixed position on the rest. The tool swings like an oar in a rowlock. This gives me more control of the edge because the tool only pivots on the rest rather than moving across or along it.

Leave beads square while the surface beneath them is shaped (top). You can use the long point of the skew chisel to define the sides of beads (center). Then flick the tool over to round the corners of small beads (bottom) with a scraping cut.

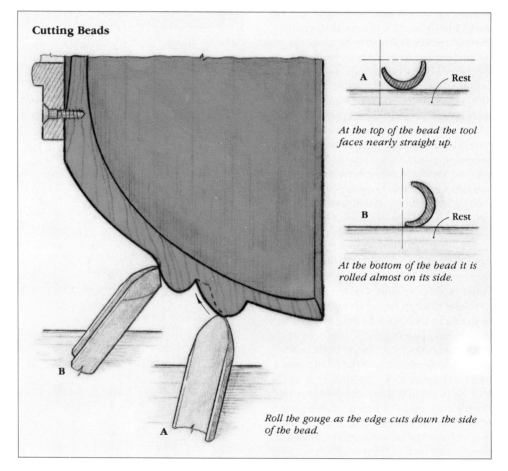

Cutting Beads

At the top of the bead the tool faces nearly straight up.

At the bottom of the bead it is rolled almost on its side.

Roll the gouge as the edge cuts down the side of the bead.

Seasoning Bowls

My approach to the problem of drying bowls is to rough them out of green wood, with a wall thickness about one tenth of the bowl's diameter; 1 in. (25mm) thick for a 10-in.- (255mm) diameter bowl. The wall should be the same thickness from the rim to the base to allow for even drying. Then I leave the bowls in a loose pile where air can circulate freely around them (out of direct sunlight) for not less than three months. This system works well for most situations. (Some of the warping takes place because tension is released when the form is hollowed, so I'll often rough-turn dry wood as well, and allow it to stabilize for a few days before turning.)

Professionals can maintain a stock of roughed bowls. Amateurs, especially when starting out, might practice their gouge technique while roughing-out bowls and then return later to finish them off when their skills have developed and they can proceed with a greater likelihood of success. In schools, students can rough standard-shaped bowls to go in a general stockpile and take others to finish that have already dried. (Always write the date on a roughed-out bowl so you know when it was done.)

Polyethylene glycol has been widely marketed as the ultimate solution to warping problems. I've never used it because so many of the professionals I've talked to who have tried it soon stopped. They discovered that the process takes about the same amount of time as air-drying but limits the finishing options. The bowl becomes semi-plastic as the water in the wood vessels is replaced by the PEG.

Since the late 1970s, many woodturners have been experimenting with the microwave oven as a means of seasoning timber. While I have flirted with attempts to speed the seasoning of roughed-out bowls, I have not found microwave seasoning worthwhile commercially and cannot recommend it to anyone as a standard practice. Most microwaves do not seem to penetrate more than 1 in. (25mm) of wood satisfactorily. So, while you can undoubtedly dry wood thinner than this, the process is time-consuming, often requiring each piece to have several short periods in and out of the oven.

I use the microwave oven to dry out my more delicate green-turned bowls (many of the bowls in the gallery were microwaved). The thickest part of these bowls lies in the foot but is still less than 1 in. (25mm). The water in the freshly felled wood heats rapidly and evenly throughout. A 3-in. (75mm) by 6-in. (150mm) bowl with a wall thickness of $\frac{3}{16}$ in. (5mm) will become hot and flexible in 2½ to 3 minutes. In this condition, it can be manipulated into another shape and held there until cool (another few minutes). I use this technique for making oval bowls (like the holly bowl on p. 145) by accentuating their natural distortion. But mostly I rely on the natural warping of the wood. To get the shape I want, I take great care in cutting the blank and then in aligning it on the lathe (usually between centers at first). I choose an even-grained piece of timber where the growth rings are symmetrical around the pith. An outward-flowing ogee shape will produce an undulating rim; a parabolic curve will become oval.

These bowls have been rough-turned out of green wood. They will be set aside to air-dry for several months before being completed.

Make a Bowl

1 Select a 4-in. (100mm) by 8-in. (205mm) block (any close-grained hardwood will do) and drill it for a center-screw faceplate. Trim the sides of the block on a bandsaw to reduce the bulk. The face of the block that is attached to the faceplate will become the top of the bowl.

2 Begin cutting off the corner and then true the base using a ½-in. (13mm) gouge. Use a light scraping cut with the lower edge for the curve (left), and a shearing cut for the base (above).

5 Develop the shape further, using a shearing back-cut. The tool is held with the top facing up and it cuts on a spur, ground on the almost vertical wing of the edge.

6 Use a ¼-in. (6mm) shallow gouge to make a shearing cut around the curve toward the foot. This is one of the few times you will be working against the grain of the wood, so make this cut gently, removing light shavings and holding the tool securely. As the cut progresses, you can detail the corner of the foot (about ¼ in. [6mm] deep) for mounting on a three-jaw chuck.

3 As wood is removed and the shape develops, smooth the curve using a shearing cut with the lower edge (above).

4 Begin to shape the foot and continue developing the curve using a scraping cut.

7 Make a scraping cut with the lower edge of the ½-in. (13mm) gouge to smooth the curve and eliminate the odd bump left by the gouge in the last step.

8 Switching back to the ¼-in. (6mm) gouge, make a shearing back-cut around the full curve. (Remember not to cut all the way off the edge of the block, or you will splinter the corner.) This cut should finish the outside curve, leaving you with a smooth, flowing shape.

10 The bowl exterior is now ready for mounting in the spigot chuck. The curve displays no lifted grain and any small ridges that remain could be sanded away or removed with a very light scraping cut.

9 If you plan to remount the bowl in a spigot chuck instead of a three-jaw chuck, transfer the diameter of the chuck to the bottom of the foot using dividers and cut a groove to accept the flange. Then shape the smaller foot using the same scraping cut employed on the larger foot.

12 Hollow the bowl using a ¼-in. (6mm) deep-fluted gouge. Make cuts from the rim to the center, from a larger to a smaller diameter, with pressure directed toward the fixing.

11 With the bowl reversed in the spigot chuck, true the face using a ½-in. (13mm) deep-fluted gouge (left). Use a drill bit (or a small gouge) to establish the depth of the bowl and make a center hole (above).

13 Refine the inside shape using gouges until it is fairly smooth and reflects the external lines of the bowl. Provide extra support for a thin wall with your hand.

14 Complete the inside by making light cuts with a curved-edge scraper. The tool is flat on the rest and cuts just above center.

15 Make a jam-fit chuck to accept the rim of the bowl so the bowl can be reversed for final shaping of the foot. True the disc face and transfer the diameter of the bowl rim to the face with dividers (left). Cut a shallow tapered groove (above right) and fit the bowl to it (right).

17 Make a finish scraping cut (left) before completing the round base with a light shearing cut (above), made against the grain.

16 Turn off the foot using a ¼-in. (6mm) shallow gouge to make a series of scraping cuts with the lower edge. Pivot the tool on the rest as the edge moves through an arc.

18 When the bowl is finished, cut it in half to see how well you've done. Then try another. Aim for sweeping curves, and use calipers to check your progress.

We are surrounded by examples of what use can do for a surface.

Consider, for example, the wooden handrails on an old staircase, the handle of a well-used garden, workshop or building tool, or the arms and seat of an old and favored chair. All have been polished by sweaty palms or grubby hands to produce a lovely patina. An indescribable surface that begs for a caress of the hand—that's what I think wood should provide.

If you are looking forward to a chapter packed with information on polishing compounds, chemical formulas and sealers, you will be disappointed. I belong to the school that believes if you want a plastic-looking bowl, you should buy a molded one. Don't splash polyurethane over a piece of wood that has done no harm to anyone. I don't even like hard-wax finishes. Synthetic finishes might do wondrous things for wood as it leaves the workshop, but it will still look the same years later. Nothing gets through the surface, so the wood fails to develop character and will never have the patina of a well-used piece left natural.

I am inclined to leave the surface of a piece unsanded and even unfinished— directly as it comes from the tool—because I know that the wood will look so good in seasoned old age. But customers, presumably attracted by (or conditioned to expect) the polished surface of high-gloss polyurethane, are not generally so keen. So I have reached a happy compromise by employing an oil-and-wax finish that enhances, but does not obscure, the sensual quality of the wood. This allows the future keeper of a piece the option of either oiling or polishing.

Abrasives

Although my oil-and-wax finish can be applied to any surface, I generally smooth the work with abrasive paper first, mainly to satisfy my customers' expectations. Abrasive papers are graded by number, according to the size of the cutting agent and its density on the paper. The papers I use normally range from 40 grit (coarse) to 220 grit (fine) and these are hand-held against the revolving wood. It is possible to do the most amazing things with coarser grits, which sometimes seem to cut as fast as chisels, though they leave a torn and scratched surface. The grits I use most are 80, 100 and 180, and 220 for some dense woods. I normally start with 80-grit paper,

A sharp tool used correctly produces a clean surface, as shown on the right side of this disc. The left side should be recut.

but this will not always cope with torn end grain on facework; for these occasions I use old, partly worn, cloth-backed sanding belts. The 40-grit belts will smooth almost anything, though they leave deep scratch marks. After the 40-grit belt, I go to 50-grit paper then to 80-, 100- and 180-grit papers. I use the 180-grit paper until it's totally worn out, at which point it will burnish the surface. I find the 180-grit finish generally satisfactory, though with some of the finer or harder woods such as African blackwood, mulga, imbuia or cocobolo, I may go on to use 220 grit or even 0000 steel wool.

A cardinal rule of sanding is: Proceed to a finer grade of paper only when all marks from previous coarser papers have been removed. You should see an even scoring pattern with no obvious deeper scratching before moving on. Unfortunately, one bit of grit is often proud of the rest and it scratches more deeply. My solution to this is to move the paper evenly and slowly across the face or along the axis of the work in a final sweep before moving on to the next grade of paper. Jabbing and dabbing increase scratching. I always use as much pressure as possible, though if you press too hard or too long in one place, the friction will produce heat cracks in almost any wood (yew and African walnut are particularly prone to this). Often it is better to sand at a lower speed than you use for turning, especially with larger facework, where peripheral speeds can be high; if the speed is too high, the sandpaper will skate over the surface rather than cut. If I'm working on a variable-speed lathe, I'll drop the speed 10% to 15%. But it is too time consuming to adjust manually the belt on my Harrison lathe, so I often wind up sanding at the same speed I use for turning.

The gradations of abrasive markings on the face of a Tasmanian myrtle disc. From the rim inward: 40, 80, 100, 180 and 220 grit.

Frequently I will wipe oil on after an initial sanding with 80-grit paper to raise the grain. The paper clogs rapidly but the muck can usually be removed by slapping the paper against the lathe bed. I never apply oil using a paper finer than 100 grit because the abrasive merely clogs and becomes unusable.

I have used garnet and aluminum-oxide papers but now prefer silicon-carbide paper, which cuts better and longer. I buy it in 9-in. (230mm) by 11-in. (275mm) sheets rather than production rolls because I want the lightest-weight backing paper possible. Production rolls have heavy backing paper more suitable for use on power sanders or with sanding blocks. These thicker papers tend to produce stiff corners and edges, which increase the likelihood of scratches, especially on concave surfaces.

I tear the sheets in quarters—each piece about 4½ in. (110mm) by 5½ in. (140mm)—and fold each one in thirds so that one cutting surface is not in contact with another and because it forms its own pad and is easier to hold. Paper folded over only once has a habit of unfolding and deteriorating more rapidly. Never wrap abrasive around a spindle or your fingers. Hold the folded sheet between your fingers and thumb and press it against the revolving wood.

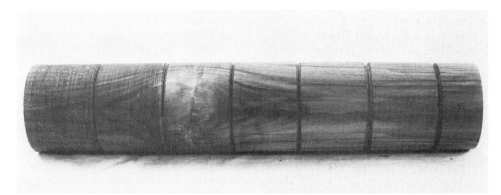

Proceed to a finer grade of paper only when all marks from previous coarser papers have been removed. Here you can see the scratches left on a sassafrass spindle from a variety of abrasives. From left to right: 24, 40, 80, 100, 180 and 220 grit, and 0000 steel wool.

Sanding a fragile holly bowl. Note that the folded sandpaper is not wrapped around any fingers and that the free hand provides support behind the thin edge of the bowl.

Any pressure on top while sanding outside surfaces should be equalled by a supporting hand on the inside.

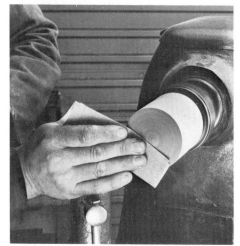

Make contact in the lower-left quadrant of the work when sanding end grain on centerwork to avoid the abrasive's being grabbed by the lathe and swept upward.

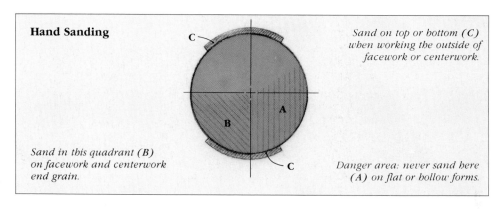

Hand Sanding

Sand on top or bottom (C) when working the outside of facework or centerwork.

Sand in this quadrant (B) on facework and centerwork end grain.

Danger area: never sand here (A) on flat or hollow forms.

Beware of letting your hand drift to the far side of the work (*A* in the drawing above) when sanding internally or on flat shapes. The upward rotation of the wood can grab the paper and carry your hand up to the top of the work's orbit. From there, your hand can shoot forward, back to the far side to meet the upward swing of the wood. Your fingers are hit end-on and bent back. The result is as if you had taken a dive onto your extended fingertips. All this occurs in a fraction of a second. I have broken three knuckles this way on two separate occasions and know others who have done the same. For safety, keep sanding pressure toward you when working on the inside and on top when working on the outside of facework. If the wood is thin, provide support with your free hand as you would when turning delicate work, as shown in the photos at top left. Centerwork is generally sanded on the top or bottom of the work (*C* in drawing) or in the lower-left quadrant (*B*) for end grain. Be careful not to allow the sandpaper to wrap around a spindle. To avoid this, hold the sheet of paper by both ends around the bottom of the work and apply pressure by lifting up, as shown below. The important point is to prevent the ends of the paper overlapping around the wood. Also, take the trouble to arrange your dust-extraction duct as close to the area being sanded as possible.

It's very easy as you sand to lose your original turned form, making the definite indefinite and insipid. Beware of rounding edges that would be better left crisp, as on a bowl or platter rim. Avoid rounding by sanding one surface first and then the other—never sand both together. But remember to soften the resultant sharp edge for safety with a quick touch of 180-grit sandpaper. Crisp does not necessarily mean sharp.

Often, when you finish sanding and run your hand back and forth across the wood surface, the end grain will feel slightly rough. This occurs because the lathe rotates in one direction and the fibers have been bent the opposite way. I usually hand-sand this with the lathe at rest, but a reversing switch on the lathe makes the job easier. If the work can rotate in the opposite direction, you can cut back all those lifted fibers easily. The sanding sequence might then run: 80 grit forward/reverse, 100 grit reverse/forward, 180 grit forward/reverse and polish normally. Problems can arise with fixings screwed onto the drive shaft; unless screwed on firmly, they'll unscrew when the lathe is reversed. I help to start the lathe in reverse rotation by spinning the handwheel (on the outboard shaft) as I switch on the machine. You could also drill and insert a pin through the threads of the fixing and the drive shaft.

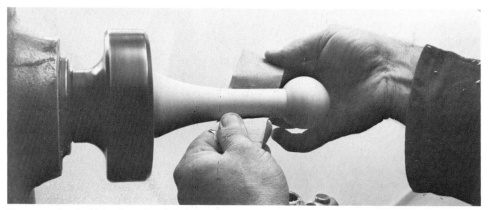

You can also hold both ends of the abrasive and apply pressure from below the work.

While I prefer the contact and control of hand-held abrasive paper against the wood, in most situations—with the exception of beads, coves, corners and other fine details—power sanding will be just as good and is always quicker. The use of power sanding tools on rotating wood is not new, but has increased dramatically in popularity in recent years.

An abrasive disc is attached to a spongy rubber backing pad mounted in an angle drill or conventional electric hand drill, as shown in the photos at lower right. The angle drill is easier to control because the body of the drill lies at a tangent to the surface being sanded. This provides better leverage than the conventional drill body, which lies at 90° to the work surface and is more likely to kick sideways.

Both abrasive and pad must be flexible to avoid deep scoring, especially in the tight curves of concave shapes. (Do not use discs held by only a center screw without adhesive—they disintegrate quickly.) On a convex surface, you can get by with a stiff backing pad or even an orbital sander. I use 2-in.- (50mm) and 3-in.- (75mm) diameter discs starting with 60 grit, if the surface is torn. More often, however, I begin with 120 grit and finish with 180 grit. These discs cut so efficiently that you can use fewer grades to achieve the same result than you'd need with hand-held abrasives.

Because the disc on the drill revolves at the same time that the wood is rotating, the position in which the disc is held against the wood will vary the cutting power and the quality of the finished surface. The wood normally revolves in only one direction—counterclockwise on the inboard side. Most drills revolve in a clockwise direction, but you can use any portion of the disc for sanding. If you use the top or bottom, the grit will cut across the path of the rotating grain, as shown at *B* and *D* in the drawing at right, leaving swirling score marks. Hand-held abrasives always leave marks in the same direction as the wood's rotation. To achieve the same effect through power sanding, you can use either side of the disc so that the grit rotates on the same path as the wood (*A* or *C* in the drawing). However, the side traveling against the wood's rotation *(C)* cuts much more quickly than the one travelling with it *(A)*. Present one side of the revolving disc to the work at, or slightly below, center height. Keep the disc moving across the surface to prevent heat build-up or excessive sanding in one spot. This gives a good finish with less obvious swirling sanding marks. When sanding the inside of facework, as in the

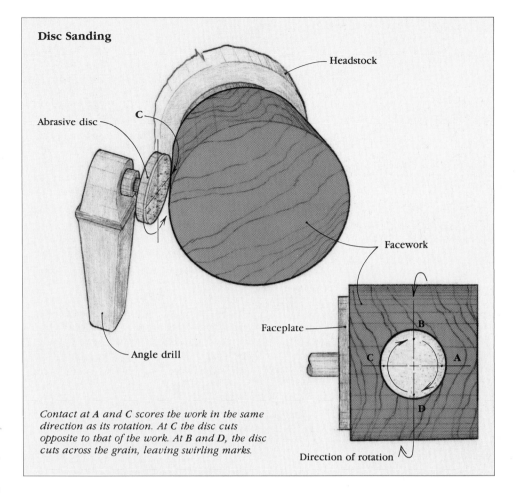

Disc Sanding

Headstock

Abrasive disc

C

Facework

Faceplate

Angle drill

Direction of rotation

Contact at A and C scores the work in the same direction as its rotation. At C the disc cuts opposite to that of the work. At B and D, the disc cuts across the grain, leaving swirling marks.

photo at bottom right, apply pressure with the bottom of the disc in the lower-left quadrant of the work, or with the top of the disc in the lower-right quadrant. Even though the disc will be cutting at a right angle to the work's rotation, if you use the sides of the disc, as for sanding the outside of the work, you risk catching the disc on the internal curves.

The major advantage of power tools, apart from speed, is that a particularly difficult area can receive special attention with much less effort than by hand. With the really rough or torn surfaces associated with spalted woods, a coarse abrasive disc—say 36 grit—is probably the only efficient way to obtain a clean surface. I use a disc mounted in the angle drill to sand bowls with free-form rims. I swing the wood on the lathe back and forth through an arc using one hand (with the lathe turned off) while the other hand holds the tool firmly in a fixed position—a relatively easy task with the angled, rather than the conventional drill. The aim is to keep the tool steady as the wood swings through an arc, so that the leading edges of an uneven rim are not cut back faster than the remainder, a common feature of over-sanding. This prevents the edges from being sanded unevenly.

In power-sanding the outside of a bowl (top), keep the abrasive disc below the centerline. When sanding the inside of a bowl (bottom), approach the work carefully with the drill tilted so that only the bottom half of the disc contacts the work in the lower-left quadrant.

Deciding upon an acceptable finish for a given situation can be a dilemma: There is no single, ideal finish for every turning. Spindles for a rush-seated chair, for example, might be incompatible with the rustic seat if they are sanded at all. Yet a miniature ebony box might be under-finished with a 180-grit surface when 220 or finer would lend the wood a superior, glowing quality, suitable for a fine, cherished object. If I am copying spindles for the antique trade, I rarely use abrasives and, on occasion, I have even used a blunt tool carelessly to match the original most closely. I've also done batches of chair spindles for cabinetmakers who varnish the end product; these I sand with 150 grit to provide a key for the final finish. In such cases, I will stop the lathe and give the spindle a final rub along its length so that the scratch marks will align with the grain. Most of my bowls are finished with 180 grit, which I feel is sufficient and suitable for their functional nature. If they're too finely sanded, people won't use them for fear of ruining the surface, which defeats their intended purpose. Only the smaller, finer or less functional, decorative pieces get a finer sanding or steel wool.

Occasionally, I'll sand a bowl hard with coarse grits (50 or 80) to remove some of the softer grain and create an undulating surface. The result is almost the same as the wear of the decades and produces a worn quality that might be hard to identify but registers in the subconscious in the same way as the well-worn hand rail or friendly tool handle.

Oil & Wax Finish

Just about everything I make is meant to be used and all the bowls have a little label saying so. In the course of their lifetimes, they will be washed and oiled or polished along with the furniture, which will enhance the wood. Most of my work gets the same treatment, be it stair rail, rolling pin, salad bowl, decorative bowl or door handle. It is sanded or not, as befits its purpose, and then oiled with vegetable oil. A coat of wax is applied on top to mix in with the oil and keep the oil in the wood during its shelf life in a gallery or store. A waxed surface is easier to maintain than an oiled surface, which attracts dust.

I use an ordinary, light cooking or salad oil because it is readily available to whomever will ultimately care for the work. The oil is applied liberally with a soft cloth to the spinning wood. If it fails to penetrate the grain thoroughly, as often happens with open-grained woods such as ash and oak, stop the lathe and rub it in. Next, I press a lump of wax firmly against the revolving wood so that it melts on with the friction, leaving a thin, but visible layer on the surface. With the work still spinning, apply a rag firmly enough to melt the wax so that it either mixes with the oil in the wood or stays in the cloth. In time, the rag will become so impregnated with oil and wax that its application alone will be sufficient. I find the best rags come from old, soft, cotton shirts or underwear. If the work is delicate, absorb the pressure of the wax and rag in much the same way that you support thin work while turning or sanding. And remember never to wrap a finishing rag around your fingers in case it gets caught by the lathe.

You can use any wax, provided it is soft and pale and opaque. Beeswax works well and a plain paraffin candle is ideal; it even has a convenient length of string down the middle to keep it from crumbling to pieces. I use soft waxes because they provide a good base for later care and whatever finish is ultimately employed. A small container might be used to hold anything from stamps to curry paste; the stamp box gets furniture polish while the curry box gets washed periodically and re-oiled. Food bowls for salads, rice or breakfast cereals will need frequent washing. These can be hand (not machine) washed in hot water, exactly as any other kitchen or table item. The intense and prolonged heat of a dishwasher could split or warp the wood. Soft wax will wash right off and the wood can be re-oiled. But hard waxes, such as carnauba, create

problems. Hard wax is fine if the wood will always be polished—though it gives too high and hard a gloss for my taste—but it doesn't like water. Water or dampness can spot the surface, which will then have to be sanded off and re-oiled. So I shall stay with my humble technique and leave the owners of my bowls to decide on their future character.

I can recall two collections of my bowls that have found very different end uses, calling for rather different treatment. One group of 6-in. (150mm) English sycamore porridge bowls is in heavy daily use, washed often, oiled occasionally. Once white, they are now a lustrous gold on the outside and a rich brown within, fading to pale at the rim. The action of the spoon moving around the contents in the bowl has sanded as well as any man-made abrasive could reasonably manage and the surface is utterly smooth. The larger salad and serving bowls in the same collection are well on their way to acquiring the same handsome finish and quality.

The second group of bowls belongs to a collector of treen. The dozens of pieces are beeswaxed regularly. They are wiped lovingly with a wax-impregnated cloth at least once a week. This lets their owner see into the woods, which have a wonderful depth and color. It is interesting to note that all have toned down to a dark gold/burnt umber or deep rose, with the grain becoming less obtrusive. In pieces over 100 years old that I have seen, the types of wood are often difficult to discern, no matter how they've been treated. They are all very dark and either reddish-brown, if polished, or grey, if left unfinished. Keep this in mind when you are busily bringing out the grain. It's a great aid at the point of sale but in the end you'll leave posterity with the shape to look at and the balance to feel—not the flashy finish.

Sanding and finishing are two of the most subjective and controversial aspects of woodturning. In general, it is better to learn to use your tools well, get a clean cut with chisel, gouge or scraper, and keep the use of abrasives to a minimum. Whatever your inclination, I suggest you experiment to produce varied surfaces rather than the uniform, flat, plastic coating that smacks of technical, more than aesthetic, achievement. Perfection can be boring.

These bowls were finished with the simple materials shown at left. Salad oil, paraffin or beeswax can be used for an attractive, reasonably durable and functional surface.

Bowl, 1979; applewood; 6 in. (150mm) x 13 in. (330mm), ⅛-in.- (3mm) thick wall; green-turned.

Bowl, 1980; elm burl; 5 in. (125mm) x 6 in. (150mm).

Scoops, 1977; radiata pine; 4 in. (100mm) x 2 in. (50mm).

Bowl, 1980; English ash; 5 in. (125mm) x 14 in. (355mm); green-turned and carved.

Bowl, 1981; holly; 3 in. (75mm) x 6 in. (150mm).

Boxes, 1984; (left to right) huon pine, sassafras, leatherwood; 2½ in. (65mm) to 3 in. (75mm) in diameter. Photo by Concept Photo, Hobart.

Bowl, 1984; leatherwood; 4½ in. (115mm) x 4½ in.; green-turned and microwaved. Photo by Concept Photo, Hobart.

Bowls and scoops, 1980; (clockwise from top left) voamboana, yew, Indian ebony (2 bowls); 2 in. (50mm) to 3 in. (75mm) in diameter. Photo by Chris Chapman.

Needle boxes, 1977; black bean (top) and celery-top pine; 3 in. (75mm) long. Photo by Richard Brecknock.

Bowl, 1980 (detail of base); ash; 18 in. (460mm) in diameter.

Bowls, 1983; Tasmanian musk burl; 2½ in. (65mm) to 4 in. (100mm) in diameter; green-turned and microwaved.

Bowl, 1983; Irish elm; 4½ in. (115mm) x 13 in. (330mm).

Bowls, 1983; laburnum; 2¾ in. (70mm) x 5 in. (125mm).

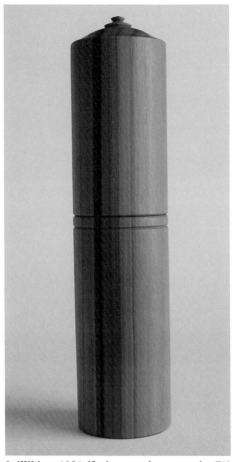

Spillikins, 1981 (facing page); putumuju; 7⅛ in. (180mm) long. Spillikin box (above); 8 in. (205mm) x 1¾ in. (45mm).

Bowl, 1981; holly; 2½ in. (65mm) x 4½ in. (115mm); green-turned and microwaved.

Bowl, 1981; English ash; 5 in. (125mm) x 18 in. (460mm).

Bowl, 1982; English elm burl; 4 in. (100mm) x 11 in. (275mm).

Plates, 1978; elm; 1¼ in. (32mm) x 10 in. (255mm). Photo by Chris Chapman.

Bowl, 1982; Lawson cypress; 6 in. (150mm) x 14 in. (355mm). Detail of patina after two years of use, washed often with hot water and detergent and oiled rarely (top right and above).

Bowls, 1984; Tasmanian horizontal scrub; 2 in. (50mm) to 2½ in. (65mm) x 4 in. (100mm).

Bowl, 1984 (top left and above); Tasmanian blackwood; 6 in. (150mm) x 11 in. (275mm). Photo by Concept Photo, Hobart.

Scoops, 1977; assorted Australian timbers; ⅝ in. (15mm) to 4 in. (100mm) in diameter. Photo by Richard Brecknock.

Boxes, 1977; celery-top pine (rear) and huon pine; 2 in. (50mm) to 4 in. (100mm) in diameter. Photo by Richard Brecknock.

Bowl, 1981 (left and above); holly; 5 in. (125mm) x 12 in. (305mm);
green-turned and microwaved.

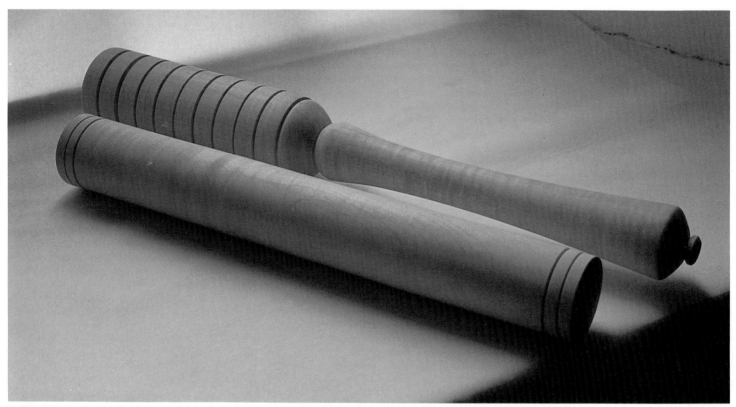

Rolling pin and meat basher, 1980; English sycamore; 12 in. (305mm) long and 14 in. (355mm) long.

Bowl, 1984; sally wattle; 5 in. (125mm) x 7 in. (180mm). Photo by Concept Photo, Hobart.

Bowls, 1981, 1982; (left) holly, 3 in. (75mm) x 7 in. (180mm), green-turned and microwaved; (right) box elder burl; 3 in. (75mm) x 8 in. (205mm). Photo by Ian D. Goodwin.

Appendix A

Troubleshooting

Problem: Symptom	Tool	Remedy
Tool chatter: Chattermarks	Chisels/gouges	Ensure bevel rubs. Try lighter, firmer cut.
	Scrapers	Keep tool flat on rest.
	All tools	Check fixing. Try lower speed. Move rest closer to work. Tighten rest. Hold tool firmly. Try stronger, heavier tool. Cut over rest support post. Provide extra support for thin work. Cut from a different angle.
Catches: Torn or lifted grain	Chisels/gouges	Ensure bevel rubs. Adjust point of cut on tool edge.
	Scrapers	Keep tool flat on rest. Angle tool so edge cuts below horizontal externally. Angle tool so edge cuts above horizontal on inside curves. Angle tool so edge cuts slightly below horizontal and at center height on the bottom of a hollow.
	All tools	Move rest closer to point of cut. Provide a solid fulcrum and prevent lateral movement. Cut from a different direction. Try a firmer and gentler cut. Adjust the cutting angle. Try a different tool. Finish with power-sander (when all else fails).
Tool won't cut	All tools	Check edge for sharpness. Adjust cutting angle.
Vibration: Tick-tick sound	All tools	Check for splits, torn grain, loose knots, wood hitting rest or lathe bed. True surface. Check for exposed fixing screws.
High-pitched sound	All tools	Provide extra support for thin work. Try a lighter cut with less pressure against the work.
Rattles and other sounds	All tools	Check lathe mountings. Check bearings. Check fixing. Tighten the tailstock. Tighten the rest. Center the work. Try a lower speed.
Abrasive scratch marks	All tools	Try a coarser grit. Try power-sander.

Appendix B

Selecting Timbers

Timbers are broadly classified into hardwoods (deciduous) and softwoods (coniferous), although you'll find plenty of soft hardwoods and hard softwoods. In general, softwoods grow more rapidly, developing wider growth rings and, therefore, more open grain. This tends to make the end grain difficult to work, so softwoods are more suitable for centerwork, such as bannister spindles, where the end grain will not need to be worked. Hardwoods generally grow more slowly and have a tighter grain. They are suitable for both facework and centerwork.

A real advantage of working in wood is that it is available almost anywhere in the world. It can be found in logs or cut into planks. If the wood is green (freshly felled), it will contain a great deal of moisture and need to be seasoned (dried out). As moisture leaves the wood, a board or log will shrink hardly at all in length, but considerably in its width, causing splits and checks. (Because checking occurs most dramatically at the ends of the wood, they are often coated with wax or paint to slow the drying process.) Wood can be air-dried naturally, allowing about one year, give or take a few months depending on the species, for every 1 in. (25mm) of wood thickness. Or wood can be kiln-dried—often with the aid of chemicals, which also help to preserve it. I prefer air-dried to kiln-dried timber because it turns better and there is no risk of inhaling unknown chemicals that might have been used in the kiln-drying process.

You can turn either green or seasoned wood, but wood becomes tougher and more difficult to work as it dries, which is why it is used green in many traditional crafts. (Chairmakers fit spindles of varying

You can cut facework discs on a bandsaw or with a hand-held jigsaw. The blank for this bowl was rough-cut out of the burl slab and then trimmed to shape before being turned.

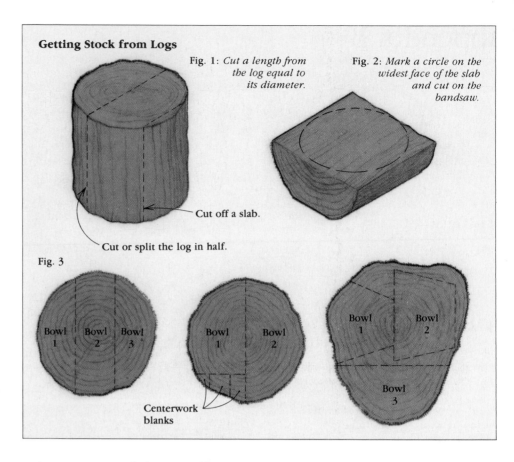

Getting Stock from Logs

Fig. 1: *Cut a length from the log equal to its diameter.*

Fig. 2: *Mark a circle on the widest face of the slab and cut on the bandsaw.*

— Cut off a slab.

Cut or split the log in half.

Fig. 3

Bowl 1 Bowl 2 Bowl 3

Bowl 1 Bowl 2

Centerwork blanks

Bowl 1 Bowl 2

Bowl 3

moisture content to chair seats and backs and the parts shrink or expand to make a tight joint.) If you turn green wood, you can expect it to change shape as it dries. Its movement can be either allowed for in the design or used to advantage.

When you begin turning, you'll want a supply of inexpensive material and plenty of it (so you won't feel guilty or inhibited about wasting it—which at first you must). But the kind of wood you look for also will depend on what you intend to make and whether it's centerwork or facework.

To practice the centerwork exercises (p. 68), you'll need a 2-in.- (50mm) to 3-in.- (75mm) diameter straight section of branch. Try to get your wood green; it is not too soon to turn it within an hour of its being felled, though you'll be sprayed with moisture as you cut. (You can get so hooked on producing long shavings that you'll forget about making anything else.) Centerwork turnings, such as small boxes, bowls or lidded containers, eggcups, candle holders, door knobs, spindles and rolling pins will require short blanks. They can be turned quickly and easily, but are best made from dry timber, so that the wood moves as little as possible in the finished piece.

You can cut facework discs out of sawn boards or round logs. For flatware such as plates, clock faces and breadboards, you'll need seasoned wood to avoid warping. Unless you have space to season boards, you'll need to buy wood that has been seasoned already. Short planks, less than 6 ft. (1.8m) long, called shorts, are often available and are usually less expensive than longer boards. Examine the wood for end splits and surface checks before you buy it. Surface checks can be removed easily in the turning, but end splits will need to be cut off. (This wastes wood, but most lumberyards will make an allowance and adjust the price.)

For deeper, larger facework, such as bowls, obtaining material can be a problem (amazing though it may seem, considering the number of trees felled). Suitable material is very scarce in most sawmills and lumberyards. In my experience, seasoned wood in excess of 8 in. (205mm) wide by 2 in. (50mm) thick is rare, as are boards over 12 in. (305mm) wide. Requests for anything in excess of 8 in. (205mm) wide by 3 in. (75mm) thick will be greeted by stares of blank amazement. And if it's available, it almost certainly won't be dry—despite what you might be told. Dry to a sawmiller tends to be around 20% moisture content, while 12% to 14% (approximating the humidity of most home interiors) is nearer the mark.

Because the wood for deep bowls takes so long to season and is easier to turn while green, turners often rough-turn bowls from unseasoned timber and true them up after they have dried and warped. All the bowls in the Gallery (pp. 132-147) were turned green. They were either dried in a microwave oven or rough-turned and set aside to be air-dried for several months (or years) before being finished. Although it's convenient to be able to cut bowl blanks from a plank, planks provide less of an opportunity to manipulate grain patterns and are more expensive than logs. I cut most of my bowl blanks straight from the log these days, following the process shown in the drawing on the facing page. Cut a length from the log equal to its diameter, stand the section on the end grain and split it down the center, or along a check. Although I use a Husqvarna chainsaw for this, an axe or splitter will do fine. The half log can go between centers or on a faceplate if you true up the flat side. Fig. 3 indicates several variations that will provide blanks of different shapes. This is the most basic way to get timber and all you need is a predatory eye. You can get blanks for bowls from a log as small as 7 in. (180mm) to 8 in. (205mm) in diameter. If you wait for whole logs to air-dry, they will often split badly, leaving you with little usable material. So I generally cut logs as soon as possible and rough them out into bowl or spindle blanks. (See p. 119 for more on rough-turning bowls and microwave seasoning.)

Wood is commercially available from sawmills, timber merchants and lumberyards or do-it-yourself stores. The last two sources will be more expensive than the first two, who are, metaphorically speaking, nearer the standing tree. If you live near a sawmill, hunt around their scrap pile and you're likely to find all you need. Merchants, too, will probably have scrap piles or an odds-and-ends section. Both sources should be able to offer expert advice on what wood is suitable for a job, which woods turn easily and which do not. They should also be able to tell you if the wood is seasoned and what its moisture content is and be able to measure it on the spot with a meter. (Whether they will bother to or not is a different matter— many large mills and yards do not like small orders.)

There are a number of companies who cater to the needs of the amateur and artist-craftsman and stock a wide range of woods, such as ebony, cocobolo, African blackwood, mulga, gidgee—the list is almost endless. Many of these woods grow in arid or tropical areas, but are imported into Europe or North America, where they are manufactured into fairly standard objects. In fact, an exhibition of woodturning these days in Sydney can be disturbingly similar to one in California, Toronto or London, with similar shapes in identical woods. That is why I generally favor using local woods: Whatever happened to national or ethnic identity?

There is a great deal of wood just lying around that can provide suitable material, especially for practice. Demolished buildings can yield vast quantities, though nails can be a problem and must be carefully removed. Urban trees that need pruning are another good source; keep your eye on the local parks-department workers and check the town dump, if it's nearby and you're allowed in. Your neighbors' backyards and gardens may also yield a considerable supply.

As a beginner, your requirements are basic. All you need is a close-grained wood that is easy to work. (Pretty patterns in the wood are wasted at this stage and highly figured grain may present more of a problem than it's worth.) Many of the ornamental or fruit trees are ideal—apple, pear, cherry, maple, privet or laburnum. But at first, you might as well try every variety of wood you can get—there's no substitute for firsthand experience and you'll soon learn what to avoid or look for. As your skills develop, you'll want more interesting material, so color and grain patterns will become more relevant.

As an amateur or budding-but-penniless professional, you could do worse than approach a going concern about their off-cuts. When I began to turn I worried that I would never collect a good stock of wood. A few months later I had a storage problem. I went around local yards buying up cheap odds and ends—almost doing the lumberyards a favor by taking what they wanted to get rid of anyway. I cut dry wood to the maximum diameter possible for discs or square lengths for centerwork, keeping all the off-cuts. Soon, I had filled a dozen sacks. Small blanks became a major storage problem when I began to concentrate on turning larger pieces. (On two occasions I have sold several tons of small blanks.) You should be able to accumulate all the wood you need without any problem—just complaints from those who share your space.

Appendix C

Make a Tool Handle

This is an excellent first centerwork project. Choose a straight-grained, knot-free hardwood, such as hickory or ash. Ensure that the long grain runs the length of the handle for maximum strength and ease of turning. A cross-grained handle could easily snap in use. To guarantee straight grain, you can split the blank out of a billet. (I've used English ash for the handle in the photos on pp. 156-157.)

Cut the stock on the tablesaw, bandsaw or by hand—to about 1½ in. (38mm) to 2 in. (50mm) square by 13 in. (330mm) long for a standard-strength tool. This will allow about ⅛ in. (3mm) thickness of wood over the diameter of the finished handle and about ¼ in. (6mm) extra for waste at both ends.

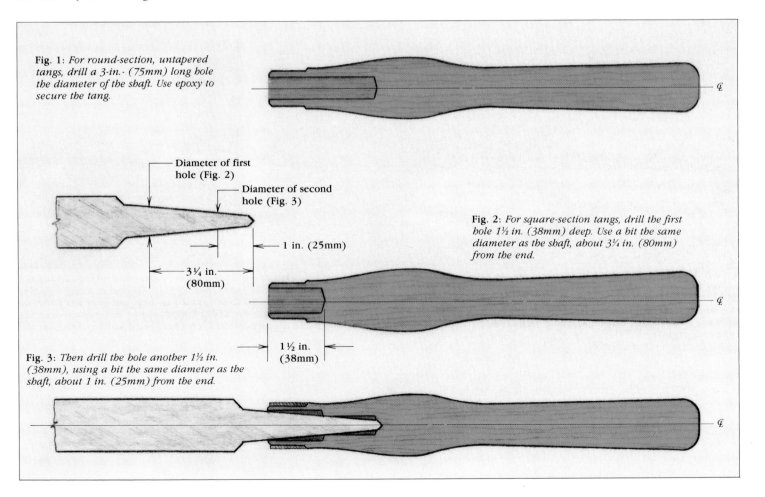

Fig. 1: *For round-section, untapered tangs, drill a 3-in.- (75mm) long hole the diameter of the shaft. Use epoxy to secure the tang.*

Diameter of first hole (Fig. 2)

Diameter of second hole (Fig. 3)

1 in. (25mm)

3¼ in. (80mm)

Fig. 2: *For square-section tangs, drill the first hole 1½ in. (38mm) deep. Use a bit the same diameter as the shaft, about 3¼ in. (80mm) from the end.*

Fig. 3: *Then drill the hole another 1½ in. (38mm), using a bit the same diameter as the shaft, about 1 in. (25mm) from the end.*

1½ in. (38mm)

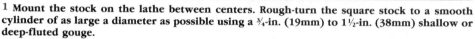

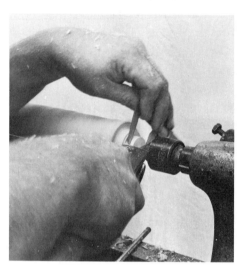

1 Mount the stock on the lathe between centers. Rough-turn the square stock to a smooth cylinder of as large a diameter as possible using a ¾-in. (19mm) to 1½-in. (38mm) shallow or deep-fluted gouge.

2 Using a 1-in. (25mm) scraper or a ¼-in. (6mm) parting tool, turn a flange to fit the ferrule. The ferrule can be a piece of 1-in.- (25mm) diameter copper or steel tubing, about 1 in. (25mm) long (be sure to file the edges smooth). Use vernier calipers to measure the inside diameter of the ferrule (top right) and turn the flange to that diameter (right). Then turn a slight chamfer on the first ¼ in. (6mm) of the flange so the ferrule will get a start over the end. The ferrule will leave a mark where it fits tightly on the wood. Turn the rest of the flange to this diameter. If the tail center is smaller than the ferrule, you can slip the ferrule over the tail center before mounting the stock and keep it there while you turn the flange. That way you won't need to stop the lathe to test the fit.

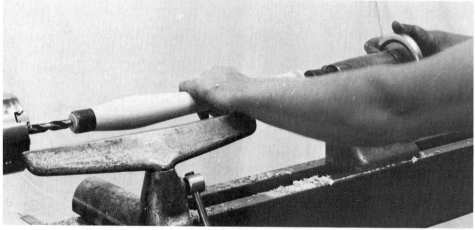

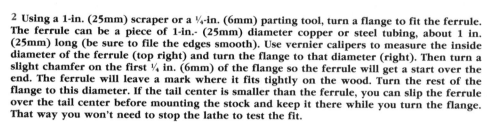

4 Drill the ferrule end to accept the tang. Mount a drill bit in a jaw chuck or Jacob's chuck. Center the handle between the drill tip and the tail center and wind in the tail center while holding the handle steady (left). (You can also push the handle onto the drill by hand, using a similar technique to the one used to drill depth holes [p. 65]. Check that you're feeding the handle parallel to the axis by easing your grip and allowing the wood to revolve slightly in your hands. The handle should center itself as you push it onto the drill.) Follow one of the sequences in the drawing on p. 155 for drilling the hole. Mount the handle between centers (or mount the ferrule end in a jaw chuck) and finish parting off the butt end (right).

3 Use the gouge to rough-out the handle and finish it with a shearing cut using a skew chisel (top left). As the shape develops, stop the lathe and test how your hand fits. Partially part off the butt end of the handle (above), leaving about ½-in. (13mm) of wood attached to the end. Leave the center mark at the ferrule end to help center the drill bit in the next step.

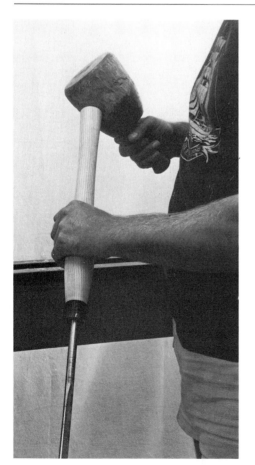

5 With the ferrule in place, push the tang of the tool firmly into the drilled hole. Then hold the handle near the ferrule and clout the butt with a mallet (left) to drive the handle onto the tang. Gouges with round-section tangs may need epoxy to ensure they stay in place. Or you can grind them with a rough, slightly stepped, square-section tang (above), so that no epoxy is needed for a good fit and you can salvage cherished handles. Square-section tangs require a stepped hole, as shown on p. 155. If the tang works loose, just clout the end of the handle again. If it still moves in the hole, tap small wedges between the flat shaft and the curved side of the hole. When the tool wears out, you can knock it from the handle and fit another.

Appendix D

Make a Screw Faceplate

Large center-screw faceplates, 6 in. (150mm) or more in diameter, are useful for turning large bowls quickly. Unfortunately, few manufacturers produce them. The largest size commonly available is about 4 in. (100mm) in diameter. Most turners I know have had to make their own, or have had one made; I've done both. Here is how to make your own.

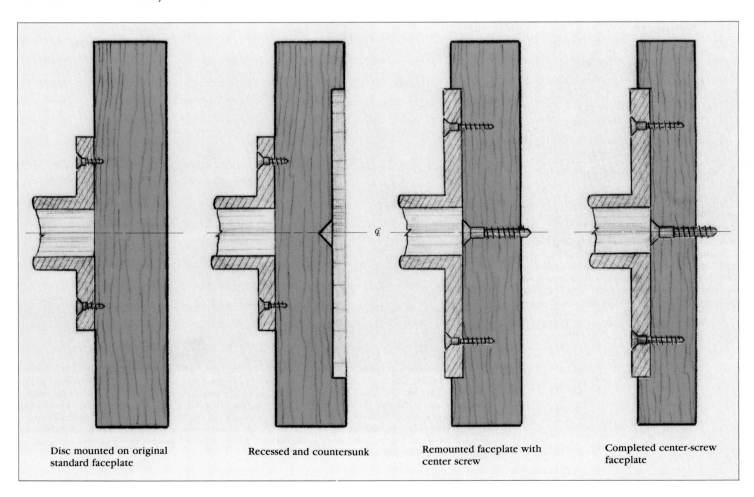

Disc mounted on original standard faceplate

Recessed and countersunk

Remounted faceplate with center screw

Completed center-screw faceplate

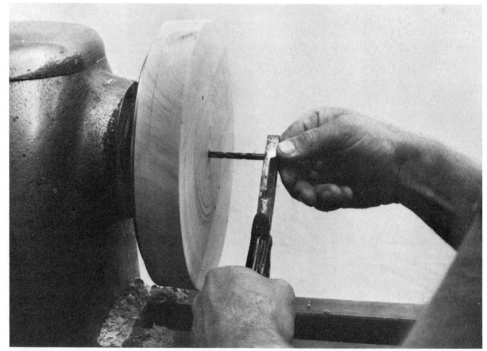

2 True the side and face of the disc using a ¼-in. (6mm) or ½-in. (13mm) gouge. Then transfer the diameter of another standard faceplate—slightly smaller than the diameter of the disc—to the face of the disc (above and left).

1 Mount a 1½-in.- (38mm) thick by 8-in.- (205mm) diameter hardwood disc on a standard faceplate with two short screws (½ in. [13mm] maximum) and screw the faceplate on the drive shaft (above). Do not use a center-screw faceplate.

4 Remove the disc from the first faceplate and install the second faceplate in the recess. Attach the faceplate with four screws penetrating the wood at least ¾ in. (19mm). Drill undersized pilot holes for the screws.

5 Mount the faceplate and disc on the lathe and true the face. Drill a center hole the diameter of a No. 12 or No. 14 wood-screw shank to meet the shallow countersink hole on the other side. You can drill the hole by hand, holding the bit with a pair of pliers (above) or in a Jacob's chuck. Or you could mount the Jacob's chuck on the tail shaft and turn the tail center in. Screw a 1½-in.- (38mm) long No. 12 or No. 14 wood screw in the center hole as tightly as possible. It should protrude about ¼ in. (6mm). I have never found it necessary to use glue to hold the screw in place; the friction is enough.

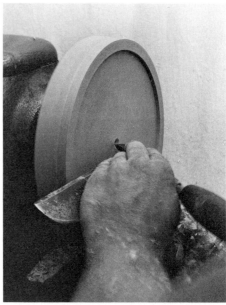

3 Turn a ⅛-in.- (3mm) to ¼-in.- (6mm) deep recess in the face of the disc to accept the second faceplate. Finish the surface using a square-edge scraper. Use a straightedge to ensure that the recess has a flat or slightly concave surface so the faceplate will not pivot (left). Then cut a shallow hole for a countersink at the center of the disc using a skew chisel (above).

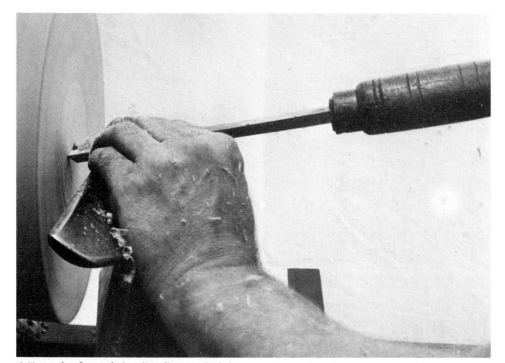

7 The center-screw faceplate is now finished. A decorative groove was turned to remove the screw holes that remained from the original fixing.

6 Turn the face of the disc flat or slightly concave so that the screw inserted through the drilled hole protrudes about ½ in. (13mm), or more if required. (Remember that the effective length of the screw can be reduced with plywood discs.) If you have difficulty cutting the wood near the base of the screw, try a scraping cut using a skew chisel or a ¼-in. (6mm) gouge. The slight concavity of the face will ensure good contact between the disc and the blank mounted on it.

Afterword

As you will discover, it is fairly easy to achieve a bowl that functions as a bowl, a box with a passably fitting lid, or a spindle covered with beads, grooves and coves. What is not so easy is to produce a really beautiful, well-balanced bowl that is a joy to hold as well as to look at, or a box with just the right degree of suction in the fit of the lid, or a slender, elegant spindle with a few beads in just the right places.

Many amateur turners will be tempted to try to earn a livelihood from the craft, spurred on by the odd sale and encouraging remarks from friends and relations. If you are one, consider the problems. Over the years I have helped a number of would-be professionals, several of whom are now reasonably successful, but it has been a struggle for them as it was for me. The problem is not in producing a salable object. For no matter how hideous or impractical a piece might be, someone somewhere will buy it. Sales are no guide to quality. But if your work is to sell readily it must be produced at the right price in a competitive market. That requires speed and speed requires practice. Old world apprentices spent five or seven years at their trade before they were regarded as fully competent and could produce their masterpiece. In today's world of instant everything this is an awesome thought, but I think that the old timers were right. It was at least five years before I developed real speed in my turning and another year or so before I had the fluent technique to convert my ideas readily into woodturnings. I provided my own apprenticeship by making lots of small, repetitive shapes: scoops, bowls, honey dippers, meat bashers, etc. I still produce many items by the hundreds and, unlike many of today's craftspeople, I do not regard them as a necessary evil. They provide the vital practice that keeps my technique sharp; I need them as a musician needs scales.

Once you've acquired the speed and skills, your problem becomes how to sell everything that you can make in a normal working day. If you want to make large, decorative salad bowls that's fine, but where do you sell 12 or 20 of them a day? Or 30 to 40 plates? Many aspiring turners have started out without considering this important aspect.

If you do take the plunge I hope you enjoy it as much as I have. And just remember as you churn the goods out, there is absolutely no reason why the speed required for production should in any way compromise the quality.

As your skill develops, beware of complacency. Aim to get things right the first time. Don't poke or jab at the wood. Any shape poked at and messed about with looks it. When you achieve flowing movements and sounds, flowing forms will follow. Never be afraid to risk ruining a job with a final cut. It is all too easy to find turnery where a shape just misses because the woodworker has settled for a surface that is more or less okay, but where one or two more cuts would have made all the difference. Too many people say "that'll do" and either don't care about achieving quality or don't want to risk an hour's work in looking for it. But it is worth pushing yourself to develop your skill so that if you want to try something technically outrageous you can tackle it with some prospect of success. I can recall a 4-in. (100mm) by 10-in. (255mm) burr elm bowl I had turned with a 1/4-in.-(6mm) thick wall that, upon inspection, I found to be less than 1/8 in. (3mm) thick near the base. (The bowl had holes in its side so it was easy to check the wall's thickness.) I held my breath and turned the whole wall down to match the thinner section. It was cut in one minute and not bludgeoned into submission with 20-grit abrasive in ten. That venture was successful. Other, smaller bowls have shattered with the final cut, but it is always worth the risk.

Decide what you want to make and go for it. Don't be satisfied with less. You will always know when you could have done better, even if others don't. Learn to be hyper-critical and enjoy the long-term results. I find I am rarely satisfied with yesterday's masterpiece because it becomes today's run-of-the-mill. The better you get, the smaller your steps forward will be, but progress is always possible. And rest assured, you will never reach perfection—but you might have glimpses of it.

Index

Editor: Laura Cehanowicz Tringali
Design Director: Roger Barnes
Associate Editors: Deborah Cannarella, Scott Landis
Associate Art Director: C. Heather Lambert
Art Assistant: Barbara Snyder
Staff Artist: Lisa Long
Copy Editor: Ceila Robbins
Indexer: Harriet Hodges
Manager of Production Services: Gary Mancini
Coordinator of Production Services: Dave DeFeo
Production Manager: Mary Galpin
System Operator: Nancy-Lou Knapp
Production Assistant: Claudia Blake Applegate, Deborah Cooper
Darkroom: Mary Ann Snieckus

Watch

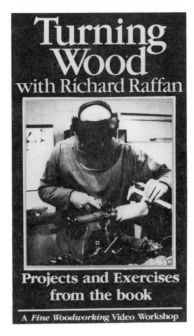

Turning Wood
with Richard Raffan

Projects and Exercises from the book

A *Fine Woodworking* Video Workshop

Richard Raffan on Videotape

To help you master the form and movement that are so important to skillful turning, Richard Raffan has put together a video workshop that demonstrates the projects and exercises from his book. Specific sections of the tape are keyed right on the screen to the relevant pages in the book, so you can both read and watch as Raffan teaches you his craft.

Raffan begins the tape by demonstrating his tool-sharpening techniques, then offers a series of gouge and skew exercises, slowing down at critical moments so you can analyze his motions. Building on these skills, Raffan then takes you step-by-step through the book's six complete projects: a tool

handle, a light-pull knob, a scoop, box, bowl and breadboard. Because each project is taped in its entirety—from mounting the stock to finishing—you'll gain a better understanding of the rhythm of woodturning, which alternates between fast, efficient stock removal and delicate, precise detailing.

This is a rare chance to work alongside a professional woodturner, and to experience the sights and sounds of woodturning first hand. As in his book, Raffan's straightforward approach and encouraging manner will help you develop new skills and increased confidence at the lathe.

117 minutes, $39.95 postpaid

Save $7.95 off the regular price

Use the coupon below to purchase Raffan's video workshop and save $7.95. Just mail the completed coupon and your payment of $32 to The Taunton Press at the address below (CT residents please add 7½% sales tax). Your tape

will be sent via UPS, so it should arrive in a week to ten days after we receive your order. All shipping and handling charges are paid by The Taunton Press. (The coupon is also good at selected retail outlets.)